THE MYSTERY OF
THE SEVEN

REBECCA WILLIAMS LOVE

WESTBOW
PRESS®
A DIVISION OF THOMAS NELSON
& ZONDERVAN

WestBow Press books may be ordered through booksellers or by contacting:

WestBow Press
A Division of Thomas Nelson & Zondervan
1663 Liberty Drive
Bloomington, IN 47403
www.westbowpress.com
844-714-3454

ISBN: 979-8-3850-4020-9 (sc)
ISBN: 979-8-3850-4019-3 (e)

Library of Congress Control Number: 2024926512

Print information available on the last page.

WestBow Press rev. date: 01/29/2025

Dedication:

To my parents, Frank and Millie Williams, whose lives inspired in me a sense of curiosity, a deep love of learning and an unshakeable faith.
To my children and grandchildren: Amanda, Jessica, Adam, JD, Titus, Ansley, David, Abeni and Annika. You are the reason I write.
To Sam, Kay, Rachel, and my Bible Study group:
thank you for your constant encouragement.
Finally, and most importantly, to my husband, Jeff.
Your belief in me gives me the courage to try.

CONTENTS

PART II
SEVEN CHURCHES

INTRODUCTION

HIDDEN TREASURE

In 2009, Terry Hebert was an unemployed metal-detector enthusiast living in Staffordshire England. Hoping to enjoy an afternoon of his favorite pastime, he knocked on the door of Fred Johnson, a local farmer and requested permission to search his field. He had no specific reason for wanting to search that particular field, but it was worth a try. Maybe he would find something worthwhile.

Fred had been reluctant in the past to allow people onto his property, but this afternoon, he decided to let Terry search, on the condition that he look for a missing wrench Fred thought he may have lost in there. Fred figured the chances of Terry finding anything were very slim. The field had been continuously farmed by his family for generations. Moreover, there was a path through the field which was used daily as a shortcut by many factory workers. If there were ever anything of value to be found in the field, it would surely have been found by now. However, Fred gave Terry permission to try, but he warned him it was likely a waste of time.

But it wasn't.

The metal detector soon began to ping and what was uncovered turned out to be the largest Anglo-Saxon treasure hoard ever discovered! The treasure was worth millions and made both men rich indeed. The amazing part was that this piece of land had been farmed for generations, yet when someone dug just a little bit deeper than anyone had ever dug before, there was this massive treasure just lying there, waiting to be found. By many estimates, the treasure had been hidden there for at least 2,500 years![1]

Now that piece of ground was not neglected, nor worthless. It had been used to feed and support that family for generations. They got their daily bread from it. But if they had really investigated it, they would have been much more than just sustained, they would have been abundantly wealthy.

I love this story. The first time I read it, my imagination was captured instantly. The parallels for us are profound. Here in my hand is my Bible. I read it every day. It was read by my parents and grandparents for generations before me. It has nurtured and sustained us all. I get my daily bread, food for my soul, from it.

But, what if there were more God wanted me to see? What if there were more He wants you to see? What if, for the person who is willing to take the time to dig just a little bit deeper than they have ever gone before, there were treasures beyond imagination, just waiting to be found? You can choose to read your verse for the day, and spend your fifteen minutes of devotional time in the morning. If you do so, you will be fed and sustained. You will find food for your soul.

But...

You could choose to go a little deeper. You could start searching scripture like one would search for hidden treasure. You could ask God to open your eyes to "behold wondrous things" out of His word[2]. And He would. You could have abundance. You would suddenly view Bible study as an adventure, and what you find would thrill your soul! I know this, because this happened to me, and this book is the story of that treasure hunt.

This Treasure Belongs To You

Some people are intimidated by deep Bible study. They feel they do not have the training or education to really understand it. But we do not need to be afraid of studying scripture for ourselves. The Bible was written to

---

[1]   *Kennedy, Maev (24 September 2009). "Largest ever hoard of Anglo-Saxon gold found in Staffordshire". The Guardian. London, UK. Retrieved 24 September 2009.*
[2]   [2] Psalm 119:118.

us and for us. This is our ground, this field belongs to us. This is a letter written to us. If God cared enough to send us a message, doesn't it make sense that He would do so in a way we could understand? And if we need help understanding, He says that He has also sent us a Teacher, the Holy Spirit, who will guide us into all truth. [3]

Deut. 29:29[4] says,

> *"The secret things belong unto the Lord our God,*
> *But those things which are revealed belong to us*
> *And to our children forever."*

If it's in the Bible, it's a revealed thing. God's word tells us that there are things which are not for us to know, but if He has written something to us – even words of prophecy – He intends for us to understand it. The Bible is not a book written for only scholars and an elite few. That kind of thinking is what plunged the world into the Dark Ages. His word is for us and to us.

Jesus also told us that every person trained in His doctrine will bring forth treasure new and old. [5] God has a treasure He wants to entrust to each generation – some revelation that people before them might not have fully understood, because it was not yet the right time for it to be revealed. We have the privilege and obligation to discover these nuggets of truth and to pass them on to our children. I do not want to be guilty of neglecting the inheritance I am supposed to leave to my children.

I'm going to be quoting a lot of scripture in this book. There is just no other way to show you where I found this treasure unless I take you to the spot where I found it and dug it out. I don't want to just share information with you, I want you to go on this journey with me.

You may or may not agree with what I share, but you can at least base your conclusions on scripture you have read for yourself. Unless otherwise noted, I am using the *King James Version*[6], however, for clarity, I may

---

[3]   John 16:13

[4]   Unless otherwise noted, all Scripture quoted is King James Version. (Original work published 1769) Public Domain

[5]   Matthew 13:52

[6]   King James Bible. Oxford University Press, 1945/1769. Public Domain

sometimes update the pronouns and verbs (not the verb itself) to modern usage.

Let me begin by giving you the back story of how I became a treasure hunter.

My Journey of Discovery

I was fortunate enough to be raised in a Christian home and to have attended a Bible college. But as a young adult, I began to be very dissatisfied with a faith that was based largely on what others told me the Bible said. It was not so much that I doubted what they told me, but that I didn't really know for myself what the Bible said. And to be honest, my daily devotional time was pretty underwhelming. I would often find my mind wandering, reading words that had become so familiar, I no longer even really heard them. I was bored and dissatisfied. I wanted something so much more from my faith.

I wanted a bold faith, one I could confidently and clearly articulate, even to scoffers. You can't get that second hand. I wanted to actually discover something for myself. So, I determined I would not only read the Bible through, but that I would really study it. And I would, to the best of my ability, get rid of all presuppositions and study the Bible with an open and studious mind. I didn't want to come at it believing that I already knew what it said, but rather I wanted to read the Bible to find out what it actually says.

The only presupposition I made was that whatever the Bible says is true. David said,

"I esteem Thy precepts concerning all things to be right." – Ps. 119:128

I determined that whatever the Bible taught is what I would believe, and whatever it did not teach, I would not believe. Even if this meant letting go of what I had previously held to be true.

I also decided that when I was investigating a particular passage or teaching, I would use every available tool to study what the Bible had to say for myself, before I read any commentary on that subject. If I just went to commentaries first, I would never find anything more than what others had already found. I did not want my understanding to be based on someone else's interpretation or investigation of God's word, but on my own study. We are encouraged to do this in scripture. Paul said,

"Study to show thyself approved unto God,
a workman who needs not to be ashamed,
rightly dividing the Word of Truth." – 2 Tim. 2:15

I John 2:27 encourages that we do not need to rely solely on others to study, but that the Spirit will guide us in our study. As a Christian, the importance of relying on the Holy Spirit to guide us cannot be stressed enough. The Lord taught me what this means fairly early in my journey of discovery.

The Truth is More Than Words

Because I had determined to let the Scriptures be my guide to truth, I began to pour over my Bible. I read and reread passages, committing many of them to memory. I learned how to use a concordance (which I will talk about later), and how to cross reference and dissect verses. I took classes on "How To Study Your Bible" and learned inductive study methods. I did my best to become a Biblical scholar.

And yet, I often stumbled over what I was learning. It all seemed to be in my head, but not in my heart. In short, I had more knowledge, but not more wisdom. My study changed what I knew, but not who I was. I couldn't honestly say that I had more love, or patience or even kindness as a result. Instead I had more guilt, because I now recognized that many attitudes and behaviors of mine were not up to God's standards. It was academic study, but it was not transformative.

This troubled me greatly and I began to pray about it. Jesus had talked about being born again, and Paul wrote about all things being new and believers being a new creation [7]. I had to be honest and admit that this was not my experience. I had the same struggles with the same thoughts; and to be frank, I was mad about it. I felt I was getting short changed. Where

---

[7]   John 3:3,7; 2 Corinthians 5:17

was the peace? Where was the joy? Where was the love and freedom? I felt more bound than ever. I knew I was missing something.... But what?

The story I am about to share with you will make some people very uncomfortable. It involves a conversation I had with the Holy Spirit. There will be some who question this whole story, doubting that the Spirit actually speaks to us. I have heard some claim that to say the Spirit speaks to you is the same as claiming extra Biblical inspiration. That is not true.

What I am describing here is not extra Biblical revelation. It is Biblical explanation from the Spirit. He was not giving me additional inspiration, he was giving me revelation of what was already written to me. All messages, and even thoughts, must be held up to the pure light of Scripture. God will never tell us anything that goes against His word or that is not confirmed in His Word. Paul said:

"But though we, or an angel from heaven, preach any other gospel unto you than that which we have preached unto you, let him be accursed." – Gal. 1:8

The Holy Spirit is the Counselor and the Teacher. The Bible can only be understood by His instruction. Trying to study the Bible apart from the Spirit will only lead us to become modern day Pharisees. It is like handing dynamite to someone who has no idea of how to properly use it. Dynamite can be very useful to those who are digging for precious gold, but it can also be incredibly destructive if used improperly.

Jesus said,

"Howbeit when He, the Spirit of truth, is come,
He will guide you into all truth." – John 16:13

Paul, speaking to the Corinthians about how to grow in our knowledge of the Lord said,

"For what man knows the things of a man,
(except by) the spirit of man which is in him?
Even so, the things of God knows no man, but the Spirit of God.
Now we have received, not the spirit of the world, But the spirit which is
of God, that we might know the things that are freely given to us of God.
Which things also we speak, not in the words which man's wisdom teaches,

But which the Holy Ghost teaches, comparing spiritual things with spiritual.
But the natural man receives not the things of the Spirit of God,
For they are foolishness unto him, neither can he know them,
Because they are spiritually discerned." – 1 Cor. 2:11-14

James tells us, *"If any of you lacks wisdom, let him ask of God, who gives to all liberally and without reproach, and it will be given to him." – James 1:5 NKJV*[8]

Following the instruction given in scripture, I decided to make it a matter of prayer, and asked God to show me what I was missing.

One morning, I woke up with a portion of scripture playing over and over in my head. It was, *"I am the Lord! That is My Name. My glory I will not share with another!"*

Now, that's kind of a weird verse to wake up to. I didn't even realize it was there at first. I just got up and began my morning routine, but I slowly became aware that this phrase was repeating over and over again in my mind, and I didn't know why. It was certainly not a verse I had ever tried to memorize, though I did recognize it.

I know that when scripture suddenly begins to play in my mind, it could be the Spirit trying to tell me something. I just didn't know what He was trying to say. So I decided to look up the verse and see what it said in context. Here is what I read:

"Thus says God, the LORD,
He that created the heavens and stretched them out.
He that spread forth the earth, and that which comes out of it,
He that gives breath unto the people upon it,
And spirit to them that walk on it.

I the LORD have called you in righteousness,
And will hold your hand, and will keep you,
And give you for a covenant of the people,
For a light to the Gentiles.

---

8   New King James Version (NKJV): (Thomas Nelson, Inc. 1982). Used by permission.

To open the blind eyes,
To bring out the prisoners from the prison,
And them that sit in darkness out of the prison house.

I am the LORD, that is My name,
And My glory I will not give to another,
Neither My praise to graven images.

Behold, the former things are come to pass,
And new things do I declare.
Before they spring forth I tell you of them." – Isaiah 42:5-9

The first part was clearly an Old Testament prophecy about Christ, and how He would be a light to the Gentiles. He would open blind eyes (physically and spiritually), and free captives. It talks about God doing new things in the earth.

Which only led me back to my current dilemma. Why wasn't I new? I sat on the edge of the bed and prayed,

"Lord, I hear Your words, and I think You
are trying to say something to me,
But I don't' know what it means.
Why is this verse playing over and over in my head?"

The thought that came to me next was in the form of a question. I sensed the Spirit asking:

"What do those words mean to you?
What sort of feelings and thoughts do they evoke?"

I felt a little surprised and even embarrassed at the question, because the thoughts that those verses evoked were not flattering. But, I figured, He already knows what I am thinking, so I may as well be honest. I said:
"Lord, to be honest, I don't' like that verse very much."

Again, I sensed the Spirit asking:

"Why? What is the story in your head when you read those words? Tell Me. What is the setting, who are the characters?"

The Spirit often talks to us in stories and parables. Jesus used parables to teach us what His kingdom was really like. In a sense, the whole Bible is a collection of stories and parables God uses to teach us. Spiritual truths are often explained and revealed through Story.

Though the Spirit had never really asked me questions like this before, I did believe it was Him speaking. I had asked Him to explain something to me, and His word says that if we lack wisdom, we can ask it of Him and He will give it. I decided to stay in the conversation, even if it seemed odd and a little uncomfortable.

I said, "Father, when I hear those words, I see a throne room. You are seated high and lifted up on Your throne, and all creation is fallen on their faces before You. And all that is as it should be. But then, from this high throne, You look down on the groveling humanity before You and declare, *"I am the Lord! That is My Name! My glory I will not share with another!"* And to be honest Lord, it feels degrading. My heart feels like it actually diminishes both You and us for You to say that."

My boldness might shock you. To be honest, it made me cringe too. But I knew that He already knew what I was thinking, and was not surprised. He asked an honest question, and He wanted an honest answer. I would never find out what He wanted to tell me if I played games and pretended to be more righteous than I was, or if I refused to engage in an honest conversation. As best as I am able, I am determined not to lie to God.

Although my response probably made you uncomfortable, and certainly made me uncomfortable, it did not seem to offend or surprise the Spirit. I felt His reply,

"In that setting, and in that story, you are right! For the king on the throne to say that to subjects that are already bowing before him would diminish them both."

I was shocked. I had been bracing for a reprimand at the least. Whatever I had expected Him to say, it wasn't that!

He then added,

"But, what if the story you are telling yourself isn't the true story? What if the words are exactly the same, but the setting is not a throne room, but a bedroom? And what if the one speaking is the King, but he is not addressing his subjects, but his bride? What if he is looking at her with all the love he has, and he knows she is holding back her love? What if he knows she is trying to figure out if she can be married to him, but still enjoy the admiration of other suitors? What if this mighty, all powerful king looks into her eyes and says, "I am the Lord. That is my name. And my glory I will not share with another. You are my wife, and I will not share you."

I felt like all the air had been sucked out of the room. Tears of awe and worship sprang to my eyes. I knew what He was talking about. Much of my life had been trying to find my comfortable lane with my faith. I wanted a relationship with Christ, but I didn't want to be weird or rejected because of it.

In the setting the Spirit described, and in the story He told, those same words became incredibly loving and powerful. They did not diminish him. The King's words elevated both him and his bride. He would be less than he was if he did not say them. She would be less if he did not say them!

The Spirit went on to say, *"You are like Eve in the garden.[9]"* I knew the word and commands of God, just as she did. Satan tried to get her to doubt what God said, but he couldn't. She was certain she knew what He said. And I was certain I knew what the Bible says. We can't be tripped up that way.

So, knowing he could not get Eve to doubt God's word, he deceived her into doubting God's character. He changed the story. He kept all the words, but changed their meaning by changing the setting and the heart of the One who spoke them. He got Eve to doubt God's love and good intentions.

I was just like the Pharisees who searched the scriptures daily, and yet did not recognize Christ when He was in front of them[10]. The Spirit impressed upon my heart, *"You know the words, but you do not know the story. Unless you know Me, My heart, and the story you are a part of, you will be deceived and defeated, even while you are reading your Bible and memorizing scriptures. You need Me to teach you what they mean."*

---

[9]   Genesis 3:1-5
[10] John 5:39

This was transformative for me! This is when I began to have interactive Bible study with the Spirit. I read, and then pause and ask the Spirit to explain it to me. I ask lots of questions, and I keep on asking them until I receive insight. Sometimes it comes immediately, but often it takes a few days of seeking. But the answers do come, and they are always thrilling. His Word is life, even when He is rebuking me!

We need to be very careful who we rely on to interpret scripture for us. Some so called Bible scholars doubt the inerrancy of scripture, or even the exclusive authority of Christ. They may be more educated and knowledgeable than many Christians, but they do not know God. Jesus said the words He speaks are spirit and life[11]. Those who do not know Him cannot understand His words because His words are spiritually discerned[12]. We cannot study scripture apart from the Spirit of God and achieve any victory, understanding or truth.

This does not mean that we don't listen to pastors, evangelists and teachers who are using their spiritual gifts to teach us. It means we have an obligation to take that teaching and compare it to scripture to see if it is correct. Early believers in Berea were called more noble than others because they studied the scripture daily to see if the teaching they received was true.[13] I am determined do the same.

It also means we must then humbly ask the Spirit to teach us and guide us to all truth. All true wisdom comes from Him.[14] Wisdom is more than knowledge. It is understanding, and it is powerful. You can memorize all kind of facts, but that doesn't mean you understand them. If you are not transformed by God's word, then you are missing the spirit of it. Don't short change yourself. Learn to ask questions, and then listen for the answer.

Often people don't hear from God because they don't really believe He will speak to them. Yet Jesus said, "My sheep hear My voice"[15]. If you are a born-again child of God, you have the ability to hear the Spirit. If you don't, either you haven't been born again, or you have not been taught to

---

[11]   John 6:63
[12]   1 Cor. 2:14
[13]   Acts 17:11
[14]   Colossians 2:3
[15]   John 10:27

expect to hear from Him. Probably because you have been taught that God doesn't speak to us anymore. And you have been taught that by someone who has never heard from God. Yet, His name is "The Word"[16], and He is still the God who speaks.

So, I began my quest for a genuine, defensible faith. I had my Bible, my inquisitive mind and a few good study tools to assist me in sifting through this precious ground. Above all I had the Holy Spirit as my Guide, Companion and Teacher. I didn't know what I would find, but I was ready for an adventure.

This book is the result of that quest. My goal in sharing what I found with you is not merely to give you information. Neither is it to win you to my point of view. Some will agree with my conclusions, some will not. I'm comfortable with that. I'm not trying to convince you, I'm hoping to provoke you. My hope and prayer is that what I share will provoke and encourage you to go on your own journey of discovery.

The Bible is a living book, breathed out by the very God whose word spoke worlds into existence. Its very words are alive and powerful[17]. We will never come to the end of our study of it, because it is not a dead, stagnant thing. Every time we dig to the bottom of its teaching, it is only to discover greater depths and heights than we ever imagined. So the one thing we need never fear is boredom!

Neither is it a "one and done" study. Our quest is a life pursuit, not a one- time journey. Every time we begin at the beginning and read to the end, we learn things we did not know before.

Some years after I began studying the Bible this way, I found myself once again at the beginning. But this time, I began to notice things I had not before, and to ask questions I had not asked before, which is where all real learning begins.

The Mystery of Seven

I was determined to study my Bible as though I were searching for hidden treasure. When one sets out to dig for gold, or hunt for treasure,

---

16   John 1:1
17   Hebrews 4:12

it is first necessary to survey the ground closely. One must learn to read the soil for certain patterns and signs that indicate that there may be more beneath one's feet than just dirt. Often gold is located deep beneath the soil, near bedrock. On the surface, however, there are clues. One must look for the presence of specific types of minerals and certain rock formations that stand out from the surroundings. If gold has been found in one place, then the presence of similar materials or conditions in another place would be good indicators that gold may be found there as well.

Repeated numbers and phrases can be such indicators in the Bible.

As I began my study of the Bible again at Genesis, I was struck afresh by the prevalence of the number seven. The number seven has been called the number of perfection or completion, and we see it figuring prominently in the works of God all throughout scripture.

God created the world in seven days[18], and all cultures and nations still measure their weeks this way. Noah was in the ark 7 days before the Flood[19]. Enoch, considered the first Old Testament prophet, and the first person raptured (or caught up to heaven), was the seventh generation from Adam[20].

Priests of the Old Testament tabernacle and temple were consecrated in a ceremony of seven days, and so was the altar[21]. When making atonement for the people, the priest was to sprinkle the blood of the sacrifice seven times before the Lord[22].

Seven priests carried the ark of God, bearing seven trumpets for seven days as the children of Israel circled Jericho seven times a day[23]! These are just a few of the Old Testament examples.

And the trend continues into the New Testament. Jesus fed the five thousand with five loaves and two fishes (which make seven)[24]. He fed the four thousand with seven loaves and a few fish, and took up seven baskets of leftovers[25]! Disciples were instructed that they should forgive each other

---

[18]   Genesis 2:1-3
[19]   Genesis 7:4-10
[20]   Genesis 5:19-24
[21]   Exodus 29:35-37
[22]   Leviticus 4:6,17
[23]   Joshua 6
[24]   Matthew 14:19-21
[25]   Matthew 15:32-39

even to seventy times seven[26]. When the work of ministering to the first church became too burdensome for the apostles, they selected seven men to serve as the first deacons [27]. We will explore the sevens of Revelation more in Part II, but suffice it to say seven is all over John's Revelation.

Hebrew Calendar

Even the Hebrew calendar is based on the number seven. I have included a Hebrew Calendar chart at the end of this chapter as a visual aid. The Hebrew people actually have two calendars in one: the Religious Calendar, and the Secular Calendar. The first month of the Secular Calendar is the seventh month of the Religious Calendar; and the seventh month of the Secular Calendar is the first month of the Religious Calendar. As a result, although there are twelve months in a year, there are two first months, and two seventh months.

This can be understood if one remembers the term "first month" is not just first in a numerical series, but first in the sense as being preeminent. One may be first in their class by being at the head of a line, or one may be first in their class by having the highest academic placement.

In this sense, Nisan is first in importance, because in that month the nation of Israel was born when it was led out of captivity at the first Passover[28]. The feast of the Passover, which includes the celebration of Firstfruits and the Feast of Unleavened Bread is observed for seven days. Thus, Nisan is the first month of the religious calendar, and the seventh month of the secular calendar.

But Tishrei is also the first month. It is the month the Jewish New Year is celebrated, making it the first in the line of months. The Feast of Tabernacles, which is celebrated in Tishrei is to be observed for seven days[29]. Tishrei is the first month of the Hebrew secular calendar, and the seventh month of the religious calendar.

---

[26] Matthew 18:22
[27] Acts 6:3
[28] Exodus 12:2,15-19
[29] Leviticus 23:24

During the course of the year, there are seven Feasts of the Lord, given through Moses, which the Hebrew people celebrate[30]. The first three occur all together in the first month of Nissan: The Feast of Passover, the Feast of Unleavened Bread, and the Feast of Firstfruits. We will look at these feasts in more detail as we come to their time on our study of the Days.

The next feast stands alone in the third month and occurs 50 days after the first Sabbath after Passover. This is the Feast of Weeks, better known as Pentecost.

The final three feasts occur in the seventh month of Tishrei. First is the Feast of Trumpets (also known as Rosh Hashanah), which is the Jewish New Year and occurs on the first day of Tishrei. On the 10th day of the month is the Day of Atonement (Yom Kippur). Finally, the Feast of Tabernacles, which is a seven day feast celebrating the ingathering of the final harvest.

It is clear that the number seven is very key in God's economy of Time. Not only are the months of the year divided into two sevens, the years themselves are divided into sevens. At the end of every seven years, Israel was to observe a year of rest (a Sabbath year)[31]. At the end of fifty years (which is seven, seven-year sequences plus one), they celebrated a year of Jubilee and the release from all debts[32].

Daniel was told that "seventy sevens" were determined for the fate of the nation of Israel[33]. If we want to understand what time it is on the prophetic kingdom calendar, the number seven is a vital key.

Wherever we see the number seven in scripture, that is a good indication that there is something more to be found. That is where we should dig for treasure!

---

[30] Leviticus 23, Deuteronomy 16
[31] Deuteronomy 15:1
[32] Leviticus 25:8-13
[33] Daniel 9:24

Hebrew Calendar

The Hebrew calendar is a based on the lunar cycle, while the Gregorian calendar is based on the solar cycle.

Hebrew Month	# Month Religious Calendar	# Month Civil Calendar	Days & Key Holy Days
Nisan	1st	7th	(30 days) March/April **Passover "Pesach"** (sundown 14th –sundown 15th) **Feast of Unleavened Bread** "Chag haMatzot" (Sundown 15th to sundown 22nd) **Feast of First Fruits** "Yom haBikkurim" (First day after the Sabbath of Passover)
Iyar	2nd	8th	(29 days) April/May
Sivan	3rd	9th	(30 days) May/June **Pentecost** Feast of Weeks "Chag Shavout" (Sundown 7 weeks and 1 day after First Fruits.)
Tammuz	4th	10th	(29 days) June/July
Av	5th	11th	(30 days) July/Aug.
Elul	6th	12th	(29 days) Aug./Sept.
Tishri	7th	1st	(30 days)Sept/ Oct. **Feast of Trumpets** "Rosh Hashanah" (New Year) (sundown Elul 29 – sundown Tishri 1) **Day of Atonement** "Yom Kippur" (sundown 9th day unto sundown 10 day) **Feast of Tabernacles** "Sukkot" (sundown 15th day until sundown 21st day)
Cheshvan	8th	2nd	(29 days) Oct./Nov.
Kislev	9th	3rd	(30 days) Nov./Dec. **Festival of Dedication** (or Lights) "Hanukkah" (Kislev 24th – Tevet 2 = 9 days)
Tevet	10th	4th	(29 days) Dec./Jan.
Shevat	11th	5th	(30 days) Jan./Feb. In leap years, an additional month is inserted here. It is called "Adar I" and has 30 days
Adar	12th	6th	(29 days) Feb./March .In leap years, this month is called "Adar II" or "Adar Beit" and has 30 days

PART I

SEVEN DAYS, SEVEN AGES

CHAPTER 1

"In The Beginning"

"In the beginning, God created the heaven and the earth."[1]

Thus begins the Holy Bible. This is the first verse, of the first chapter, of the first book of the Bible. It is the thesis statement of the whole Bible. Everything the Bible has to say will build upon this statement. Genesis does not try to prove the existence of God, nor does it offer proofs that He is the creator of the universe. It begins with the flat statement that God is, and that He created everything. Those who doubt or want to argue that point need read no further until they have cleared up their doubts, for the Bible will have nothing more to say to them.

This is how God's revelation works. God makes a statement, and you are left to receive it or not. If you receive it, you can proceed forward and go on to new revelations. If, however, you do not receive it, you may as well go find some other use of your time, for God's Word will have nothing more it can say to you. If you reject the notion that the universe was created, and that God is its creator, nothing else the Bible has to say will have any validity, for everything in Scripture flows from God's authority, as Creator, to rule supreme over His creation. If however, you have made it past that first great statement and are prepared to receive it, the adventure has only just begun!

One day in January, a number of years ago, I was starting my yearly journey to read the Bible through. I had traveled this path many times

---

[1]   Genesis 1:1

before. But as I was reading through Genesis' account of creation, I began to wonder, "So what does this mean to me?"

Why was it important for me to know that on the third day God created plants, and on the fourth day He created the sun, moon and stars? Couldn't it just have read, "In the beginning, God created the heavens and the earth", and left it at that? Why was it necessary for me to know the order of creation and the days? One thing I was sure of is that there was a reason. God is not random. He does not waste words.

Knowing that there was likely something wonderful to dig into, I first assembled my tools. When one begins prospecting for gold, there are certain tools that are invaluable in sifting through material to reveal treasure.

The Bible was originally written in Hebrew and Greek, so those tools included a good Hebrew/Greek concordance (I use the same *Strong's Exhaustive Concordance* I had way back in Bible college). I do have a number of good Bible commentaries, but I don't use those until I have exhausted my own study.

The Aleph-Tav

Using the Hebrew Concordance, let's take a closer look at that first sentence of Genesis.

In English, Genesis 1:1 has ten words, but in the original Hebrew, this verse has just seven words (there's that number again). A literal translation reads:

"(In the beginning) created God (et) (the heaven) and (the earth)."

Hebrew reads right to left – not left to right as English does. The fourth word in the first sentence of the Hebrew Bible is "et"[2]. It consists of the first letter of the Hebrew alphabet (Aleph), and the last letter (Tau).

John J. Parsons writes in *Hebrew for Christians*:

"In <u>Or Torah,</u> Rabbi Dov Ber, the Maggid of Mezritch, explained first words of Torah:"Bereshit Bara Elohim Et – 'In the beginning God created et'

---

2   James Strong, *The New Strong's Exhaustive Concordance of the Bible* (Nashville: T. Nelson, 1990), H853.

(Gen. 1:1). Note that 'et' is an untranslatable word used to indicate that a definite direct object is next (thus there needs to be an 'et' before the heavens and the earth). But Dov Ber points out that 'et' is spelled – Aleph-Tav, …Aleph is the first letter of the Hebrew alphabet and Tav the last, so, he reasoned, in the beginning God created the Alpeh-Tav. Since God did this before creating the heavens and the earth, the letters are considered to be the primordial 'building blocks' of all creation."[3]

Revelation 1:8 tells us Jesus is the "Alpha and Omega, the Beginning and the End" The words Alpha and Omega are the first and last letters of the Greek alphabet, and are the Greek translation of Hebrew Aleph- Tav. There is not an English equivalent for "et", but in Hebrew it is used as a connecting word, connecting what goes before with what comes after. In this case Elohim (God), with His creation.

Not only is every word of the Bible purposeful, even the language of the Bible is significant. Hebrews is the most fascinating language. It is rich in so many unique ways. Unlike English, Hebrew letters have more than just sounds. They actually have meanings, pictographs, and numeric value. Not just every word, but every letter has meaning! As one combines the meanings of each letter in a word, the definition of the word is revealed in its spelling.

I have included a Hebrew Alphabet Chart at the end of this chapter. It shows the letters, their names, meanings and numeric values. I hope it will be helpful tool for you as we go along.

Let's look now at the first letter: Aleph. The word meaning for Aleph is "first, strong". Its early pictograph resembled a bull.

When the children of Israel made the golden calf to worship, it is because of this association: Aleph means both "Lord" and "bull". The bull represents strength. Not a wild strength, like a lion, but strength that is willing to be yoked, offering itself in the service of others. When bulls were sacrificed, it represented loving the Lord with all your strength. It was also a picture of Christ offering himself for His people. The Baals (false gods, lords) of the Old Testament were often represented as bulls. But the Baals required those who served them to be sacrificed instead of themselves. Satan ever tries to first imitate, and then twist what God does.

---

3   John J. Parsons, "Hebrew For Christians", hebrew4christians.com

The meaning for Tav is "sign of the covenant", and its pictograph looks like a cross. So "et" literally translates to "first, strong sign of the covenant."

In this little word, we find the Aleph (bull or ox) and the Tav (cross) – Christ, the Humble Servant.

> *"And being found in appearance as a man,*
> *He humbled Himself and became obedient unto death,*
> *even the death of the cross." – Phil. 2:8*

When a man was walking to be crucified, he carried his own cross. The base of the cross was fixed in the ground at the place of crucifixion, so it was only the crossbeam that the man carried. He would carry this beam across his shoulders, much as an ox would carry the yoke across his shoulders. Thus, the bull or ox is a picture of Christ being the One who humbled Himself and became obedient to the death of the cross.

So right there in the very middle of the first sentence of the Bible, we see the "first, strong sign of the covenant", which is the Lord (bull) and the cross. Christ, the humble Servant, slain from the foundation of the world[4]. Isn't that amazing!

The bull and the cross. The Aleph and the Tav. The beginning and the end. Messiah -Christ. How awesome is that!

The End From The Beginning

Because there is no English equivalent for the word "et", the translators left it out, and yet, if it is allowed to remain, and it is read just as it is written in the Hebrew, the first sentence of the Bible would read:

> "In the beginning God created 'the beginning and the end',
> the heaven and the earth."

That sheds a much broader light on the text. It is a statement that is further echoed in other scriptures, making it consistent with the testimony of the Bible as a whole.

---

[4]   Rev. 13:8.

Isaiah 46:9-10 says,

"Remember the former things of old, for I Am God, there is no other;
I Am God, and there is none like Me,
Declaring the end from the beginning,
and from ancient times things that are not yet done..."

And from Isaiah 40:21,

"Have you not known? Have you not heard?
Has it not been told you from the beginning?
Have you not understood from the foundations of the earth?"

Genesis 2:4 reads:

"These are the generations of the heavens and of the earth
When they were created,
In the day that the LORD God made the earth and heavens.."

Some translations read "generations", and others read "history", but in either case, it implies more than just the past history. They had no past history on the day they were created. The word means "the whole History" – the whole story. The Hebrew word used here is "toldot", and is defined as: "Descendants, results, proceedings, generations, genealogies; account of men and their descendants; course of history; begetting or account of heaven".[5]

In the creation story, God was also giving us the history – all generations – of Heaven and earth, before it happened! It is a snapshot of all that He is going to do!

Remember, everything God instructed to be written in the record of the Bible is for a reason. There are no idle words in the Bible. Every word of God is inspired and has meaning. It is consistent with God's character and His Word that He would be declaring how it all would end, even while He was telling us how it all began. God is in total control of His creation

---

[5]   James Strong, *The New Strong's Exhaustive Concordance of the Bible* (Nashville: T. Nelson, 1990), H8435.

and always has been. Everything that has ever been thought or done was known by God before He laid the foundation of the earth. He knows, and has always known, exactly how everything would play out. There are no unforeseen circumstances, no mysteries, to Him. And He has chosen to let us in on some of His secrets.

"Surely the Lord God does nothing,
Unless He reveals His secret to His servants the prophets". – Amos 3:7NKJV

"But there is a God in heaven who reveals secrets…" – Dan. 2:28

A Day As A Thousand Years

In both the Old and New Testaments, we are told that a day with the Lord is as a thousand years, and a thousand years as a day.

"For a thousand years in Your sight are like yesterday when it is past,
and like a watch in the night." – Psalm 90:4

"But, beloved, do not forget this one thing,
that with the Lord one day is as a thousand years,
and a thousand years as one day."- 2 Peter 3:8 NKJV

When God repeats Himself, and we are told not to forget this "one thing", it would be a good idea to pay close attention. God is telling us something important about time, and about how God measures it. When Peter made this statement, he was speaking about end time events. If we want to correctly understand the prophecies from God, we need to learn to measure time the way God does.

The most obvious mention of days is found in the very first pages of the Bible. The seven days of creation. The most obvious mention of a thousand years is found in the last book of the Bible. Revelation tells us that creation will culminate in the Thousand Year reign of Christ[6].

This present mystery, of which we are a part, will be revealed when we understand the relationship between days and thousand-year periods of

---

[6]   Rev. 20:6.

time. Each day of creation is not just revealing something God did once, long ago. It reveals what God has been doing, and is presently doing, every day since creation. It also reveals what God will do next, and when! In the days of creation, God is giving us His entire plan for the ages of time.

Romans 1:20 tells us

"For the invisible things of Him from the
creation of the world are clearly seen,
Being understood by the things that are made."

As we pay close attention to the Creation story in Genesis, we will begin to see a fuller picture of God's plan for the Ages. There is a reason, and a pattern, to every moment of creation.

The Seventh Day

Concerning Time, the very first day God blessed and sanctified (set apart for holy purposes), was the seventh day, or the Sabbath. Sabbath means "rest". Genesis 2:2-3 tell us that on the seventh day, God "rested" from all His work of creation. In this context, rest does not mean to recoup after exertion, but rather to cease working. His work of creation was complete. God blessed the Sabbath, and desired that it be remembered throughout all generations. Long before the Law was given to Moses on the mountain, the Sabbath was sanctified by God. There was something God was saying to man through the Sabbath – a promise made and a hope given – that He didn't want us to ever forget.

Spiritually, of course, the Sabbath was pointing toward the rest from works that Christ, the Lord of the Sabbath, would bring to us. But a multidimensional God speaks a multidimensional word. God "is and was, and is to come"[7] – and His word has past, present and future application as well. In the Sabbath, there was something more God was trying to reveal to those who would care to look.

We know from the Creation Story, that the first week ended in a Day of Rest: The Sabbath. Revelation tells us that there is a Thousand Year time

---

[7]   Rev. 1:8

of rest coming at the end of the ages. Here again is that key correlation: a Day is as a Thousand Years, and a Thousand Years are as a Day.

Bearing all this in mind, a closer look at the seven days of creation is in order. We also need to make a careful study of each thousand-year period of time since then. This is not as daunting a task as it might first seem. Genesis records in very specific detail the exact years of time each of the key generations lived, starting with Adam and continuing until well after Jacob. The events recorded in Genesis alone span a couple of thousand years.

Without Form And Void

But before we look at the specific days of creation, let's look at the first two verses of Genesis 1, because before we get past them, we will run into our first mystery. Since we are trying to discover what God is showing us about time, we have to at least address the arguments about the age of the earth, and the seven literal days of creation.

"In the beginning God created the heaven and the earth.
And the earth was without form and void; and darkness
was upon the face of the deep. And the Spirit of God
moved upon the face of the waters." – Gen. 1:1,2

Genesis 1:1 tells us that God created everything in the beginning, but by Genesis 1:2 something seems to have gone awry. Before God speaks "light", the state of the earth is "without form and void".

The phrase "without form and void" comes from two Hebrew words: "tou bou". The phrase means "formlessness, confusion, wasteland, chaos, vanity, to be empty, a vacancy, undistinguishable ruin, emptiness, void."[8]

Yet Isaiah tells us:

"For thus says the Lord that created the heavens; God himself
that formed the earth and made it; he hath established it,
he created it not in vain, he formed it to be inhabited: I am
the LORD; and there is none else." – Isaiah 45:18

---

[8]   James Strong, *The New Strong's Exhaustive Concordance of the Bible* (Nashville: T. Nelson, 1990), H8414, H922.

This says that God did not create the world "in vain". The word used for "in vain" here is "tou", the same word used in Genesis 1. It means: "to lie waste; a desolation, a worthless thing, in confusion, empty place, without form, nothingness, naught, vain vanity, waste, wilderness."[9] Isaiah says God did not create the world in this condition. Yet, that is the condition in which we find the world at the beginning of the Genesis week. What then is the solution to this apparent contradiction?

Some believe that there is a space or gap between Genesis 1:1 and Genesis 1:2.

This theory is that after God created the heaven and earth, something went so terribly wrong that God destroyed it all and started fresh. The Genesis week is therefore the story of this new creation.

Supporting this idea are the Old Testament prophets Jeremiah, and Isaiah. Both describe the state of the earth after a cataclysmic judgment from God.

"I beheld the earth, and lo, it was without form, and void; and the heavens, and they had no light." – Jeremiah 4:23

"Behold, the Lord makes the earth empty and makes it waste, and turns it upside down, and scatters abroad the inhabitants thereof." – Isaiah 24:1

Both Genesis 1:2 and Jeremiah 4:23 use this exact phrase ("without form and void"). Two inductive Bible study methods; The Law of First Mention (which teaches that to understand a concept in its most basic form, one must study the first time it is mentioned) and the Law of Equivalence of Expression (which teaches that when an identical word or phrase is used two different places, they should be studied together), point us to the possibility that there was a former dispensation of creation which was destroyed due to evil. Both Ezek. 28:12-15 and Isa. 14:12-14 speak of the time when Satan was first created as an anointed angel, but then lost his place in heaven due to pride and rebellion. These passages could be referring to a former state of creation that predates Genesis 1:2.

We know from Job 38:4-7, that the heavenly angels were created before the earth, because we are told that they sang for joy at the creation of the

---

9   Ibid.H8414.

earth. Certainly, the fall of Lucifer seems to have predated the creation week because immediately in Genesis 3 we see him coming in the form of a serpent into the garden to lead Adam and Eve astray. Whatever happened, it happened before then for sure.

This would explain Satan's particular hatred of Adam and Eve. Especially as they were created "lower" than he[10]. If he were jealous and resentful of them being given the domain which was once his, that would be a strong motive for him wanting to destroy them. He desires to get that domain and authority back.

This theory would also explain the apparent age of the earth being much greater than 6,000 -7,000 years old, which would be its age if there were no missing gap of time. If there were a previous creation that was destroyed, and Genesis 1:2 is describing the state it fell into due to judgement, that would reconcile this problem.

However, there are some scholars who flatly reject this notion. They believe the world was created in 7 literal days (with one day of rest), and there is no gap between Genesis 1:1 and Genesis 1:2. It is important to keep in mind that in each of the camps represented by these two views are some very learned, intelligent, faith-filled people.

For myself, I believe that God created the world as we now know it, in seven literal days. The inclusion of the phrase "the morning and the evening" to define day leaves no doubt of this. I also believe that there was a previous creation which was destroyed before Genesis 1:2. This is known as the Gap theory, and Rev. C.I. Scofield, who edited the Scofield Bible, is a leading proponent of this theory. He wrote;

"Jer. 4:23-26, Isa. 24:1 and 45:18, clearly indicate that the earth had undergone a cataclysmic change as the result of a divine judgment. The face of the earth bears everywhere the marks of such a catastrophe. There are not wanting intimations which connect it with a previous testing and fall of angels."[11]

---

[10] Psalm 8:5

[11] Rev. C.I. Scofield, D.D., "Scofield Reference Edition Bible", King James Version, Genesis 1:2, footnote 3

In the end, we can only know for certain what the Bible specifically tells us. We know that God is light and in Him is no darkness at all[12]. We know that He does not create chaos, nor, according to I Corinthians 14:33 is He the author of confusion. And yet, that appears to be the state of the earth in Genesis 1:2. And that is the state of the world as Genesis 1:3 opens – beginning the week of creation. Whatever it is that we need to know in order to fulfill our purpose and calling, it can be found from Genesis 1:1 forward.

What We Know For Certain

From Genesis, we can know for certain that God created the heaven and the earth. Secondly, from the text we know that before the first day of the creation week, the world was in darkness, without form, and void. Therefore, there was a world, and water present before Genesis 1:3, which was the first day of creation, according to the text.

The Mystery of "Let There Be"

God began each day of creation with the command, "Let there be…" and there was. His will was done on earth just as He spoke it in heaven. *"And God said, "Let there be light", and there was light." – Gen. 1:3*

As I was meditating on this phrase "Let there be", a passage from John 14 came to mind.

"Let not your heart be troubled. You believe in God, believe also in Me."
- John 14:1

I have always loved this verse for the comfort Christ was offering. But to be honest I have also always struggled with it. Because my heart and mind have so often been troubled. But when Christ speaks this, He is not expressing a desire for us not to be troubled, any more than God was merely expressing a desire for a little light on the subject when He said, "Let

---

[12]   I John 1:5

there be light." It is the same God, speaking the same word. I wondered why it was that when He spoke it in Genesis, there was an explosion of light, yet when I read those words in John, I find in me only the wish that they were so. I want to share with you how God demonstrated the mystery and power of "Let there be" in my own life.

A number of years ago, I found myself in a situation that severely troubled me. I'm not proud to say that I completely lost it and was nearly on the verge of hysteria. The exact situation is not important, but it was one in which I felt very helpless and frightened. I began to rant and rave in frantic prayer, though it was much more like a terrified tantrum than prayer.

Suddenly, I felt the Holy Spirit speak to me. He said, "*Quiet yourself*". The verse that came to mind was Psalm 131:2, which speaks of quieting oneself as a weaned child would.

I would love to tell you that I immediately calmed down, but it had the opposite effect. I went from being frightened to being angry. How could the Lord be so cruel as to imply that all I needed to do was calm down? I don't know if you have noticed, but saying those words to an upset person is like throwing gasoline on a fire.

I said, "Lord, do You think I WANT to be upset? Don't You think I would be calm if I were capable of it? How am I supposed to be calm?"

Again, the gentle voice of the Holy Spirit spoke. He said, "*Choose to.*"

Choose to? Really?! I thought, "That's ridiculous! As if I could just choose how I feel!" I happened to be in the bathroom while all this was going on (the only room in the house with a lock on the door for privacy), and I remember looking into the mirror at my red, tear stained face. Just to prove to the Lord that this would not work (yet also really hoping it could work), I said, "Ok, Lord. Then I choose to!"

It was like a warm, soothing blanket suddenly descended on my spirit and engulfed my whole being! I literally felt the fear, hysteria and despair just dissolve away. It was replaced with an overwhelming sense of calm and well-being. I suddenly knew everything was going to be ok. And it was.

Because I happened to be looking in the mirror when this occurred, I saw the instant change that came over my face. I looked into my startled, wide-eyed reflection and said, "Really?! That's it?! That's really IS all I have to do? Just choose to?"

The Holy Spirit then showed me that it really is that simple, and yet it isn't. The power did not come from me choosing to obey. Rather, the power to obey came with the command. Choosing to obey is what allowed me to access the power to be calm. I had been trying to get calm for awhile, and my wanting to be calm, and trying to be calm got me nowhere. But when God tells us to do something (and He never makes suggestions, they are commands), He also imparts the power to do it. I had the power to choose to be calm, not because I wanted to, but because God told me to. With the command comes the power.

So, when God says, "Let the peace of God rule in your heart"[13], He is not making a suggestion that we be peaceful. He is also not telling us to pull ourselves together and exercise our own self-control and behave. He is speaking with the same creative, authoritative voice and power that created the universe. He is imparting peace, even in our storms. He is not just commanding, something – He is bestowing something. We must choose to receive it.

I wanted to share this with you so you would understand the personal importance of this kind of Bible study. It isn't just to learn cool things, or discover mysteries. We are meant to meditate on what we learn and ask ourselves, "So what does this mean to me? How is this to be applied to my life?" If you don't know, then ask Him! God loves to be asked questions. We used to sing with the kids in Sunday school,

"Call to Me, and I will answer you
And tell you great and unsearchable things you
do not know." – Jer. 33:3 NIV[14]

The importance of asking questions cannot be over stressed if we want to discover the hidden and wonderful truths of God. This is the system of receiving the Lord has set up.

"And I say unto you,
Ask, and it shall be given you.
Seek, and you shall find.
Knock and it shall be opened unto you." – Luke 11:9

---

[13] Col. 3:15
[14] The Holy Bible, New International Version (NIV): Biblica, Inc.(Copyright 1973,1978, 1984, 2001). All rights reserved worldwide. Used by permission.

Seven Days, Seven Ages

After getting this far in my study, I now was ready to take a closer look at the seven days of creation and line them up with the ages of Time, just to see what I would find. I honestly just went into this much like Terry Hebert went into that field in England; with curiosity, but not with any real expectation of what I would find. I didn't even know at this point whether there were seven ages or not. I just thought I'd start charting it all out and see where it would lead me.

When I say I charted it all out, I literally mean that. I made dozens and dozens of charts before I was through. I have included abbreviated versions of a few of them in this book. I'll direct you to them as they become pertinent. I started by charting out the Days of Creation, and then overlaying the thousand year periods of time.

On the charts I have included, I started the count of the Ages of Time with Adam's creation at year 1, and counted forward from there. Each Age is a thousand years. I also give the years in BC and AD. All the dates are approximate, but as near as can be figured with the information available to me.

Hebrew Alphabet Chart

Letter	Pictograph	Meaning	Numeric Value
Aleph	Ox head	Strength, Power, Leader, First	1
Beth	Tent floorplan	Tent, House, Inside, Family	2
Gimel	Camel neck	Foot, Camel, Pride, Lifted up	3
Dalet / Daleth	Door	Door, Pathway, Move through, Way of life	4
Hey / He	Man with raise arms	Behold! Show, Reveal, Breath	5
Vav / Vau	Tent peg	Secure, Hook, Add, Nail	6
Zayin	Plow	Plow, Weapon, Sword, Cut off Pierce	7
Chet / Het / Cheth	Tent wall	Outside, Divide, Half, Separation	8
Tet / Teth	Basket	Surround, Contain, Basket, Snake, Mud	9
Yud / Yod	Closed Hand	Work, Throw, Worship, Deed	10
Kaph / Kaf	Open Palm	Open, Allow, Wing, Hand,	20
Lamed	Shepherd Staff	Teach, Yoke, Bind, Control	30
Mem	Water	Chaos, Mighty, blood, Multitude	40
Nun	Seed	Continue, Heir, Son, Seed, Fish, Activity, Life	50
Samech	Thorn	Grab, Hate, Protect, Staff, Support, Prop	60
Ayin	Eye	Know, See, Experience, Understand, Fountain	70
Pey / Phe	Mouth	Mouth, Opening, Word, Speak, Here	80
Tsadhe / Tsaddi	Fish Hook	Pull in, Inescapable, Desire, Trouble, Harvest, Hunt	90
Qoph / Koph	Back of Head	Behind, Last, Final, the Least	100
Reysh / Resh	A Head	A Person, Highest, Most Important, Chief	200
Sin / Shin	Teeth	Sharp, Peak, Devour, Destroy	300
Tav / Tau	A Mark	Mark, Sign, Cross, Ownership, Seal, Covenant, Last	400

Other Resources for Hebrew Alaphabet:

Jewish Virtual Library
www.jewishvirtuallibrary.org

Hebrew 4 Christians
www.hebrew4christians.com

CHAPTER 2

DAY ONE – Light & Dark

"Then God said, 'Let there be light', and there was light.
And God saw the light, that it was good: and God divided the light from
the darkness. God called the light Day, and the darkness He called Night.
And the evening and the morning were the first day." -Genesis 1:3-5

On the first day of creation, God called forth the Light from Darkness, and divided the two. Each day ever afterward would begin in darkness, and end in light (the evening and the morning were the first day). The Biblical day is measured from evening to evening (or sundown to sundown). This differs from the way many westerners tend to think of days as being measured from morning to morning.

The fact that the days begin in darkness, and precede to light is the exact opposite of the Law of Entropy, which we observe in nature. Unless acted upon by an outside force (such as an intelligent, creative mind), all things in nature move from order to disorder. Order cannot emerge from disorder on its own; that is a scientific impossibility. People who assert that faith is anti-science, and then go on to embrace a theory that violates scientific laws are a puzzle to me. Even if you have matter (which also cannot come from nothing), nothing in this universe could exist unless something or someone (God), acted upon it to create intentional, intelligent, order. On the first day of creation, we see order and light erupting from disorder and darkness. This is a supernatural, creative act.

FIRST AGE OF TIME: THE DAY OF LIGHT AND DARK

The first thousand years of Time (which is the First Age) as recorded in Genesis, encompassed the lives of Adam, Cain, Abel, Seth and Enoch. It spanned the years of time from Adam, in year 1 of creation, until Enoch (the seventh generation from Adam) was "taken" in year 987. During those years, 9 generations were born, from Adam to Lamech, the father of Noah. You will find a Timeline of the first Day at the end of this chapter, which may help you to visualize the events of this first thousand years.

This understanding of a day as a thousand years gives greater clarity to God's warning to Adam in the garden. Adam was told not to eat of the Tree of Knowledge of Good and Evil, and that in the "day" he did so, he would die[1]. Since Adam died at the age of 930 years, long after he left the garden of Eden, some have imagined a discrepancy in scripture.

To explain this seeming discrepancy, I was taught in Bible college that what God meant was that Adam would die spiritually the day he ate of the tree. I have also heard others teach that in the day Adam ate of the tree, he was under penalty of death, so that ever after he was a "dead man walking", or as good as dead.

Both of these are true in a sense, but they are not the whole truth. God actually does mean exactly what He says. In God's economy of time, Adam actually did die the same Day he sinned. No man has ever lived to a thousand years.

I have found time and time again that seeming discrepancies in scripture are really opportunities to dig deeper, and see something I did not see before. We don't need to make excuses for God or His word, we need to study and understand it more deeply. All the clues are there.

At the end of this chapter, you will find a timeline for this First Age of Time entitled "The Days of Adam". It illustrates the first generations of Genesis and key events that define this age. I include similar timelines at the end of each chapter on the different ages.

---

[1] Gen. 2:9,15-17

The Sons of Adam: Good and Evil

Included in this period of time are the generations known as the "sons of God" and the "daughters of man"[2]. These are mentioned in Genesis 6 as a generation of people who lived on the earth prior to the Flood. This brings us to yet another mystery for us to look into.

There are two main schools of thought regarding what these terms mean. One view teaches that "sons of God" is a reference to the line of Seth, who was born to Adam and Eve after Cain killed Abel. In this theory, the "daughters of man" are actually the ungodly line of Cain, who murdered Abel. Thus the Bible is saying the ungodly daughters of Cain (daughters of man) married the godly sons of Seth (sons of God).

Certainly, the chronicle of the first thousand years focuses largely on the descendants of these two brothers. What actually happened in the first family? Why would the descendants of Cain be considered evil and those of Seth be considered godly?

Although the story is familiar to many readers, we will take a brief moment to recap. Adam and Eve, after leaving the Garden of Eden had two sons: Cain, the oldest, and Abel the youngest. As the boys grew, they chose different occupations. Cain became a farmer, and Abel became a shepherd.

"And in the process of time, it came to pass that Cain brought an offering of the fruit of the ground to the Lord.
Abel also brought the firstborn of his flock and of their fat.
And the Lord respected Abel and his offering,
but He did not respect Cain and his offering.
And Cain was very angry...
and it came to pass, when they were in the field,
that Cain rose up against Abel his brother and killed him." – Gen. 4:3-8

As a result of this first murder, Cain was banished from his family, and Eve eventually had another son, named Seth. Eve said, after the birth of Seth, *"For God has appointed another seed for me instead of Abel"*[3].

---

[2]   Gen. 6:1-4

[3]   Gen. 4:25

Apparently, Abel was murdered before either Cain or Abel had children, because Gen 4:16-17 says, *"Then Cain went out from the presence of the Lord and dwelt in the land of Nod on the east of Eden. And Cain knew his wife, and she conceived and bore Enoch."*

It was said after the birth of Seth's son, Enos *"Then men began to call on the name of the Lord"*[4]. Of both Enoch and Noah it was said that they walked with God[5]. By the way, this Enoch is not the same as Cain's son, nor Seth's son. Enoch was apparently a popular name then. The Enoch which walked with God was born in the seventh generation after Adam and was Seth's great, great, great grandson.

In the chart below, on one side we see the righteous descendants of Seth. It includes Enoch, who walked with God, and who was "taken" at around year 987. Also shown are Methuselah, who died the year of the flood; and Lamech, Noah's father, who died three years before the flood.

On the other side is seen the unrighteous descendants of Cain including Lamech (different one from Noah's father), who also committed murder. You will notice several names which were common to both lines. Notice also the "darkness" came first. Cain, who killed righteous Abel, was the firstborn.

Adam's Generations
2 Lines of Sons

Cain (murderer of Abel)	Generation #2	Seth (given instead of Abel)
Enoch	3	Enosh
Irad	4	Kenan
Mehujael	5	Mahalalel
Methushael	6	Jared
Lamech (murderer – Gen.4:23-24)	7	Enoch (walked with God – taken)
Jabel, Jubal, Tubal-Cain, Naamah	8	Methuselah (oldest man)
	9	Lamech
	10	Noah (walked with God)

---

4   Gen. 4:26

5   Gen. 5:24; 6:9

So, we see that the first thousand years (Day or Age of Time), is characterized by the separation of Light and Dark- those who walk with God and those who do not.

But there is another interpretation to what is meant by the term "sons of God".

Sons of God and Daughters of Men

The second view is that "sons of God" is a reference to angels. Fallen angels specifically. This is what the text says:

"And it came to pass, when men began to multiply on the face of the earth,
and daughters were born unto them,
that the sons of God saw the daughters of men that they were fair,
and they took them wives of all which they chose.
And the Lord said, "My Spirit shall not always strive with man,
for that he also is flesh, yet his days shall be an hundred and twenty years."

There were giants in the earth in those days, and also after that,
when the sons of God came in unto the daughters of men,
and they bare children to them,
the same became mighty men which were of old, men of renown."
— Genesis 6:1-4

This is certainly mysterious, and one of the most controversial portions of scripture in the Bible. As I said, some contend this is talking about two human families intermarrying. But others believe that a clear distinction is made in the text between humans and these sons of god. They believe this is talking about some other life form — not of the earth, intermarrying with earthly humans. Very strange indeed! Although there is controversy over what the phrase actually means, there is clearly a distinction made between "sons of God" and "daughters of men". How do we find the truth?

An important Bible study rule I have learned is: Whenever possible, let scripture interpret scripture. There are two ways to do this. The first is to define terms. We have already begun to become familiar with this tool. We go back to the original Hebrew and see exactly what words were used, and what they mean. And the second is to see where else in Scripture that word or phrase is used (the Law of Equivalence of Expression), and see what further insight that can bring. This is like assaying a sample stone, and surveying land.

Let's turn to the Strong's Exhaustive Concordance of the Bible[6] to define a couple of words and terms. The term "Sons of God" is made up of two Hebrew words:

"Sons" is from the Hebrew word "Ben". It is a masculine noun meaning "Son, grandson, child, member of a group in the widest sense of literal and figurative relationship"[7]. As one might call the founding fathers "Sons of Liberty".

"Of God" is the Hebrew word "Elohim". It is a plural masculine noun meaning "Rulers, judges, divine ones, angels, gods, works or special possessions of God, God."[8] Of the 2,606 times it is used in scripture, 2,346 times it is translated, "God" and is a direct reference to the creator God. [9]

Now that we have definitions, let's look to see where else in scripture that phrase is used.

"Now there was a day when the sons of God
Came to present themselves before the LORD,
And Satan came also among them.
And the LORD said unto Satan,
'Where are you coming from?'
Then Satan answered the LORD and said,
'From going to and fro in the earth,
And from walking up and down in it." – Job 1:6-7

"Again there was a day when the sons of God
Came to present themselves before the LORD,
And Satan came also among them
To present himself before the LORD." – Job 2:1

"Where were you when I laid the foundations of the earth?...

6   James Strong, *Strong's Exhaustive Concordance of the Bible* (Iowa Falls: World Bible Publishers).

7   James Strong, *The New Strong's Exhaustive Concordance of the Bible* (Nashville: T. Nelson, 1990), H1121.

8   Ibid. H430

9   Gen. 1:1

When the morning stars sang together,
And all the sons of God shouted for joy." – Job 38:4,7

These verses clearly refer to angelic beings that appear before the throne of God in Heaven as "sons of God". The fact that these "sons of God" sang and shouted for joy on the day God laid the foundations of the earth shows that they are not humans, as human beings had not yet been created. They are angelic beings. There can be no other understanding of them. Together with Genesis 6, these are the only instances in the Old Testament where this phrase is used.

The phrase is often used in the New Testament, however, but the language there is Greek or Aramaic, so in the King James Bible, there is no direct way to compare them. However, in the Septuagint (Greek translation of the Old Testament), the word "angels" is used in Gen. 6[10].

This phrase is used in the New Testament to refer to those who are "led by the Spirit of God."[11]. That would be a reference to people who are "born again" and now have the spirit of God. However, that condition could not exist until after Christ's atoning death and resurrection. At the time the Old Testament was being written, the phrase was ever only used to refer to angelic, or heavenly beings – never to mortals.

Are "Sons of God" Godly Men?

A verse that is often cited in support of the view that "sons of God" means godly men is Luke 3:38

> *"Which was the son of Enos, which was the son of Seth,*
> *which was the son of Adam, which was the son of God."*

They believe that what the Bible is teaching is that the sons of Adam (through Seth, Adam's godly son) were intermarrying with the daughters of Cain.

There are a couple of problems with this view. First, although Adam was called "the son of God" in Luke, he never was called that in the Old

---

[10]   ((CCAT)) Septuagint (LXX) Greek Old Testament data files, Blue Letter Bible.
[11]   Romans 8:14

Testament. To say that "sons of God" means "sons of Adam" seems to me to be a stretch. One not made anywhere else in the Old Testament. Furthermore, Cain and Seth were both sons of Adam.

The phrase is consistently used – in both the Old and New Testaments – to refer to direct creations of God. Adam was a direct creation of God, but his sons would not be, as they were born of their earthly parents; they were "sons of Adam". Angels are direct creations of God, as they are not born, but created. Those who are born again in the New Testament are called sons and daughters of God, because they are born of the Spirit and are a "new creation"[12]. Jesus is the "Son of God" because He was directly created by God, through the virgin birth – not born of an earthly man.

Are "Sons of God" Fallen Angels?

There are many Bible scholars who say, based on the Hebrew and how this phrase is used in the Old Testament, that Gen. 6 is saying that angels left their "first estate"[13] (heaven), and came down and married human women. "Giants" and "mighty men of old" are Old Testament terms referring to the resulting offspring. We will look at this more on Day 2, but this intermarrying was given as a key reason for the Great Flood of Noah's day.

The book of Jude speaks of angels who did not keep their "first estate". That phrase "first estate" comes from the Greek word "arche", and it means, "beginning, origin, that by which anything begins to be; the first place, principality, rule, authority."[14]

The same word is used in John 1:1 when he says, *"In the beginning (arche) was the Word, and the Word was with God, and the Word was God."* It is the same word translated "principalities" in Eph. 6:12:

> *"For we wrestle not against flesh and blood, but against principalities, against powers, against the rulers of the darkness of this world, against spiritual wickedness in high places."*

---

[12]   2 Cor. 5:17

[13]   Jude 1:6

[14]   James Strong, *The New Strong's Exhaustive Concordance of the Bible* (Nashville: T. Nelson, 1990), G746

The New Living Translation of the Bible puts it this way, *"For we are not fighting against flesh and blood enemies, but against evil rulers and authorities of the unseen world, against mighty powers in this dark world, and against evil spirits in the heavenly places."*[15]

Excerpts from The Book of Enoch

There is another source we can look to that might help: the Book of Enoch. Jude himself cites the Book of Enoch when speaking on this topic. The Book of Enoch, although not considered scripture, is nevertheless not only quoted in the Bible, it was widely read and accepted as truth in the first century. There are many books of science and history which, while not scripture, nevertheless contain valuable information from which we may learn.

Jude's readers would have been very familiar with the book and Jude's references to it. The phrase "sons of God" was not unique to the Bible. Ancient people would have had a definite understanding as to what the phrase meant. Here, then is what the Book of Enoch has to say on this subject:

6:1-3 "And it came to pass when the children of men had multiplied that in those days were born unto them beautiful and comely daughters and the angels, the children of heaven, saw and lusted after them, and said to one another, "Come, let us choose us wives from among the children of men, and beget us children..." (200 of them participated)

7:3 "...and they took unto themselves wives... and they became pregnant, and they bore great giants..."

15:8-12 "And now, the giants, who are produced from the spirits and flesh shall be called evil spirits upon the earth, and on the earth shall be their dwelling. Evil spirits have proceeded from their bodies, because they are born from men and from the holy Watchers is their beginning and primal origin... and the spirits of the giants afflict, oppress, destroy, attack, do battle, and work destruction on the earth, and cause trouble. They take no food, but nevertheless

---

[15]   Eph.6:12 NLT

hunger and thirst, and cause offences. And these spirits shall rise up against the children of men and against women, because they had proceeded from them."[16]

It is clear that the Book of Enoch teaches that the angels who did not keep their first estate, were fallen angels who left their place in heaven in order to mate with human women. This is Enoch's explanation of the origin of demons. They are the disembodied spirits of the giants. According to this book, these events happened during the time of Jared, the fifth generation from Adam.

Old Testament saints, as well as those in the early New Testament church, all understood the phrase "sons of God" to mean angels. The idea that this was referring to godly men did not come into vogue until the middle of the first century, many hundreds, even thousands of years after this was written.

The early church writers, including Justin Martyr, Josephus, Tertullian, and Jerome, just to name a few, all held the view that these "sons of God" were fallen angels, as did Jude.

Frederick Filby, who researched and wrote many books on this subject, concluded his discussion of the teachings of the early church fathers by stating that:

> *"...although the whole subject is mysterious, the evidence for the 'angel' interpretation is much the stronger and that it is not only consistent with the early Hebrew mode of expression, but provides the adequate impetus for that great moral decline which brought the Flood."*[17]

Jude said he wanted to remind his readers of certain things they once well knew. He then mentions these fallen angels in verse 6. Whatever our current view of the book of Enoch is, in Jude's day, it was commonly read and believed by the early church. Otherwise, it would have made no sense for Jude to cite that work in his arguments.

---

[16] Schnieders, Paul C., Charles, Robert H. *The Books of Enoch: Complete Edition—* 3rd Ed. (Las Vegas, Nev., 2012)

[17] Roger Forster & Paul Marston, *Reason & Faith: Do Modern Science and Christian Faith Really Conflict?* (Eastbourn: Monarch Publications, 1989), 358

The alternative view did not come into popularity until around the fourth century with the writings of Augustine.[18] It was around this time in history that the Book of Enoch was officially rejected from the cannon of Scripture, and thus, its views on this subject were also rejected. Robert I. Bradshaw in his work *Creationism and the Early Church* stated: *"The influence of the Book of Enoch and the popularity of the Septuagint (which translated "sons of God" as "angels") in the early church may explain why no Christian writer challenged the view that the Sons of God were angels until the third century AD."*[19]

The Nephilim

The term "Nephilim" is an Hebrew word which refers to the offspring which was produced by these fallen angels and human women. Genesis 6:4 refers to these beings as giants.

> *"There were giants in the earth in those days,*
> *And also after that,*
> *When the sons of God came in unto the daughters of men,*
> *And they bare children to them,*
> *The same became mighty men which were of old,*
> *Men of renown." – Gen. 6:4*

The word translated here as "giants" is the Hebrew word "Napil" or Nephilim (the suffix "im" in Hebrew is a plural). The word literally means "fallen ones, rebels, apostates."[20] It was translated as giants because, from many other Old Testament scriptures, it is clear that they literally were giants.

> *"And there we saw the giants,*
> *The sons of Anak,*

---

[18]   Robert I. Bradshaw, *Creationism and the Early Church*. Chapter 5 *The 'Sons of God'*. 1998.robibradshaw.com

[19]   Ibid.

[20]   James Strong, *The New Strong's Exhaustive Concordance of the Bible* (Nashville: T. Nelson, 1990), H5303

Which come of the giants:
And we were in our own sight as grasshoppers,
And so we were in their sight." – Num 13:33

"For only Og, king of Bashan, remained of the remnant of giants,
Behold, his bedstead was a bedstead of iron,
...nine cubits (13 feet) was the length thereof
And four cubits (6 feet) the breadth of it." – Deut. 3:11

"And there went out a champion out of the camp of the Philistines,
Named Goliath, of Gath, Whose height was six cubits and a span
(9.75 feet or 3 meters)." – 1 Sam. 17:4

I believe this is the true origin of the myths of gods and demigods that are found in every ancient culture and religion. So, what was actually going on in Genesis 6?

The Nature of Angels

One of the main arguments used by those who determine that "sons of God" is really a reference to sons of Adam, and not to fallen angels, is that they believe angels can't procreate. They cite Jesus as their source. But is that what He said? Let's look at what He actually said:

"For in the resurrection they neither marry, nor are given in marriage,
but are as the angels of God in heaven."- Matt. 22:30

"For when they shall rise from the dead,
they neither marry nor are given in marriage,
But are as the angels which are in heaven." – Mark 12:25

What Jesus actually said is that angels do not marry. It is a correct assumption that if the angels in Heaven do not engage in marital relations, they therefore do not procreate. However, He did not say that they are incapable of the act of procreation.

He also expressly stated that He was speaking of heavenly angels. Fallen angels engage in many activities that Heavenly angels do not. Heavenly Angels who are not fallen and remain in their "first estate" do not engage in this activity. Why?

Angels, were not meant to procreate because they are eternal, immortal, spiritual beings. Procreation was given to those who are on in the earth, and mortal (this includes plants and the animal kingdom), as a means to continue their species and fill the earth. When we are in Heaven, and in our immortal form, we will no longer engage in marriage and procreation either. Not because those are immoral activities, but because there will no longer be a need for them. We will be immortal, and we will be in perfect unity and oneness at all times. This is what Jesus taught.

When God set creation in order, He ordained that everything; every tree, plant, animal and human, was to reproduce "after its own kind". To mix species was an abomination to God. In the Old Testament Law, not even clothing was to be made of both plant and animal material.

"You shall keep My statues.
Thou shalt not let thy cattle gender with a diverse kind:
Thou shalt not sow thy field with mingled seed;
Neither shall a garment mingled of linen and woolen come upon thee."
– Lev. 16:32

What are angels? According to the Bible, they are powerful, spiritual beings. Angels can be present without being seen, or they may appear in human form when necessary. Hebrews 13:2 says that we may even interact with angels thinking they are just other humans. But despite appearing in human form, angels and humans are not the same "kind".

The Bible is clear that Heaven is a real place, where real beings exist. We know that it is possible for humans, even in the flesh, to go there because Enoch, Elisha, and Jesus were all taken there in physical form. However, in order to dwell there, it is necessary for mortal bodies to be changed, according to 1 Corinthians 15:53. Heaven must then be a place that exists in a different dimension than earth.

Angelic beings (whether they be holy or fallen) may sometimes be referred to as extra-terrestrials (by humans, not the Bible), but the truth is that they are "extra" or "trans – dimensional". They can inhabit the same room as you do without you being aware of them. But they are aware of you.

The Watchers

Daniel refers to angels as "the watchers"[21]. Psalm 91:11 tells us that they watch over us to protect us. But the book of Job indicates that there are angelic beings who are not so benign. They also watch us. These are the fallen angels, or demonic, satanic spirits. 1 Peter 1:12 indicates that angels are not only watching, but are curious about us and our relationship with the Lord.

Genesis 6:2 says that these fallen angels took wives of all they chose. The Hebrew word translated here "took" is "laqah". It literally means "to take, get, lay hold of, seize, snatch, take away."[22] The implication is that they abducted these women.

What would Satan's (and his minion's) purposes be in trying to pollute the human race, and procreating with humans? They likely had many reasons. We know Satan is motivated by a desire to be worshipped, and a lust to acquire wealth and power[23]. Even a casual study of satanic activity or worship will reveal a preoccupation with sexual perversion. Satanic worship has an emphasis on sensuality and gratification of fleshly appetites of all kinds. Satan and satanic beings seem enslaved to the need for physical sensation and gratification. Those in their power are as well.[24]

I believe that this event is what inspired the myths of gods and demigods that we find in so many cultures and religions. According to scripture, Satan has a great desire to be worshipped as God[25]. Representing themselves as beings from heaven, and as gods, these fallen creatures deceived and seduced humans into worshipping them.

---

[21] Daniel 4:13,17,23
[22] James Strong, *The New Strong's Exhaustive Concordance of the Bible* (Nashville: T. Nelson, 1990), H3947
[23] Isa. 14:12-15
[24] Eph. 2:2-3
[25] Isa. 14:13-14

But, probably the most compelling motivation Satan would have had stems from the prophecy against him spoken by the Lord in the Garden of Eden:

> *"And the LORD God said unto the serpent,*
> *'Because you have done this, you are cursed above all cattle,*
> *And above every beast of the field...*
> *And I will put enmity between you and the woman,*
> *And between your seed and her seed,*
> *And it shall bruise your head,*
> *And you shall bruise his heel." – Gen. 3:14-15*

Perhaps Satan foolishly thought that if he could pollute the human race with his own "seed", this prophecy could not be fulfilled. Or perhaps he realized that, as a woman does not have "seed", that God was planning to send His own Son, born through the woman, and this Son would destroy all the kingdom of Satan.

Satan always tries to get there first, and by doing so, to thwart God's plan. He did so with Abraham, beguiling him into creating a son through a surrogate, rather than waiting on the Lord to fulfill His promise of giving them a son. The resulting brokenness and hurt this act did to his family is still being played out in the world today through the hatred between the descendants of Ishmael (Islamic nations) and those of Isaac (Israel). He did so with David, tempting him many times to take the crown promised him through his own effort. He did so with Christ in the wilderness, and again in the garden, hoping to prevent Him from securing the kingdom. He tempted Christ with the possibility of receiving the kingdom without suffering. One thing we can be sure of, whenever God makes a promise to us, and singles us out for blessing, Satan will try to get there first and cause us to question, doubt or even act against that promise. Abraham thought he was helping God fulfill His promise, instead his actions delayed it by many years.

Whichever view one holds (that sons of God are fallen angels, or that they are godly men), the point remains that this first Day of Time was dominated by two opposing groups of people, who could also be characterized as "dark and light".

Day 1 - The Days of Adam

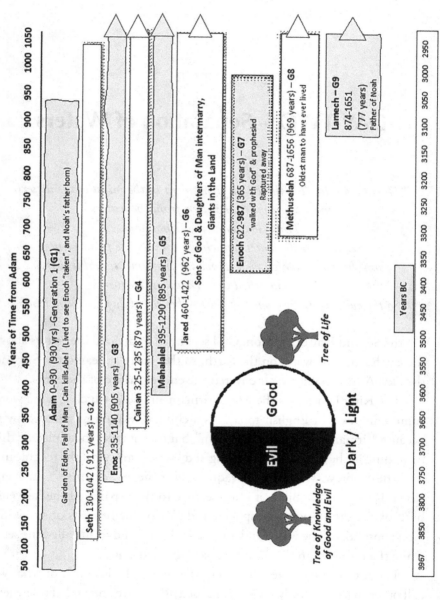

Years of Time from Adam

50 100 150 200 250 300 350 400 450 500 550 600 650 700 750 800 850 900 950 1000 1050

Adam 0-930 (930 yrs) –Generation 1 (G1)
Garden of Eden, Fall of Man, Cain kills Abel (Lived to see Enoch "taken", and Noah's father born)

Seth 130-1042 (912 years) – G2

Enos 235-1140 (905 years) – G3

Cainan 325-1235 (879 years) – G4

Mahalalel 395-1290 (895 years) – G5

Jared 460-1422 (962 years) – G6
Sons of God & Daughters of Man intermarry, Giants in the Land

Enoch 622-987 (365 years) – G7
"walked with God" & prophesied
Raptured away

Methuselah 687-1656 (969 years) – G8
Oldest man to have ever lived

Lamech – G9
874-1651
(777 years)
Father of Noah

Tree of Knowledge of Good and Evil

Tree of Life

Evil   Good

Dark / Light

Years BC

3967 3850 3800 3750 3700 3650 3600 3550 3500 3450 3400 3350 3300 3250 3200 3150 3100 3050 3000 2950

CHAPTER 3

DAY TWO – Separation of Waters

"Then God said, 'Let there be a firmament in the midst of the waters,
and let it divide the waters from the waters.'
Thus God made the firmament,
and divided the waters which were under the firmament
from the waters which were above the firmament; and it was so.
And God called the firmament Heaven.
So the evening and the morning were the second day." – Gen. 1:6-8

On the Second Day of creation, God separated or divided the waters above the earth from the water on the earth, so that there appeared the Sea and the Sky. At this point, water covered the entire surface of the earth.

The King James uses the word "firmament" here, which is not a word commonly used in English today. As a child, I was always puzzled by it because "firmament" sounds like "firm", but then it talks about placing this firm thing in the sky. It was confusing and I wasn't sure what the text meant.

The Hebrew word here is "raqia" and it means "expanse"[1]. In every case it is used in the Bible, it is a reference to the expanse of the heavens, both of the sky in our atmosphere, and also of the heavens of space. So God consolidates the water under the skies into liquid form called the seas, while the moisture in the air becomes cloud and mist.

The text also indicates that there is water in the heavens, or what we call outer space. It is only recently that scientists have concluded that there

---

[1]   James Strong, *The New Strong's Exhaustive Concordance of the Bible* (Nashville: T. Nelson, 1990), H7549

is an abundance of water in space, counter to what had been believed and taught for many years.[2]

THE SECOND AGE OF TIME: THE DAY OF WATERS

In prophetic language, waters symbolically represent the nations or peoples of the earth.

> *"And he said unto me, The waters which you saw, ...*
> *are peoples, and multitudes, and nations, and tongues." – Rev. 17:15*

In this second Age of Time, there were two main divisions that took place. First, we see the whole world covered in water by the Great Flood of Noah's time. The Second division was that of nations and tongues.

Noah was born 1056 years from Adam, and the Great Flood occurred in the year 1656. This could be thought of as mid-day of the Second Day or Age. Please refer to the Day Two – The Days of Noah chart at the end of this chapter.

Just as on the second day of creation God divided the waters on the earth from the waters above the earth, in the second thousand years of History, God used the Flood to divide the sons of God (waters from the heavens), from intermarrying with mankind (waters of earth).

Secondly, we see the division of nations and languages at the Tower of Babel. We cannot pinpoint the exact time this happened, but we are told:

> *"And unto Eber were born two sons:*
> *the name of one was Peleg;*
> *for in his days was the earth divided." – Gen. 10:25*

The name Peleg literally means "division"[3]. Peleg was born 1756 years from Adam, and died in year 1996. Since he was named in commemoration

---

2   Orbital Today.com; *"Is There Water in Space? An Extensive FAQ"*- Orbital Today (Oct. 8, 2022)

3   James Strong, *The New Strong's Exhaustive Concordance of the Bible* (Nashville: T. Nelson, 1990), H6389.

of the division of nations, it likely happened around the year 1756 from Adam. This would be roughly 2,500 BC.

In the same Age, there was the emergence of nations (symbolically "waters"), and the division of peoples through the confusion of languages. People now began to spread over the earth and fill it.

So, we see that the Second Day or Age of Time (second 1,000 years of time), was literally and figuratively characterized by water covering the earth (the Great Flood), and the division of waters, which symbolically are the nations. If one had taken a snapshot of the earth on the second day of creation, and in the second Age of Time, they would have looked identical: nothing but sky and sea.

Let's take a closer look at these two events.

The Great Flood

"And it came to pass, when men began to multiply on the face of the earth,
and daughters were born unto them,
That the sons of God saw the daughters of men that they were fair;
and they took them wives of all which they chose.
And the Lord said, My spirit shall not always strive with man, for that
he also is flesh: yet his days shall be an hundred and twenty years.

There were giants in the earth in those days; and also after
that, when the sons of God came in unto the daughters of
men, and they bare children to them, the same became mighty
men which were of old, men of renown. – Gen. 6:1-4

In the last chapter, we discussed at length Gen. 6:1-4, in which the state of humanity just before the Flood is described. The view that fallen angels intermarried with mankind, thus corrupting the human race, explains another strange phrase used in Gen.6:9 where it says that Noah was a man "perfect in his generation".

"But Noah found grace in the eyes of the LORD.
These are the generations of Noah: Noah was a just man, and perfect
in his generations, and Noah walked with God." – Gen. 6:8-9

The Hebrew word translated "perfect" here means: "complete, whole, sound, healthful, unimpaired, innocent, having integrity, what is complete or entirely in accord with truth"[4]. This word occurs 91 times in Scripture and is variously translated as: "without blemish, perfect, upright, without spot, uprightly, whole, sincerely, complete, full". The text is not implying that Noah was perfect, as no human being could be. Neither is this a commentary on his character, though in the same passage we are also told that Noah was a "just man" (lawful, righteous), and that he walked with God.

When we are told Noah was perfect, it was in reference to his "generations". It means Noah's family was not corrupted by this intermingling of different kinds of blood. One thing God insisted on, from the very beginning, was that everything should reproduce "after its own kind". The mixing of fallen angles and men in marriage would be an abomination.

In verse 5, directly after we were told about the sons of god intermarrying with the daughters of men, the Bible says:

> "And GOD saw that the wickedness of man was great in
> the earth, And that every imagination of the thoughts of
> his heart was only evil continually." – Gen. 6:5

It is clear from the text that there is a connection between this wickedness and the intermarrying. It is also clear that this event was a compelling factor in God's decision to send the flood. Noah's non-contamination by this intermarrying, and lawlessness, was expressly given as the reason he was selected to be spared and to preserve humankind.

The result of the fallen creatures intermarrying with humans was a world filled with violence, depravity and evil. Whatever was going on, it not only corrupted the human race, but the animal kingdom as well. We know this because God found it necessary to not only cleanse the world of the human race, but also of all the land creatures, and even birds. God declared:

> "And behold, I, even I, do bring a flood of waters upon the earth
> To destroy all flesh, wherein is the breath of life, from under heaven,

---

[4]   James Strong, *The New Strong's Exhaustive Concordance of the Bible* (Nashville: T. Nelson, 1990), H8549.

and everything that is in the earth shall die...
All in whose nostrils was the breath of life,
of all that was in the dry land, died." - Genesis 6:17, 22

The Apostle Paul wrote in Ephesians 2:2 that Satan is "the prince of the power of the air, the spirit that now works in the children of disobedience." The Flood, intended to cleanse this evil from the earth, was targeted specifically at "all in whose nostrils was the breath of life". It is no coincidence that those who breathed air were also those who came under the satanic influence of the prince of the power of the air.

Hybrid Creatures

In the mythology of every ancient culture, the so-called gods which came down to earth and intermarried with humans, were often depicted as being part human and part animal. Among them are the jackal headed Anubis, and the cat headed Bast of Egypt. There were hybrid beings such as the minotaur (man's body with a bull's head), the centaur (part man, part horse), and the satyr (part man, part goat). According to the book of Enoch, the corruption of creation by fallen angels was not limited to humans, but also violated animals and birds. This (according to the book of Enoch) was why even the animal kingdom had to be wiped clean.

Jesus told us that in the end times (in which we are living, as we shall see), it would again be "as in the days of Noah".

"And as it was in the days of Noah,
So shall it be also in the days of the Son of man." – Luke 17:26

Whatever was going on then, will be going on now.

I do not believe that it is coincidental that the subject of otherworldly beings interfering with mankind is gaining popularity and credence. Whatever one's thoughts are on the subject, there can be no argument that the topic is widely known in every culture of the world, and is widely accepted as truth by the majority of people in this country. In a poll done by The Pew Research Center and published in June of 2021 it was stated:

"As an unprecedented U.S. intelligence report brings new attention to the phenomenon of unidentified flying objects, about two-thirds of Americans (65%) say their best guess is that intelligent life exists on other planets, …A smaller but still sizable share of the public (51%) says that UFOs reported by people in the military are likely evidence of intelligent life outside Earth. "[5]

Deception

The Bible tells us that the predominate characteristic of Satan is that he is a deceiver. Jesus said of him;

> *"He was a murderer from the beginning,*
> *And abode not in the truth, because there is no truth in him.*
> *When he speaks a lie, he speaks of his own,*
> *For he is a liar, and the father of it."* – John 8:44

Satan, the "prince of this world"[6], is a master deceiver, and he controls the narrative the world believes. As Prince of the power of the Air, he also controls the airwaves, and the media which passes through it. He is the original Spin Doctor. We cannot trust to appearances. He has even attempted to appear as an angel of light[7], but he is all darkness.

Whatever was really going on in Noah's time, and in ours, one thing we can be certain of is that the enemy is lying to the world about it. Just as these beings represented themselves as sons of God in Noah's day, there is a growing deception about other worldly beings in our time. I believe these are not beings from some other world, but from another dimension. The Bible clearly teaches that our world is regularly visited by both demonic, and angelic beings. These are not gods, for there is only one God. However, they are beings superior in strength, knowledge and age to humans.

Equally troubling is the genetic pollution of species. Scientists are experimenting with DNA splicing of plants, to create new, hybrid species.

---

[5]   Courtney Kennedy & Arnold Lau, www. Pewresearchcenter.org. (June 30,2021)
       "Most Americans Believe in Intelligent Life Beyond Earth"
[6]   John 12:31; 14:30; 16:11.
[7]   2 Cor. 11:14.

Much of our food supply now is grown from hybridized plants and seeds (GMOs). One study stated "It is estimated that up to 80% of processed foods contain GMOs."[8] There have even been successful efforts to splice plant and animal DNA, as well as human/animal DNA. The fields of cloning, AI and even transhumanism are among the most prolific studies in science today. I'm not saying all these things are evil, though some are. I can't always tell where the lines are concerning what is good advancement, what is dangerous, and that is part of the problem. I'm not sure anyone really knows.

Where there is deception, there is confusion. Confusion is always a hallmark of Satan's handiwork. There was certainly confusion of the natural order in Noah's day, and in our day as well. Today people are confused over climate change, medicine, politics, ethnicity and even gender! We are definitely confused over truth and what it even means. Lines are being blurred in every area of society. What we used to prosecute, we now defend and celebrate. All of these things involve confusion of the natural order and a turning upside down of ancient mores.

The prophet Isaiah, speaking of conditions in the end times wrote:

"We know we have rebelled and have denied the LORD.
We have turned our backs on our God.
We know how unfair and oppressive we have been,
Carefully planning our deceitful lies.
Our courts oppose the righteous,
And justice is nowhere to be found.
Truth stumbles in the streets and honesty has been outlawed.
Yes, truth is gone, and anyone who renounces evil
is attacked." – Isa. 59:13-15 NLT

"Woe to them that call evil good, and good evil.
That put darkness for light, and light for darkness.
That put bitter for sweet, and sweet for bitter!" – Isa. 5:20

In our day, as in Noah's time, deception and confusion rule in nearly every arena to a profound degree. What used to be given and obvious is now doubted and denied. Truth is now considered subjective, and each person can decide on their own truth.

---

8   Are GMOs in My Food? Farm Aid 2016, www.farmaid.org

We will look more closely at all this on Day Six, but clearly, whatever was going in Noah's day, the result was a creation so corrupted that God could allow neither the human race, nor the animal kingdom, to continue as it was. And it will happen again in our time.

The Seventeenth Day of the Seventh Month

Before we leave the discussion of Noah, I want to point out another wonderful gem hidden in the story of the Great Flood. Bear in mind, every detail in Scripture is full of meaning, even down to the days and dates on which events occur.

Genesis 6 and 7 tell the story of how God instructed Noah to build an ark that would preserve the lives of his family and of every kind of animal from the flood that was coming. The ark is symbolic of Christ, who saves all who enter in to the salvation He offers.

"I am the door. By Me if any man enter in,
He shall be saved, and shall go in and out and find pasture." – John 10:9

Noah entered the ark and passed safely through the flood waters to a new life. This is symbolic of those who enter Christ and follow Him in baptism into a new life.

"...those who disobeyed God long ago
when God waited patiently while Noah was building his boat.
Only eight people were saved from drowning in that terrible flood.
And that water is a picture of baptism, which now saves you,
not by removing dirt from your body,
but as a response to God from a clean conscience.
It is effective because of the resurrection of Jesus
Christ." – 1 Peter 3:20-21 NLT

We are told in Gen. 7:11 that Noah and all his family entered the ark in "the second month, the seventeenth day of the month." Referring back to our Hebrew calendar, you may recall that there are two first months. However, the system of the Hebrew religious calendar was not instigated until the first

Passover at the time of the Exodus in Moses' day. At the time of Noah, there was only one calendar in use. On that calendar, the first month, in which the new year is celebrated, is the month *Tishri*, which occurs in Sept/Oct. The second month of the yearly calendar is *Cheshvan* (Oct./Nov.).

Scripture then goes on to tell us that it rained for forty days and nights. The waters rose continually until they covered even the highest mountains. For one hundred and fifty days (five months) the ark sailed on an endless sea, unbroken by any sign of land. Visually, it was just like the second day of Genesis.

"And the waters returned from off the earth continually,
And after the end of the hundred and fifty days the waters were abated.
And the ark rested in the seventh month,
On the seventeenth day of the month,
Upon the mountains of Ararat." – Gen. 8:3-4

The seventh month is the month *Nisan*.

After 40 days, Noah opened the window of the ark and sent out a raven and a dove, which returned to him, finding no place to rest[9]. After another seven days, Noah sent the dove out again.

"And he stayed yet another seven days,
and again he sent forth the dove out of the ark. And the dove came in to
him in the evening. And lo, in her mouth was an olive leaf plucked off.
So Noah knew that the waters were abated from off the earth." – Gen. 8:11

Even to this day the dove with an olive branch in its beak is a symbol of peace and hope.

Why is it important for us to know the exact day the ark "rested" after the flood? What else happened, historically, on the seventeenth day of Nisan? Asking questions like these is key to unlocking all kinds of hidden treasure, and this instance is no exception.

But I'm not going to show you just yet. If you're like me, this will probably drive you crazy, but there is a reason why we aren't going to chase that down right now. I promise we will return to it, and I hope you will find it as thrilling as I did.

---

[9]   Gen.8:6-9

For now, just make note of that date: the 17th of Nisan, and its association with coming out of the flood and the beginning of a new life. Keep it in mind. We will see it again in the Days to come.

Nimrod And The Tower of Babel

The second major division of the second age of time is described in Genesis 11. There we find the account of the Tower of Babel. After the great flood, the whole earth spoke one common language. Perhaps as they discussed the cataclysmic event that had so recently nearly wiped out the entire population of earth, they began to thank they should do something to prevent God from doing such a thing again. They decided that they should build a tower.

It could be they thought if they got high enough, they could survive any future flood. It is clearly stated however that their motive was to "*build a city and a tower whose top is in the heavens; let us make a name for ourselves, lest we be scattered abroad over the face of the whole earth.*" (Gen. 11:4).

Now the Lord had given them a command to be fruitful and fill the earth. It seems clear that their whole action and intent was to defy the command of God. God decided to help them obey.

> *And the LORD said, "Indeed the people are one and they all*
> *have one language, and this is what they begin to do.*
> *Now nothing that they propose to do will be withheld from them.*
> *Come, let Us go down and there confuse their language,*
> *that they may not understand one another's speech."*
> *So the LORD scattered them abroad from there over the face of all the earth,*
> *and they ceased building the city.*
> *Therefore its name is called Babel,*
> *because there the LORD confused the language of all the earth;*
> *and from there the LORD scattered them abroad over*
> *the face of all the earth. – Gen. 11: 6-9 NKJV*

Genesis 10:5 tells us that God separated them into their lands, according to their languages, families and nations. If you look at the Days of Noah Chart at the end of this chapter, you will notice that it only took the people of the earth 101 years after the Flood to get into such a state that God had to separate us once again!

God did not step in because there was ever any real danger of man reaching into heaven (the highest heaven, the abode of God) through their own efforts. Note that the Lord had to "go down" to deal with them. The Lord must ever always stoop down to deal with us, His ways are far higher. The Lord did not stop them in order to save Heaven from men. He stepped in to save men from themselves. Basically, He said, "If this is what they are beginning to do, there is nothing they won't do." He separated them to keep them from turning back into the society He had to destroy in the flood.

What made people decide to build this tower? Who put them up to it, and why did they go along with it? We have a likely answer in Genesis 10.

> *"Now this is the genealogy of the sons of Noah: Shem, Ham, and Japheth. And sons were born to them after the flood...*
> *The sons of Ham were Cush, Mizraim, Put, and Canaan... Cush begot Nimrod, and he began to be a mighty one in the earth.*
> *He was a mighty hunter before the Lord,*
> *Therefore it is said, 'Like Nimrod the mighty hunter before the Lord.'*
> *And the beginning of his kingdom was Babel." – Gen. 10:1, 6-10*

Although individuals are certainly capable of all kinds of mischief and depravity, it reaches a whole new level when they band together under a magnetic, unifying leader. Unity without righteousness is a very great evil and has led to the worst atrocities mankind has ever perpetrated.

Nimrod was the third generation from Noah, but he was born to Ham after his other sons, and at the same time the fourth generation was being born (we'll see the significance of this when we come to the fourth day). You can see him on the Days of Noah Chart. He was the first world ruler, uniting the earth under one government, one language, one purpose and one religion.

The name "Nimrod" means "rebellion, mighty one"[10]. The Bible says he was a "mighty hunter before the Lord". This sounds nice, until you dig a little deeper and understand what that really means.

---

[10] James Strong, *The New Strong's Exhaustive Concordance of the Bible* (Nashville: T. Nelson, 1990), H5248.

The word translated "mighty" here is the Hebrew word "gibor". It means "strong, mighty, champion, chief, giant"[11]. It is the same world used in Gen. 6:4 of the giants where it calls them "mighty men of old, men of renown". The Bible tells us there were giants in the land before the flood, and also afterward. It is possible that Nimrod was somehow connected with these fallen creatures. It is certain that he was of the same spirit and mind as they, as we shall see.

James Boice, in his commentary states,

> *"This is not talking about Nimrod's ability to hunt wild game. He was not a hunter of animals. He was a hunter of men – a warrior."*[12]

Chuck Smith, in his commentary on this portion of scripture writes,

> *"It should be translated, 'he was a mighty tyrant in the face of the Lord'. The hunting was the hunting of men's souls. Nimrod became a leader in apostasy, developer of a great religious system later to become known as the Babylonian religious system, or "mystery Babylon". That whole religious system was begun by Nimrod... it was he who inspired the people to build this tower that would reach into haven... the tower really was literally not to reach into heaven, but the tower was to worship. It was an observatory where they would go and worship the stars, the constellations and so forth. And many such towers have been uncovered in the archaeological diggings there in the Babylonian plain."*[13]

Joshua 10:13 and 2 Samuel 1:18 both make mention of *The Book of Jasher*, referencing it as an historical record of early times. It fills in some additional details about Nimrod. According to Jasher, Nimrod was very long lived, ruling from the time of the Tower of Babel until the days of Esau. This is very plausible considering Eber, of the same generation, lived to be 464 years old (see the Days of Noah Chart).

---

[11]   Ibid. H1368.

[12]   Boice, James Montgomery "Genesis: An Expositional Commentary" Volumes 1,2, and 3 (Grand Rapids, Michigan: Zondervan, 1987)

[13]   Smith, Chuck, Verse by Verse Study of Gen. 10-12 (C2000), Blue Letter Bible Commentaries.

Here are a few excerpts from the *Book of Jasher* regarding Nimrod:

"And Cush, the son of Ham, the son of Noah, took a wife in those days
In his old age, and she bare a son, and they called his name Nimrod...
At that time the sons of men began to rebel and transgress against God,
And the child grew up, and his father loved him exceedingly,
for he was the son of his old age...
And he became their lord and king, and they all dwelt with him in the city
of Shinar, and Nimrod reigned in the earth over all the sons of Noah,
and they were all under his power.
And all the earth was of one tongue and words of union,
but Nimrod did not go in the ways of the Lord, and
he was more wicked than all the men that were before
him, from the days of the flood until those days.
And he made gods of wood and stone, and he bowed down to them,
and he rebelled against the Lord, and taught all his subjects
and the people of the earth his wicked ways...
And Terah, the son of Nahor, prince of Nimrod's host,
was in those days very great in the sight of the king and his subjects,
and the king and princes loved him, and they elevated him very high...
and the wife of Terah conceived and bare him a son in those days.
Terah was seventy years old when he begat him, and Terah called the name
of his son that was born to him 'Abram' because the king had raised him in
those days, and dignified him above all his princes that were with him."
– Jasher 7:23, 45-47, 49-51[14]

This account agrees with scripture in that Abraham was born to Terah when Terah was seventy[15]. The name "Abram" means "exalted father or prince"[16], so it is feasible that Terah served in some high capacity in Nimrod's court. God called Abram out of Ur of the Chaldees[17], which was part of the kingdom of Babel, over which Nimrod ruled.

---

[14] The Book of Jasher, Copyright 2009 by IAP, Printed in Scotts Valley, Ca – USA, Anonym.

[15] Gen. 11:26

[16] James Strong, *The New Strong's Exhaustive Concordance of the Bible* (Nashville: T. Nelson, 1990), H87

[17] Gen. 11:31

The book of Joshua in the Bible also verifies that Terah was an idolater:

"And Joshua said to all the people,
'Thus says the LORD God of Israel:
Your fathers, including Terah, the father of Abraham
And the father of Nahor,
Dwelt on the other side of the River in old times,
And they served other gods." – Joshua 24:2

The book of Jasher also lends greater insight to the phrase in Gen. 11:28, *"And Haran died before his father Terah in his native land, in Ur of the Chaldeans."* According to Jasher, Terah betrayed his son Haran (father of Lot and Sarah), to Nimrod, resulting in Haran being executed in front of his father. The word translated "before" his father could certainly be translated to mean "in front of", not just previous to his father[18]. In fact, it was this incident that led to Terah taking his family and fleeing Ur.

It is certain that it was Nimrod who led the people of the earth to unite together in one purpose: to build the tower of Babel. Here is what the book of Jasher has to say about that:

"And the building of the tower was unto them a transgression and a sin…
and whilst they were building against the Lord God of heaven,
they imagined in their hearts to war against
him (in retaliation for the Flood)
and to ascend into heaven.
And all these people and all the families divided themselves into three parts:
The first said, 'We will ascend into heaven and fight against Him'.
The second said, 'We will ascend into heaven
and place our own gods there and serve them.'
And the third part said, 'We will ascend into heaven
and smite Him with bows and spears.'
And God knew all their works and all their
evil thoughts, and He saw the city,
and the tower which they were building." – Jasher 9:25-26

---

[18] James Strong, *The New Strong's Exhaustive Concordance of the Bible* (Nashville: T. Nelson, 1990), H6440

This sounds very much like the words of Lucifer recorded in Isaiah:

"How you are fallen from heaven,
O Lucifer, son of the morning!
How you are cut down to the ground,
You who weakened the nations!
For you have said in your heart:
'I will ascend into heaven,
I will exalt my throne above the stars of God;
I will also sit on the mount of the congregation
On the farthest sides of the north;
I will ascend above the heights of the clouds,
I will be like the Most High.'" – Isaiah 14:12-14

The spirit that moved Nimrod and the nations to build Babel was certainly the same as that of the fallen sons of God, whose interference with man first produced the mighty men of old before the flood. It seems likely this is where the "also afterward" of Genesis 6:4 occurred, as the same phrase is used of both the giants and Nimrod.

As in the days of Noah, there is now once again a great push to conquer space. The desire to not only explore the solar system, but even to colonize it, is a very popular idea today. It is possible that the tower of Babel was not a building whose height reached space, but a tower whose purpose was to look into the heavens. Not just to observe the heavens, but to somehow serve as a base from which the heavens could be conquered. That is what their stated purpose was. I am not suggesting that all space exploration is somehow evil, but I am noticing that in Noah's day, mankind was very interested in and occupied with the idea of conquering space, and so are we in this day and age. I do note that in Scripture, the Lord God gave the earth to man, not the outer heavens. When we travel into the outer heavens, we leave our allotted domain and travel into territory which God never gave to us. When the Bible talks about "trespasses", this is what it means: that someone has gone beyond their rightful boundary and ventured into territory (spiritual, emotional or physical) that they have no right to be in.

The point of all this is that in the days of Noah, the whole earth was united under one despotic world ruler. They had a one world government, one religious system, one purpose, and one language. Jesus says that just before His return the world would again find itself "as in the days of Noah"[19]. We will not go into a study of it here, but the New Testament, and especially the book of Revelation, speaks of a one-world ruler who will arise and unite the earth under a one-world government. He is called the Anti-Christ, and the Beast. He will also instigate a one-world religion under the leadership of the False Prophet, and establish the mark of the beast. He will be a man possessed by the Dragon, who is identified as Satan[20].

This is what the world was like in the days of Noah, and it will be again.

To summarize, in the second day of creation there was division of waters (above and below), and water covered the earth. And so it was in the second age of time: the days of Noah.

---

[19]   Matt. 24:37, Luke 17:26
[20]   Rev. 12:9; 13:2

Day 2 - The Days of Noah

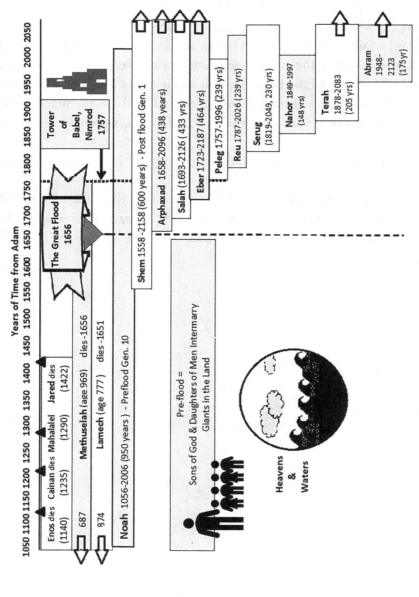

Heavens & Waters

Pre-flood =
Sons of God & Daughters of Men Intermarry
Giants in the Land

Years of Time from Adam

1050 1100 1150 1200 1250 1300 1350 1400 1450 1500 1550 1600 1650 1700 1750 1800 1850 1900 1950 2000 2050

Enos dies (1140)
Cainan dies (1235)
Mahalalel (1290)
Jared dies (1422)
Methuselah (age 969) dies -1656
Lamech (age 777) dies -1651
Noah 1056-2006 (950 years) - Preflood Gen. 10
687
874

The Great Flood 1656

Tower of Babel, Nimrod 1757

Shem 1558 -2158 (600 years) - Post flood Gen. 1
Arphaxad 1658-2096 (438 years)
Salah (1693-2126 (433 yrs)
Eber 1723-2187 (464 yrs)
Peleg 1757-1996 (239 yrs)
Reu 1787-2026 (239 yrs)
Serug (1819-2049, 230 yrs)
Nahor 1849-1997 (148 yrs)
Terah 1878-2083 (205 yrs)
Abram 1948-2123 (175yr)

Approx Years B.C.

2950 2900 2850 2800 2750 2700 2650 2600 2550 2500 2450 2400 2350 2300 2250 2200 2150 2100 2050 2000 1950

CHAPTER 4

DAY THREE- Land and Seed

"And God said, Let the waters under the heaven
be gathered together unto one place,
and let the dry land appear: and it was so.
And God called the dry land Earth;
and the gathering together of the waters called he Seas:
and God saw that it was good.
And God said, Let the earth bring forth grass,
the herb yielding seed, and the fruit tree yielding fruit after his kind,
whose seed is in itself, upon the earth: and it was so.
And the earth brought forth grass, and herb yielding seed after his kind,
and the tree yielding fruit, whose seed was in itself, after his kind:
and God saw that it was good.
And the evening and the morning were the third day." – Gen. 1:9-13

On the third day of creation, God caused dry land to appear out of the seas. It took Science thousands of years to discover what God told us in the first chapter of the Bible. The first life on earth came up from the seas. He not only created all plant life, but specifically designed it so that everything would reproduce "after its own kind", through its seed. I feel confident that in another thousand years Science will have discovered this truth as well, although currently they are still stumped on life evolving from one kind into another. The key words for this day are: seas, land, seed.

Three is the number associated with resurrection life, and with the Holy Spirit, who is the third person of the Trinity. Jonah came out of the whale on the third day. Christ rose from the grave on the third day. On the third day of creation, land came up out of the seas, and plants came up out of the ground.

THE THIRD AGE OF TIME: THE DAY OF LAND AND SEED

In the Third Age of Time, a man named Abram was born into the kingdom ruled by Nimrod. At the age of seventy-five, Abram was called to leave his nation and go to a land that God would show him. (See Day 3: The Days of Abraham, Moses and Judges Chart). Remember, the seas represent nations, and Abraham was called to come out and be separate from the nations. To him, God promised a "seed" (or offspring), and land. So in this thousand years, God is establishing this seed of Abraham in the promised land. This is the emergence of the nation of Israel. First the seas, then the land. First the nations, then the seed of Israel. First the land, then the Promised Land.

Just as an interesting note; studying Day 3-The Day of Abraham, Moses and the Judges Chart, we see that Abraham, through whom the nation of Israel would be born, was born in the year 1948 from Adam. I do not think it is coincidental that the modern nation of Israel was born in the year 1948 from Christ, the "second Adam"[1]. It is astonishing and wonderful to see the sovereign hand of God even in the timing of events in human history.

This Third Day begins with Abram being called out of the nations in the year 2023 (from Adam) to a land that God would show him. Later God establishes His covenant with Abraham and promises him all the land he walks through, and also promises that it will belong to his seed forever.

"Now the Lord had said unto Abram, Get out of your country,
and from your kindred, and from your father's house,
and go to a land that I will shew you."– Gen. 12:1-3

"And the Lord said unto Abram, …
all the land which you see, to you will I give it,
and to your seed forever…– Gen.13:14-17

---

[1]   1 Cor. 15:45

"I will take you from among the nations, gather you out of all countries, and bring you into your own land." – Ezekiel 36:24

The verses from Ezekiel are referring to God's re-gathering of Israel after they had gone into captivity, but they clearly establish that God's intent concerning the nation of Israel is that they were to be a seed that He would separate from the nations and plant in the land He promised to them.

After Abraham dies, four generations pass, and then the family of Israel (for it was not yet a nation), goes into the land of Egypt. There they multiply and serve Pharaoh for four more generations. Then, 430 years after God confirmed the covenant with Abraham, God sent Moses to lead the children of Israel out of Egypt and into the Promised Land[2]. The Exodus occurred around the year 2463 from Adam. (See "Calculating the Year of the Exodus" at the end of this chapter).

In this Age God called Abraham out of Ur, Jacob out of Syria, and Israel out of Egypt. It was a millennia of establishing a Seed in the Land. It would encompass the times of Abraham, Isaac, Jacob, the birth of the patriarchs of the 12 Hebrew tribes. It is the time of Moses and the 2nd "calling out" of the children of Israel into the Promised Land. It encompassed the establishment of Israel as a nation through The Times of the Judges, which was a span of 450 years[3] from Moses through Samuel, who ruled Israel after the death of Joshua and Moses.

During all this time, the two main things that we see happening are the establishment of a "seed" (nation of Israel) in a "land" (Promised land of Israel). Just like what God did in the third day of creation. Isn't that amazing?!

There are so many amazing events that occurred on this Day of Time. We will discuss some of them in Part 2 of this book, but for now, I have chosen to just focus on highlighting the broad themes of the Land and the Seed. All of the stories from this Age are about how God planted the seed of promise in Abraham's heart. God watched over that seed until it became a much longed for child, and then a family, and finally, nation! When the time was right, exactly according to the prophecy God gave

---

[2]   Exodus 12:40
[3]   Acts 13:20

Abraham, He led this nation on an incredible journey to plant the seed in the Promised Land.

Which leads us back to the 17th of Nisan.

The Seventeenth Day of Nisan

The Feast of Passover

A thousand years after the Great Flood, God's chosen people would again be selected to pass through the waters and emerge on the other side as a new nation. After 430 years of waiting, and four generations of slavery, God sent Moses to lead Israel out of Egypt into the promised land. At the time of the Exodus from Egypt, God instructed Moses and the children of Israel to apply the blood of the Passover Lamb to their doorposts.[4] That night, all the firstborn of men and animals in the nation of Egypt died, and the children of Israel packed up and fled the country. God parted the waters of the Red Sea, and they all passed through the flood safely. Exodus 12-14 tells the story of what happened that night, and in the days that followed.

The night of the first Passover was the 14th of Nisan (a month known as Abib in ancient times). The Passover Lamb was killed at sunset the 14th of Abib (Nisan). Remember, the Hebrew day begins at sunset, so just as one day was ending, and another was begging, the lamb is sacrificed. It's blood was to be applied to the doorposts and lintel of the house (forming the shape of a cross), and the whole household was to enter in and be safe.

Later that night, around midnight, the Angel of Death passed through the land and killed all the firstborn of men and animals. But when he saw the blood on the doorposts, he passed over that house. Pharaoh, and all Egypt, were so horrified at the loss of their firstborn, they told the children of Israel to leave that very night. So, that night, the night of Nisan 14, the Angel of Death passed over the people of Israel, and they made their exodus from Egypt. They made their first camp at Etham, on the edge of the wilderness[5].

---

4   Exodus 12
5   Exodus 13:20

The next day, the 15th of Nisan, the people were on the move again. They had to eat their bread unleavened because they left in such haste that there was no time to leaven the dough and let it rise. The seven day Feast of Unleavened Bread is celebrated by the Hebrew people to this day in commemoration of this event. The Lord, leading them by a pillar of cloud by day, and a pillar of fire by night, led them to turn back from the wilderness and camp by the Red Sea[6].

Within a day or two, Pharaoh and Egypt had a change of heart. He amassed his army and set off in pursuit. As night fell, the Egyptians overtook the children of Israel camping by the Red Sea, and both sides expected a massacre. They were both right, but not in a way either side expected.

While the Angel of the Lord guarded them from behind, God divided the waters of the Red Sea, and the children of Israel passed all night through the waters on dry ground[7]. In the morning, after all the Israelites were safely across, the Egyptians entered the gulf, but the waters returned and drowned them all.

When did this happen? According to Numbers 33:5-8, the people of Israel crossed through the "flood" on dry ground, the 17th of Nisan! Given the text, and the distances involved, it could not have happened any sooner. The same day Noah's ark safely came through the flood!

Traditionally, the Jews celebrate this event on the 21st of Nisan, which is the last night of the Feast of Unleavened bread. The thinking is that once Pharaoh and his army were destroyed, there was no more need for haste, and so the people could again take the time to leaven their dough. However, according to Exodus 15:22-27, they were continuing to travel for three more days after crossing the Red Sea before they camped at Marah, where God healed the waters. That would bring them to the 21st and the end of the week, which the Feast of Unleavened Bread commemorates.

The Lord later instructed Israel that after they came into the Promised Land, on the first day after the Sabbath of the week of Passover, they were to celebrate the Feast of Firstfruits[8]. On this day they were to celebrate the Lord bringing them into the Promised land, and wave a sheaf of the

---

[6] Exodus 14:2
[7] Exodus 14:20-24
[8] Lev. 23

firstfruits of the land before the Lord. It was like saying, "You did it! You kept Your promise and have blessed us just like You said, and here is the proof!"

But that is not the end of the story of the 17th of Nisan.

Remember Noah's dove that returned with the olive branch in its beak 47 days later? Well in the book of Leviticus, the children of Israel were given another Feast to observe yearly.

"From the day after the Sabbath
— the day you bring the bundle of grain to be lifted up as a special offering —
count off seven full weeks.
Keep counting until the day after the seventh Sabbath, fifty days later.
Then present an offering of new grain to the Lord.
From wherever you live, bring two loaves of bread
to be lifted up before the Lord a special offering...
That same day will be proclaimed an official day for holy assembly,
a day on which you do no ordinary work.
This is a permanent law for you, and it must be observed from
generation to generation wherever you live." — Lev. 23:15-17,21 NLT

This is what is known as the Feast of Weeks (because they count off the weeks), or what the church knows as Pentecost.

According to the Genesis text, 47 days after the ark came to rest, the dove returned with an olive branch in her beak. This would be fifty days after the 14th of Nisan (which would come to be known as Passover). Pentecost is always on a Sunday, no matter what day of the week Passover occurs, because it must always be the day after the Sabbath of that week.

But we'll save that part of the story for the next Day.

Calculating the Date of Exodus to 2463 Years from Adam

Gen. 13:14-17 Age 75+ Covenant Made	Gen. 15:13-18 Age 85 Covenant Confirmed	Gen. 17 Age 99 Covenant Confirmed	Ex. 12:40-41 430 years later The Exodus
"And the Lord said unto Abram, after that Lot was separated from him, 'Lift up now thine eyes and look from the place you are northward, southward, eastward, and westward. For all the land which you see I will give it to you and to your seed forever. And I will make your seed as the dust of the earth… Arise, walk through the land in the length of it and in the breadth of it, for I will give it to you."	"And He said unto Abram, 'Know of a surety that your seed shall be a stranger in a land that is not theirs, and shall serve them, and they shall afflict them 400 years….But in the 4th generation they shall come here again… In the same day the Lord made a covenant with Abram saying, "Unto your seed have I given this land…" *400 year prophecy made *4th generation will return	"Behold My covenant is with you, and you shall be a father of many nations, neither shall your name any more be called 'Abram, but your name shall be Abraham'… I will give unto you, and to your seed after you, the land wherein you are a stranger,… this is My covenant,… every man child among you shall be circumcised…In the selfsame day was Abram circumcised." *Name changed *Sign of circumcision given	"Now the sojourning of the children of Israel, who dwelt in Egypt, was 430 years. And it came to pass at the end of the 430 years, even the selfsame day, it came to pass, that all the host of the Lord went up from the land of Egypt." Generations

Entered: Born In Egypt:
1st Jacob -130   5th Ram
2nd Judah -42   6th Amminidab
3rd Pharez-22   7th Nashon
4th Hezron   8th Salmon

Acts 7:6-8
"And God spoke on this wise, 'That his seed (Abraham's) should sojourn in a strange land, and that they should bring them into bondage and entreat them evil 400 years… and after that they shall come forth and serve Me in this place. And He gave him the covenant of circumcision…"

Gal. 3:16-17
"Now to Abraham and his seed were the promises made… and this I say, that the covenant that was confirmed before of God in Christ, the Law, which was 430 years after, cannot disannul…"

430 years dated from:
1. The confirmation of the covenant made at age 85, and age 99
2. At age 85, is when God 1st said they would be strangers in land, be afflicted, and come back to Promised land after 400 years. I used this date. Abraham was born 1948 years after Adam, add 85 to that, and then 430, and you get 2463.
3. After 4 generations of bondage, Israel returned to the Land, just as was foretold to Abraham 430 years earlier.

Day 3 - The Day of Abraham, Moses & the Judges

Years of Time from Adam

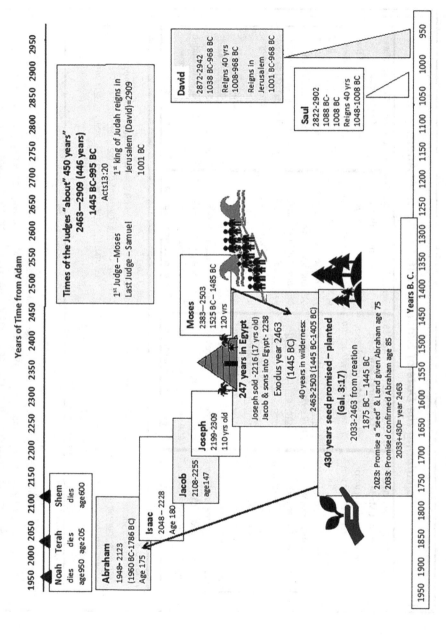

1950 2000 2050 2100 2150 2200 2250 2300 2350 2400 2450 2500 2550 2600 2650 2700 2750 2800 2850 2900 2950

Noah **Terah** **Shem**
dies dies dies
age950 age205 age600

Abraham
1948- 2123
(1960 BC-1786 BC)
Age 175

Isaac
2048 – 2228
Age 180

Jacob
2108-2255
age147

Joseph
2199-2309
110 yrs old

Moses
2383–2503
1525 BC – 1485 BC
120 yrs

247 years in Egypt
Joseph sold - 2216 (17 yrs old)
Jacob & sons into Egypt- 2238
Exodus year 2463
(1445 BC)
40 years in wilderness:
2463-2503 (1445 BC-1405 BC)

430 years seed promised – planted
(Gal. 3:17)
2033-2463 from creation
1875 BC – 1445 BC
2023: Promise a "Seed" & Land given Abraham age 75
2033: Promised confirmed Abraham age 85
2033+430= year 2463

Times of the Judges "about" 450 years"
2463–2909 (446 years)
1445 BC-995 BC
Acts13:20

1st Judge –Moses   1st King of Judah reigns in
Last Judge – Samuel   Jerusalem (David)=2909
                          1001 BC

David
2872-2942
1038 BC-968 BC
Reigns 40 yrs
1008-968 BC
Reigns in
Jerusalem
1001 BC-968 BC

Saul
2822-2902
1088 BC-
1008 BC
Reigns 40 yrs
1048-1008 BC

Years B. C.

1950 1900 1850 1800 1750 1700 1650 1600 1550 1500 1450 1400 1350 1300 1250 1200 1150 1100 1050 1000 950

CHAPTER 5

DAY FOUR – The Sun, Moon & Stars

"And God said, Let there be lights in the firmament of the heaven
to divide the day from the night;
and let them be for signs, and for seasons, and for days, and years:
And let them be for lights in the firmament of the heaven
to give light upon the earth:
and it was so.
And God made two great lights; the greater light to rule the day,
and the lesser light to rule the night:
he made the stars also. And God set them in the firmament of the heaven
to give light upon the earth, and to rule over the day and over the night,
and to divide the light from the darkness:
and God saw that it was good.
And the evening and the morning were the fourth day." - Gen. 1:14-19

There are a couple of new concepts we see introduced on day 4.

First of all, notice that God not only created the sun, moon, and stars, but for the first time, we see Him assigning a specific task or purpose to His creation. The stated reasons God gave for creating the sun, moon and stars were for them to be for signs, for seasons, for days and years. They were to rule the day and night, and divide light from darkness.

The Rule of Four

On the fourth day, we have the concept of rule or authority clearly established. God, who has all authority, bestows authority upon His creation. He is the One who appoints authority, and He clearly spells out the dominion or realm in which each authority is to function. Although light and dark, day and night are mentioned as being created or called into being on Day 1, we see the authority to rule over them being appointed to the heavenly bodies on day 4.

These heavenly bodies were also to be for signs and seasons. The Hebrew word for "signs" used here is "owth". It means: " a signal, a beacon, a monument, evidence, mark, token, miracle, omen."[1] None of this is talking about astrology, which is forbidden in scripture.[2] Rather they are signs in the sense the Psalmist speaks of when he says, "*The heavens declare the glory of God. Day unto day they show His handiwork.*"[3]. God is going to use them to reveal something.

We know God sent a special star to guide the wise men at Christ's birth[4]. Additionally, we are told that at the end times, there will be signs in the sun, moon and stars[5]. In the book of Revelation, the apostle John sees signs in the heavens which reveal God's work on earth.[6]

In a very literal sense, our world is ruled by the sun, moon and stars. The sun and moon control the ability for life to exist on this planet. The tides, and thus the weather, along with the measurement of days, seasons and years are all marked by the movements of these heavenly bodies.

Because the heavenly bodies were given authority to rule the day and night on day four of creation, the number four is associated with rule and authority. There are four seasons in a year, four major directions on a compass, and four 4 dimensions that rule time and space (length, width, depth, time). There were four rivers that went out of Eden to water the whole earth. In heaven, there are 4 cherubim which are continually before

---

[1] James Strong, *The New Strong's Exhaustive Concordance of the Bible* (Nashville: T. Nelson, 1990), H226.

[2] Lev. 19:26, Isaiah 47:13-15

[3] Psalm 19:1

[4] Matt. 2:2-10

[5] Luke 21:25

[6] Rev. 12

the throne of God. Judah, the fourth son of Isaac is the tribe from which the Kings of Israel came, and through which Christ, the King of Kings was born.

There is an ancient prophecy of Christ which reads:

> *"I shall see him, but not now: I shall behold him, but not nigh:*
> *there shall come a Star out of Jacob,*
> *and a Scepter shall rise out of Israel." – Num. 24:17*

It is beautifully fitting, therefore, that the birth of The King, the Star out of Jacob, was announced by The Star of Bethlehem, and rejoiced over by angels, whom the book of Revelation symbolically refers to as stars[7].

Even the Hebrew calendar reflects this Rule of 4. Our 4th month (April) is the 1st month (Nissan) of the Jewish religious calendar. Our 1st month is the 4th month of the Jewish civil calendar (Tevet). The 4th is First! The 4th position is the first in Rule. The fourth generation from Noah produced Eber (who ruled the generations of Seth), and Nimrod (who was a mighty ruler in the earth and the 1st king of Babylon and Assyria).

THE FOURTH AGE OF TIME: THE DAY OF KINGS AND PROPHETS

So what happened in the fourth thousand years of History?

In the Fourth Age of History, (3000 to 4000 years after Adam), we see the emergence of the kings of Israel, and the ministry of the prophets. The heavenly bodies were specifically given to "rule" the day and night, and for "signs". Kings rule, and prophets know how to read the signs of the times. Thus, this age is known as the Times of Kings and Prophets. Although Saul was the first king of Israel, he was not of the ruling tribe of Judah. Although David was the first king of Judah, he did not rule in Jerusalem until his seventh year of reign. To be very specific, I believe this Age of Kings begins the first time the King of Judah enters the temple of the Lord in Jerusalem. This occurred in 967 BC when king Solomon (the fourth son of David born in Jerusalem) begins to build the temple in Jerusalem[8].

---

[7]   Rev. 1:20
[8]   1 Kings 6:1, 37-38

This Age concludes a thousand years later when the last king of Judah, Jesus Christ, rides into Jerusalem on a donkey, being declared the "son of David" (a Messianic title for the kings of Judah)[9]. He would later be crucified under a banner declaring Him to be the King of the Jews[10]. One week before His crucifixion, Jesus entered Jerusalem, went to the temple and cleared it. We celebrate this today as Palm Sunday. This occurred in 33 A.D., exactly a thousand years after Solomon dedicated the first temple. Just as Solomon was the first king of Judah to enter the temple, Jesus would be the last. Within a few years, this last temple would be utterly destroyed by Rome in 70 A.D.

This Age of Kings and Prophets may also be measured from when the first prophet, Samuel, anointed the first king of Judah, David. It extends until the final prophet, John the Baptist, baptized the final King, Jesus. Jesus Himself identified John the Baptist's ministry as pivotal in the changing of the times.

"And from the days of John the Baptist until now
The kingdom of heaven suffers violence...
For all the prophets and the law prophesied until John." – Matthew 11:12-13

In John's days, and in Christ's, there would be a changing of the times to a new Day. Just as the Passover lamb was sacrificed in the evening as one day ends, and another begins, Christ would be sacrificed at the changing of the times from Day Four to Day Five.

Another alternative to measuring this fourth millennia of time is to begin approximately 2909 years after Adam (the year David, the first king of Judah entered Jerusalem for the first time), and count until Jesus, the last king of Judah entered Jerusalem for the first time as a baby. This would be about 1001 B.C. until 1 A.D. If this all sounds confusing, remember, the Days are roughly marked by thousand-year periods of time, but they are determined not by a date on the calendar, but by events. The Day of Prophets and Kings begins when the first prophet anoints the first king of Judah, and ends when the last Old Testament prophet proclaims the last king of Judah. Jesus said no one could know the day or hour of His second

---

[9]   Matt. 21:2-9
[10] Matt. 27:37, Mark 15:26, Luke 23:38, John 19:14-21

coming, but rather, the new Day will begin when He returns, no matter what that calendar date might be.

2943 years from Adam, Solomon, became the first king of Judah to enter the temple at Jerusalem. He did so for the first time in 967 B.C. If this event did indeed mark the beginning of the Fourth Day of time, it would then end the Passion Week of Christ. On that week, Jesus Christ rode into Jerusalem on a donkey while the crowd waved palm branches, and hailed Him as the Son of David. He was crucified one week later under a banner proclaiming Him King of the Jews. This fulfilled the prophecy of Zechariah;

> *"Rejoice, O people of Zion!*
> *Shout in triumph, O people of Jerusalem!*
> *Look, your king is coming to you.*
> *He is righteous and victorious,*
> *Yet he is humble, riding on a donkey." – Zechariah 9:9 (NLT)*

From 967 BC to 33 AD is exactly 1,000 years!

The Rule of the Day and of the Night

What parallels can be seen between the rules of the Kings of Judah, and the rule of the sun, moon and stars? David, the first king of Judah, began his reign in Hebron where he reigned for six years. In his seventh year as king, he began to reign in Jerusalem in 1001 BC. After 30 years, he arranged for his son, Solomon, to be crowned king. They co-reigned for three years, during which time David made certain the throne and kingdom would be secure after his death.[11] In 968 BC, David died after reigning 33 years in Jerusalem. Solomon (fourth son of David born in Jerusalem) then began his solo reign. In his fourth year on the throne, he began to build the temple in Jerusalem[12]. This would be the year 967 BC. The reigns of David and Solomon are considered to be the golden age of the kings. Under their rule, the kingdom was established, enemies defeated, and the temple was built. There was unity, and eventually peace and prosperity. It was a bright day.

---

[11]   1 Chron. 29
[12]   2 Chron.3:2, 1 Kings 6:1

After Solomon's reign however, the nation of Israel was divided into two kingdoms[13]. The northern kingdom consisted of ten tribes which rejected the line of Judah for their king. They also abandoned the worship of God at the temple in Jerusalem, setting up various high places to worship in Samaria, which their northern kingdom came to be known as[14]. The southern kingdom came to be known as Judah. Their kings continued to be of the line of David, and they continued to worship God in the temple at Jerusalem, at least for a time.

After about 420 years of the reign of Kings, both kingdoms were conquered and went into captivity. Israel (Samaria) was conquered by the Assyrians[15]. About 130 years later, Judah was conquered by Nebuchadnezzar and went into Babylonian captivity[16]. Does the name Babylon ring any bells? We have seen it before, and we will see it again.

Just as on the fourth day of creation in which God created the sun, moon, and stars to rule the day and night, these two kingdoms became like metaphors of Day and Night. Judah remained loyal to the Davidic line and the worship of the true God, while Samaria turned away from the light, and fell into the darkness of idolatry.

Children of Israel as Stars in Heaven

In addition, the 12 tribes of Israel are often prophetically referred to as stars.

God told Abraham in Gen. 15:15;

> "*Look now toward heaven, and tell the stars,*
> *if thou be able to number them:*
> *and he said unto him, So shall thy seed be.*"

Also, in Deut. 1:10; "*The Lord your God hath multiplied you, and, behold, ye are this day as the stars of heaven for multitude.*"

---

[13]   2 Chron.10:16-19, 1 Kings 12:17-20
[14]   1 Kings 12:26-33
[15]   2 Kings 17
[16]   2 Kings 25

In Gen. 37:9, Joseph was telling his family about the dream God had given him.

> *"And he dreamed yet another dream, and told it his brethren, and said,*
> *'Behold, I have dreamed a dream more;*
> *and, behold, the sun and the moon and the*
> *eleven stars made obeisance to me."*

The interpretation was that his father, mother, and his 11 brothers (the whole family of Israel) would bow to him. Thus we see Jacob, whose name was changed to Israel[17], represented as the sun, and the patriarchs of the tribes of Israel represented as stars.

In the Book of Revelation, Israel is depicted as a woman with a crown of 12 stars on her head, which would be the 12 tribes. She gives birth to a male child (Christ) who is caught up to God and His throne.

> *"And there appeared a great wonder in heaven;*
> *a woman clothed with the sun,*
> *and the moon under her feet, and upon her head a crown of twelve stars:*
> *And she being with child cried, travailing in*
> *birth, and pained to be delivered.*
> *… and the dragon stood before the woman which was ready to be delivered,*
> *for to devour her child as soon as it was born.*
> *And she brought forth a man child, who was to*
> *rule all nations with a rod of iron:*
> *and her child was caught up unto God, and to his throne. - Rev. 12:1-5*

Therefore, it is consistent with scripture that the sun, moon and stars are a reference to the nation of Israel, its tribes and kings. Further, just as the lights in the Heavens were given to rule and as signs, so we see the Bright, Morning Star (Christ), evidencing many signs when He was here:

> *"And Simeon blessed them, and said unto Mary his mother,*
> *Behold, this child is set for the fall and rising again of many in Israel;*
> *and for a sign which shall be spoken against." – Luke 2:34*

---

[17] Gen. 13:28

"Ye men of Israel, hear these words; Jesus of Nazareth,
a man approved of God among you by miracles and wonders and signs,
which God did by him in the midst of you, as
ye yourselves also know:" - Acts 2:22

"And many other signs truly did Jesus in the presence of his disciples,
which are not written in this book:"
- John 20:30

"I Jesus have sent mine angel to testify unto you these things in the churches.
I am the root and the offspring of David,
and the bright and morning star." – Rev. 22:16

"I Am the Light of the World." – John 9:5,8:12

The Time of the Prophets

The heavenly bodies were given to rule the day and night, and for signs. As kings represent those who rule and reign over Israel, prophets deal with signs. After the time of the Kings, the prophets continued to warn and minister to the dispersed people of Israel and Judah. Then after 70 years of captivity, as was foretold by the prophet Jeremiah[18], Judah returned to their land. It was during this time that the prophet Daniel had his visions and spoke of a future time when great kingdoms would rise and fall.

Daniel chapter 2 tells of a vision in which it was foretold that four great world powers would rise one after another. First would be Babylon, which ruled over Judah for 70 years. The Babylonians were then conquered by the second kingdom: the Medes and Persians. They ruled in the holy land for 200 years. Next would come the kingdom of Greece, which conquered Jerusalem in 333 B.C. and ruled until the Romans took Jerusalem in 63 B.C. These are the great powers that dominated the world, Jerusalem, and the Holy Land during the final 400 years of the Fourth Age of History. It all unfolded exactly as Daniel foretold, and Rome was the power which ruled Jerusalem and the Holy Land during the time of Christ.

---

[18]   Jeremiah 25:11-12; 29:10

Daniel actually lived to see the first part of this prophecy fulfilled. He served in Nebuchadnezzar's court, and through the reigns of subsequent kings of Babylon. He was still there when Belshazzar, the final king of Babylon, was conquered by Cyrus the Great. This event was foreshadowed by the handwriting on the wall incident recorded in Daniel 5.

The 2,300 Days of Daniel 8

Daniel chapter 8 tells of a more detailed vision Daniel was given of the future time when the kingdom of Greece would displace the Medes and Persians. The vision was very specifically about the holy city of Jerusalem. In this vision, the king of Greece (represented by a goat), would cross the river and defeat the ram (Persia). This part of the vision was fulfilled roughly 200 years later when, in 333 B.C., Alexander the Great, the first king of Greece, defeated Darius III, the ruler of the Persian empire. Just as the vision foretold, Alexander charged across the Pinarus River to shatter the Persian army. They would meet in battle two more times, but the fate of Darius was sealed from this first decisive defeat.

In the second part of the vision, the first king (Alexander the Great) dies, and his kingdom is broken into four kingdoms, ruled by four kings (represented by horns in the vision). This is exactly what happened. Later, out of one of these kingdoms, a king would arise that would destroy the holy city and the temple, and put an end to the daily sacrifices.

The Jews believe this was fulfilled when Antiochus IV (Epiphanes), the king of Syria (which was one of the four kingdoms which splintered off of Greece), captured Jerusalem in 167 B.C. and desecrated the Temple by offering the sacrifice of a pig on an altar to Zeus[19].

Others believe it was fulfilled in 70 A.D. when Titus, the Roman general under emperor Vespasian, destroyed Jerusalem, and the temple. From that time to this, there has been no temple for the Jewish people. As is true for many prophecies, there can be more than one fulfillment. There will come a time in the future when this will all unfold again.

---

[19] The First Book of the Maccabees, The Apocrypha or Deuterocanonical Books of the Bible. July 7, 2011, Halcyon Press Ltd. 1 Maccabees.

In his vision, Daniel hears the question asked, *"How long shall be the vision concerning the daily sacrifice, and the transgression of desolation, to give both the sanctuary and the host to be trodden under foot?"*[20]

And the answer was given; *"And he said unto me, 'Unto two thousand and three hundred days; then shall the sanctuary be cleansed."*[21]

So, the question was, "How long will the vision last? How long will both the sanctuary (holy, or sanctified place), and the host (Judah – the Jewish people) be trodden under foot? The holy place for the Jews has always been Jerusalem and the temple mount.

The answer was 2,300 days. In Daniel chapter 9, a week is a prophetic reference to a period of 7 years. In that reckoning, a day would be equal to a year. So, to be consistent, 2,300 days, prophetically, means 2,300 years.

We know when the 2,300 years began, because they start where the vision does; when the rough goat (Alexander the Great, the first king of Greece), crossed the river to defeat the ram (the king of Persia). This happened in 333 B.C. In all the many centuries since then, the city of Jerusalem has been repeatedly destroyed and trampled upon by one nation after another.

If you count 2,300 years from 333 B.C., you come to 1967 A.D. In June 1967, the nation of Israel fought the Six Day War. At that time, the Jews (once more reborn as the nation of Israel in 1948) entered Jerusalem and proclaimed "The temple mount is in our hands!"[22] The temple mount is the holy place. For 2,300 the Jews had not been a sovereign nation in control of the holy city. But they are now. And all this was foretold by Daniel in around 500 B.C.! We are living in prophetic times!

The Old Testament books of the prophets cover the period of time from Samuel, the first prophet[23], until John the Baptist, who was the final Old Testament prophet[24]. Luke 3 tells us that John baptized Jesus in the 15th year of Tiberius Caesar, which would be about 29AD- 30 AD. From

---

[20]   Daniel 8:13

[21]   Daniel 8:14

[22]   "Mordechai "Motta" Gur (May6, 1930-July16, 1995) was an Israeli politician and the 10th Chief of Staff of the Israel Defense Forces. During the Six-Day War (1967), he commanded the brigade that penetrated the Old City of Jerusalem and broadcast the famous words, 'The Temple Mount is in our hands!'"- Wikipedia, 2012, Mordechai Gur.

[23]   1 Sam. 3:20

[24]   Matt. 11:13

scripture, we know that John was beheaded near of the beginning of Christ's three year ministry, which began then.

Final Prophet and King

Thus, Day Four of History started with the first king of Judah to enter the temple at Jerusalem, and ended with the last King of Judah to do so. It began in the ministry of Samuel, the first Old Testament prophet, and would end with the ministry of the final Old Testament prophet, John the Baptist. This day's crowning glory was the birth of the last king of Judah, Jesus – the King of Kings, the Bright and Morning Star, the Son of God and Ruler of Heaven and Earth. His birth would be announced by the Star of Bethlehem, and the singing of angels, which Revelation 1 tells us are also symbolized by stars.

In the Midst of Years

Another awesome fact is that the 4th day is in the exact middle of the seven day week. The first sentence of the Bible is just seven words long, and the fourth word is the word "et", which is spelled "Aleph, Tav" – the first letter of the Hebrew alphabet, and the last letter. Literally, "the beginning and the end", "the Alpha and Omega", "the First and the Last". All of which are titles used of Christ in scripture! The fourth word points directly to what would happen the fourth Day of History – the coming of the Messiah.

The prophet Habakkuk wrote:

> *"O LORD, revive Your work in the midst of the years!*
> *In the midst of the years make it known;*
> *In wrath remember mercy."- Hab. 3:2*

And it was literally in the midst of years that Christ came and made known God's finished work of salvation! What a wonder and thrill God's Word is!

This picture of Christ in the midst was beautifully illustrated in the Old Testament temple in the form of the Menorah.

Christ in the Menorah

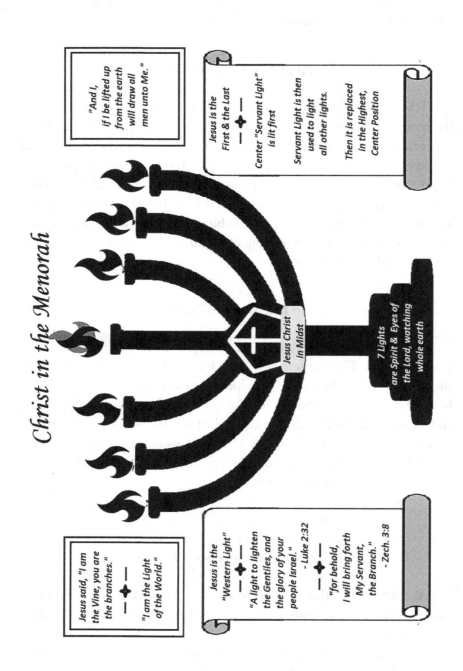

"And I,
if I be lifted up
from the earth
will draw all
men unto Me."

Jesus is the
First & the Last

Center "Servant Light"
is lit first

Servant Light is then
used to light
all other lights.

Then it is replaced
in the Highest,
Center Position

Jesus said, "I am
the Vine, you are
the branches."

"I am the Light
of the World."

Jesus is the
"Western Light"

"A light to lighten
the Gentiles, and
the glory of your
people Israel."
- Luke 2:32

"for behold,
I will bring forth
My Servant,
the Branch."
- Zech. 3:8

Jesus Christ
in Midst

7 Lights
are Spirit & Eyes of
the Lord, watching
whole earth

The Menorah

One of the most compelling instances of the number seven, in both the Old and New Testaments is the Menorah.

The menorah is a lampstand having seven lights on seven arms, which branch out from a central stem. It is the symbol of faith to the Hebrew people, much as the cross is to those of the Christian faith. It is seen throughout the Bible, Old and New Testaments. God instructed Israel to place a menorah in the Holy place of the tabernacle and temple. Zechariah saw a vision of a menorah, which was identified as the Word of God and as the Lord of all the earth[25]. In the first chapter of the book of Revelation, we see Christ standing in the midst of seven lamps – a visual of a menorah.

A Picture of Christ

The design for the menorah was given to Moses with very exacting detail, and it was to be the light for the tabernacle of the covenant[26]. We see this imagery of Christ as the center and His people as branches over and over in scripture.

"I am the vine,
You are the branches.:" – John 15:5

"...Behold, a candlestick all of gold,
With a bowl upon the top of it,
And his seven lamps thereon,,
And seven pipes to the seven lamps, which are upon the top thereof...
They are the eyes of the Lord,
Which run to and fro through the whole earth." – Zech. 4:2, 10

As we have seen, the number seven is very significant in scripture, and it is always associated with Christ. The seven-armed menorah was prominent in the tabernacle and the temple, which were are pattern or image of heavenly things.[27]

---

[25] Zech. 4:2, 6, 10.
[26] Exodus 25:31-40; 27:17-24
[27] Heb. 8:5

The Servant Light

In the daily temple ceremony, the center light of the menorah – called the "shamash" or "Servant Light" – is lit first and from it all other lights are lit. In their work *Lost In Translation Vol. 1*, John Klein and Adam Spears wrote:

"The center lamp is referred to as the "ner tamid" or "eternal light (Lev. 24:2). This particular light is also called the "shemesh", or "servant", because it was used to rekindle the remaining six lights on the menorah whenever they were trimmed. The Hebres word for "sun" is also shemesh, and the sun is considered the servant-light to the natural world. The sun was created the fourth day just as the shemesh holds the fourth position on a menorah. Ancient Hebrew rabbis have suggested that this shemesh position represents Messiah."[28]

Christ, the Messiah, is called the Servant in Zechariah's prophecy.

"…for behold, I will bring forth My Servant, the Branch." – Zech. 3:8

Jesus, though He was Christ, stooped to serve others, even washing the feet of His disciples.

"For even the Son of man came not to be ministered unto,
But to minister, and to give His life a ransom for many." – Mark 10:45

"If I then, your Lord and Master, have washed your feet,
You also ought to wash one another's feet…
The servant is not greater than his lord…" – John 13:14,16

Lit With Olive Oil

The original menorah did not use candles, which are consumed when burned, but olive oil (a picture of the burning bush that appeared to Moses which burned but was not consumed. This is also a picture of the Holy Spirit which appeared on the heads of the disciples as tongues of fire

---

[28] John Klein & Adam Spears, *Lost In Translation Vol 1* (chapter 5, Menorah), P.111-112

on Pentecost)[29]. The Holy Spirit (symbolized by the olive oil) was first poured out in full on Christ, and then on His church at Pentecost. Christ resurrected first, and afterward so will all those who are His.

The Western Light

The central light is also known as the Western Light. The original design for the menorah was a lampstand topped with bowls containing oil. There was a spout in which a wick was placed, and this was lit to provide light. The bowls were positioned so that they all faced the central light, so the three on the right faced inward toward the center, and the three on the left also faced toward the center. The center light was turned so that it faced the Holy of Holies, which contained the ark of the Presence of God. Since the opening to the Holy place was in the east, the ark was placed in the west. The center light faced the ark, it therefore faced the west, thus "The Western Light". This is also a picture of Christ.

"And He said, 'It is a light thing that You should be My servant
to raise up the tribes of Jacob,
To restore the preserved of Israel:
I will also give You for a light to the Gentiles,
That You may be My salvation unto the end of the earth."- Isa. 49:6

"A light to lighten the Gentiles,
And the glory of your people Israel." – Luke 2:32

The term Gentiles is a Hebrew word for the non-Jewish nations of the earth, who are represented as being western lands.

The First and the Last

The central light (in the fourth position) – the servant light – was lit first with coals taken the altar. Then it is lifted out (or lifted up) and used to light all the other lights in order from right to left.

---

[29]   Acts 2:3

"When you have lifted up the Son of Man,
Then shall you know that I am He." – John 8:28

"And I, if I be lifted up from the earth,
Will draw all men unto me." – John 12:32

Then it is placed back in its place. This makes this light the first and the last, which is a description Jesus used of Himself in Revelation 1:17.

Christ (The Light of the World) left His place in Heaven, was lifted up on the cross. After He was lifted up into Heaven at His resurrection, He sent His Spirit to His disciples on Pentecost. Just as the Servant Light lit all the other lights (Jesus said to His disciples, "You are the light of the world"[30].), and then returned to His place, Jesus sent the Holy Spirit in the form of fire to light His disciples when He was lifted up into Heaven[31].

The middle position – the fourth position – the Servant Light – represents Christ.

As I progressed in this study I am sharing with you, the image of the Menorah came up again and again. I believe it can be used almost as a map of creation and time. It is the visual God gave to unfold some of His most wonderful mysteries to us. In a way, it is a two dimensional representation of both the solar system (with many lights revolving around one central light), and an atom (with its electrons revolving around a central nucleus).

One hallmark of Truth, is that it holds true in both the macro and micro. Truth looks the same in a microscope and a telescope. God has created the world in such a way that if you discover something to be true in one place, it will also be true in another. For example, the Law of Sowing and Reaping holds true whether one is talking about agriculture or relationships. Truth just is. Truth doesn't change with the position or opinion of the observer. Only what is false alters according to perspective.

---

[30] Mat. 5:14
[31] Acts 2:1-4

The Passion Week of Christ

Before we leave our exploration of this Fourth Day, we need to take a closer look at the final week of this Day.

About 2500 years after the Flood, and about 1500 years after the events of the Exodus and the first Passover, Jesus made His entrance in history.

"...For even Christ, our Passover, is sacrificed for us." – 1 Cor.5:7

The final week of Christ's life on earth before the cross was the week of Passover.

Let's walk through that week together.

According to John 12:1, six days before the Passover, Jesus was in Bethany. John 12:12 -13 then says,

> *"On the next day much people that were come to the feast,*
> *when they heard that Jesus was coming to Jerusalem,*
> *took branches of palm trees and went forth to meet him,*
> *and cried, 'Hosanna: Blessed is the King of Israel*
> *that comes in the name of the Lord."*

This is what has come to be known as the Triumphal Entry of Christ. Traditionally, the church celebrates this event on Palm Sunday, the week before Easter, and it is considered the first event of the Passion Week of Christ. It was the 9th of Nisan.

The 10th of Nisan is the day the Passover lamb is selected and presented to the priests. For the next four days, the lamb was to be closely examined to assure that it was without flaw or fault[32].

For the next four days, the scriptures tell us that Jesus went daily to the temple, where He was repeatedly examined by the Pharisees, Sadducees, and chief rulers. They were looking for some fault they could accuse Him of, but were unable to find any[33].

---

[32] Ex. 12:3
[33] Mat. 22:15-46; Mark14; Luke 19-20

Two days before the Passover (13 Nisan), Simon the Leper hosted a feast in Christ's honor and Lazarus and his sisters were present. After the dinner, Mary anointed His feet with oil and Judas became very angry about it. The text seems to indicate that this event may have been what pushed him over the edge and made Judas decide to sell Jesus out[34].

The day before Passover, Jesus sent His disciples to prepare the feast in Jerusalem. Passover is celebrated at sunset "between the two evenings" on the 14th of Nisan. That means it was celebrated at sundown in the afternoon of the 14th Nisan. However, in the Old Testament, the original Passover, as God instructed, was kept at the beginning of 14 Nisan[35].

"In actuality, then, there were really two Passover observances happening at the time of Jesus: one led by the priests at the Temple and the other observed by the people in their homes. These separate observances were also at different times: The Temple-kept Passover was observed late in the afternoon of Abib 14, while the home-kept Passover was kept at the beginning of Abib 14. As the gospels show, Jesus and His disciples ate the Passover in a home rather than at the Temple, observing it the evening before the priests did at the Temple. In other words, Jesus kept it as Abib 14 began, while the priests kept it as Abib 14 ended."[36]- David Grabbe

That evening, at sunset (the beginning of the 14th), Jesus ate the Passover with His disciples. After dinner, they went to the Garden of Gethsemane on the Mount of Olives. Jesus prayed three times for this cup of suffering to pass from Him, but also prayed, *"Nevertheless, not My will, but Thy will be done."*[37]. That same night, Jesus was arrested and taken to the chief priests to be examined.

In the morning (Friday, still the 14th,), Jesus was sent to Pontius Pilate, and then to Herod. Both men examined Him and declared, "I find no fault in Him."[38]. Despite being declared innocent, Jesus was crucified at noon. For three hours, there was darkness over the land, just as there had been in Egypt at the first Passover[39].

---

[34]   Mat. 26:6-16; John 12:2-7; Luke22:1-6; Mark 14:1-11.

[35]   Ex.12:6-20

[36]   David C. Grabbe: *What the Bible says About Two Passover Observances at Time of Jesus* (Bible Tools.org)

[37]   Mat. 26:39

[38]   John 18:38; 19:4,6

[39]   Mat. 27:45

At 3 PM, just as the priests were sacrificing the Passover Lamb "between the evenings" at the temple, Christ died[40]. It was still the 14th of Nisan, and He was buried before sunset in order that the Jews could celebrate the Sabbath the next day. It was a very special Sabbath that year.

That year, the first day of the feast of Unleavened Bread, (the day after Passover and a Sabbath) was on a Saturday, which was also the Sabbath of the week. This is known as a "high Sabbath".

"The Jews therefore, because it was the preparation,
That the bodies should not remain upon the cross on the Sabbath day
(for that Sabbath day was an high day),…" – John 19:31

The Dilemma of Good Friday

Jesus said;

"For as Jonah was three days and three nights in the whale's belly,
So shall the Son of man be three days and three nights
in the heart of the earth."- Matt.12:40

How does a Friday crucifixion reconcile with those words? The answer is found by a careful reading of what Jesus actually said. He did not say He would be three nights in the grave, He said He would be three nights "in the heart of the earth".

When I was in Jerusalem, one of the tours we took was to the court of the high priest, where Jesus would have been examined on the night He was arrested. Although the original is no more, the general location and layout of the court are still there. Afterward, they took us to view a replica of the prison where condemned prisoners would have been kept on the night before their execution. It is literally just a hole cut out of the rocky ground. Condemned prisoners were lowered into this tomb-like cell through a hole in the ceiling. There is no door, or windows; no other openings, or light of any kind. The first night Jesus spent in the heart of the earth, He was still alive, though already beaten and abused. He was entombed alive. This was night one of the torment He endured for you and me.

---

[40]   Matt. 27:44-50

While we stood in somber silence in that hole, someone began to read the prophetic words of Psalm 88, which foretells the sufferings of Christ on that fateful night:

O LORD God of my salvation, I have cried day and night before you.
Let my prayer come before you, incline your ear unto my cry.
For my soul is full of troubles, my life is drawn nigh unto the grave.
I am counted with them that go down into the pit.
I am as a man that has no strength.
Free among the dead, like the slain that lie in the grave, whom
you remember no more, and they are cut off from your hand.
You have laid me in the lowest pit, in the darkness, in the deeps.
Your wrath lies hard upon me, and you have
afflicted me with all your waves. Selah.
You have put away my acquaintance far from me. You
have made me an abomination unto them. I am shut
up, and I cannot come forth..." – Psalm 88:1-8

As we were climbing out of that pit, people from another group began to hum "Amazing Grace". There were many people there, from all parts of the earth, speaking different languages. We could not communicate with one another, but when someone began to hum that blessed song, we all joined in. We did not need words to worship together. It was one of the most moving, sacred moments I have experienced.

The Year Christ Died

Being fairly confident that Christ died on a Friday, how can we know the year in which He died? There are a few clues given in scripture. We can know the crucifixion of Christ had to have happened between the years of 26 A.D. to 37 A.D., because those are the years in which Pontius Pilate was governor[41].

---

[41]   Helen K. Bond. *Pontius Pilate in History and Interpretation.* (Cambridge University Press. 1998) p.8

Also, the crucifixion had to have happened after 29 A.D., because Luke 3:1,23 tells us that John baptized Jesus in the 15th year of the reign of Tiberius Caesar (who reigned from 14 A.D. until 37 A.D.)[42]. After His baptism, Jesus (who was then about age 30[43]), began His ministry, which lasted for about three years. This narrows the possibilities down to year 32 A.D. at the earliest, to year 34 A.D.at the latest.

These are the Dates and days on which the new moons, and Passover occurred in those years[44]:

Passover & New Moons 31 AD - 34 AD

YEAR	NEW MOON	14TH NISAN (PASSOVER)	DAY OF WEEK
31 A.D.	12 March	27 March	Tuesday
32 A.D.	29 March	13 April	Sunday
33 A.D.	19 March	3 April	Friday
34 A.D.	9 March	24 March	Wednesday

Looking at this chart, we can rule out years 31 and 32 A.D. because we know that Jesus rose from the dead after three days, on a Sunday[45]. Therefore, He could not have been crucified on a Tuesday or a Sunday.

"Four dates have been proposed by scholars as the historical date of the crucifixion of Christ, but only one – Friday, April 3, in the year 33 AD – is backed up by astronomical history, two Oxford University scientists say."[46]

Which places the crucifixion of Jesus at the age of 33 on Friday, April 3, 33 A.D., at 3 PM.

---

[42] https://en.m.wikipedia.org

[43] Luke 3:23

[44] Colin Humphreys & W. Waddington. (1992). *The Jewish Calendar, A Lunar Eclipse and the Date of Christ's Crucifixion.* (Tyndale Bulletin. 43.10.5375/001c.30487

[45] Mark 16:9; Luke 24:1; John 20:1

[46] Thomas O'Toole. The Washington Post. *Oxford Scholars Consult the Stars for Date of Crucifixion to 33 A.D.,* (April 20, 1984).

The Seventeenth Day of Nisan

Remember the 17th of Nisan?

On the day after the Sabbath of the Passover (always a Sunday), the Jews celebrate the final holy day of the Passover week – the Feast of Firstfruits. On that day, the high priest was to come before the Lord with a lamb of the first year without blemish, and wave two sheaves of grain before the Lord. These would be the very first of the harvest for the year[47].

On that Sunday morning, the 16th Nisan, the very first Easter Sunday, Jesus presented Himself to Mary outside the empty tomb.

> *"Jesus said unto her,*
> *'Do not cling to Me, for I have not yet ascended to My Father.*
> *But go to My brethren and say to them, 'I am ascending to My Father*
> *and your Father, and to My God and your God." – John 20:17 NKJV*

Jesus, the high priest of our faith, still had a priestly function to carry out on our behalf.

> *"So Christ has now become the High Priest*
> *over all the good things that have come.*
> *He has entered that greater, more perfect Tabernacle in heaven,*
> *Which was not made by human hands and is*
> *not a part of this created world,*
> *With His own blood, Not the blood of goats and calves,*
> *He entered the Most Holy Place once for all time*
> *and secured our redemption forever." – Hebrews 9:11-12 NLT*

This is what the scene looked like in Heaven when Jesus made His triumphal entry there on that first Easter Sunday:

> *"And I saw in the right hand of Him that sat on the throne*
> *a book written within and on the backside, sealed with seven seals.*
> *And I saw a strong angel proclaiming with a loud voice,*
> *'Who is worthy to open the book, and to loose the seals thereof?'*

---

[47] Lev. 23:10-12

And no man in heaven, nor in the earth, neither under the earth,
was able to open the book, neither to look thereon.
And I wept much, because no man was found worthy
to open and to read the book, neither to look thereon.

And one of the elders said to me, 'Weep not. Behold, the
Lion of the tribe of Juda, the Root of David, has prevailed
to open the book, and to loose the seven seals.'

And I beheld, and Lo, in the midst of the throne, and of the four beasts,
and in the midst of the elders, stood a Lamb as it had been slain,...
And they sang a new song, saying,
'You are worthy to take the book, and to open the seals thereof.
For You were slain, and have redeemed us to God by Your blood
out of every kindred, and tongue, and people, and nation...
And I beheld, and I heard the voice of many angels round about the throne,
and the beasts and the elders,
and the number of them was ten thousand times ten thousand,
and thousands of thousands,
Saying with a loud voice,
'Worthy is the Lamb that was slain to receive power,
and riches, and wisdom, and strength and honor,
and glory and blessing!" – Rev. 5:1-12

As the High Priest of our faith, Christ presented Himself before the throne of God, having already offered Himself as the Passover Lamb, and He waved before the Lord the sheath of firstfruit. What was this "sheath of firstfruit" He presented?

"And the graves were opened,
And many bodies of the saints which slept arose,
And came out of the graves after His resurrection,
And went into the holy city,
And appeared unto many." – Matthew. 27:52-53

"But now is Christ risen from the dead,
And become the firstfruits of them that slept...
But every man in his own order:
Christ the firstfruits,
Afterward they that are Christ's at His coming." – 1 Cor. 15:20,23

Although we are not specifically told in scripture what happened to these saints who rose from the grave when Christ resurrected, early church teaching was that they ascended into heaven as well.

"(They were raised), Not to converse again, as heretofore, with men, but to accompany Christ, that raised them, into heaven; and to be as so many ocular demonstrations of Christ's quickening power." -John Trapp[48]

"These first miracles wrought in connection with the death of Christ were typical of spiritual wonders that will be continued till he comes again... (they were) quickened, and come out from among the dead, and go unto the holy city, the New Jerusalem." – Charles Spurgeon[49]

These first saints to resurrect from the dead with Christ became the firstfruits of a greater harvest which is still to come!

After Jesus appeared to Mary Sunday morning, He walked with 2 disciples on the road as they traveled to Emmaus[50]. That is about seven miles from Jerusalem. That evening, as they were about to eat, they suddenly recognized that the one speaking with them was Jesus! They no sooner realized this than He disappeared from them. They left that same hour and traveled all the way back to Jerusalem. It must have been dark by the time they arrived. That means it was now the 17th of Nisan.

They found the rest of the disciples gathered in the upper room. Everyone was filled with excitement, wonder, and even confusion. Suddenly, Jesus appeared in the room, though the doors were closed and locked. He spoke with them, displaying His hands and feet, proving that it really was Himself.

---

[48]   John Trapp, *A Commentary on the Old and New Testaments Vol. 5* (Eureka, California: Tanski Publications, 1997)

[49]   Charles Haddon Spurgeon, *Commentary on Matthew: The Gospel of the Kingdom.* (London: Passmore and Alabaster, Paternoster Buildings, 1893)

[50]   Luke 24:13-51

After eating with them, He led them out of the upper room towards Bethany, which is beyond the Mt. of Olives. As He came to the top, He ascended into Heaven before their eyes.

This was the 17th day of Nisan. The day the Ark came to rest on the mountains after the flood. A day which showed the promise of new life, after terrible death. The day God brought the children of Israel through the flood and safely into the Promised Land. Free from bondage, slavery and death. The day Christ rested from His redemptive work and rose from the mountain into Heaven, bringing His "sheaves" with Him.

But that's not all!

Remember that dove with the olive branch? When Jesus was baptized, the Holy Spirit lit upon Him as He came up out of the water (remember, the flood was a picture of baptism)[51]. So we see the dove is symbolic of the Holy Spirit.

After Jesus' resurrection, He was seen on earth for 40 days, meeting with the apostles and speaking to them about the kingdom of God[52]. After the 40 days (43 days from Passover), Jesus told the apostles to wait in Jerusalem until He had sent them the Holy Spirit, and then He ascended in the clouds into Heaven for the final time.

Seven days later;

"And when the day of Pentecost was fully come,
They were all with one accord in one place,
And suddenly there came a sound from heaven as of a rushing, mighty wind,
And it filled all the house where they were sitting... and they
were all filled with the Holy Ghost..." – Acts 2:1-2, 4

On the same day Noah first sent out the dove, and it returned to him, Jesus ascended into Heaven. And on the same day that Noah sent the dove again and it returned to him with an olive branch in its beak, was the day the Lord sent the Holy Spirit from Heaven, bearing "gifts" to men on the day of Pentecost. Just as the dove signaled the end of Noah's ordeal and the beginning of new life; the coming of the Holy Spirit signaled the beginning of new life for believers, and a New Day on our kingdom calendar. If all of this doesn't thrill you, you are unthrillable!

---

51   Mat. 3:16; Mark 1:10; Luke 3:22; John 1:32
52   Acts 1:2-3, 9-11

Day 4 - The Day of Kings & Prophets

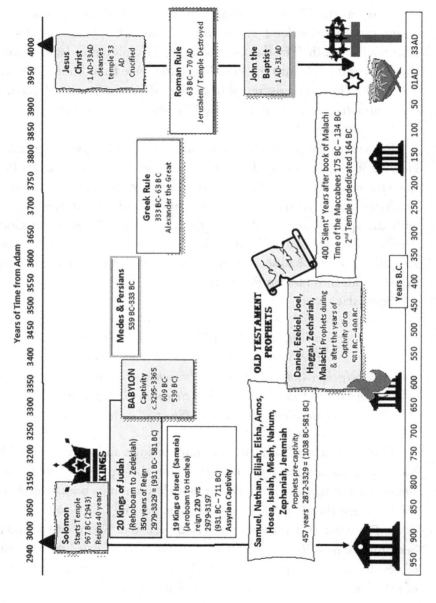

Years of Time from Adam

2940 3000 3050 3100 3150 3200 3250 3300 3350 3400 3450 3500 3550 3600 3650 3700 3750 3800 3850 3900 3950 4000

Solomon
Starts Temple
967 BC (2943)
Reigns 40 years

KINGS

20 Kings of Judah
(Rehoboam to Zedekiah)
350 years of Reign
2979-3329 = (931 BC - 581 BC)

19 Kings of Israel (Samaria)
(Jeroboam to Hoshea)
reign 220 yrs
2979-3197
(931 BC - 711 BC)
Assyrian Captivity

BABYLON
Captivity
c.3295-3365
609 BC -
539 BC)

Medes & Persians
539 BC-333 BC

Greek Rule
333 BC - 63 BC
Alexander the Great

Roman Rule
63 BC - 70 AD
Jerusalem / Temple Destroyed

Jesus Christ
1 AD-33AD
cleanses
temple 33
AD
Crucified

John the Baptist
1 AD-31 AD

OLD TESTAMENT PROPHETS

Samuel, Nathan, Elijah, Elsha, Amos,
Hosea, Isaiah, Micah, Nahum,
Zephaniah, Jeremiah
Prophets pre-captivity
457 years 2872-3329 = (1038 BC-581 BC)

Daniel, Ezekiel, Joel,
Haggai, Zechariah,
Malachi Prophets during
& after the years of
Captivity circa
581 BC - 400 BC

400 "Silent" Years after book of Malachi
Time of the Maccabees 175 BC - 134 BC
2nd Temple rededicated 164 BC

Years B.C.

950 900 850 800 750 700 650 600 550 500 450 400 350 300 250 200 150 100 50 01AD 33AD

CHAPTER 6

DAY FIVE – Day of Fish and Birds

"Then God said, "Let the waters abound with
an abundance of living creatures,
and let birds fly above the earth
across the face of the firmament of the heavens."
So God created great sea creatures and every living thing that moves,
with which the waters abounded, according to their kind,
and every winged bird according to its kind. And God saw that it was good.
And God blessed them, saying, "Be fruitful and multiply,
and fill the waters in the seas, and let birds multiply on the earth."
So the evening and the morning were the fifth day."
- Gen. 1:20-23

The Fifth Day of Creation, God created fish and birds: Every kind of aquatic life, and every kind of bird.

Responsibility along with Blessing is a new concept introduced on this day of creation. In a sense, each day as God surveyed His work and pronounced it "good", God was giving His blessing on His creation. But this day, the fish and birds were given a blessing and a command, to be fruitful and multiply. While plant life had seed in itself, it was not given any command or instruction – reproduction would occur without any act of will on its part. But being fruitful is an action which the animals must perform – it would not be automatic. God blessed them and gave them a responsibility at the same time.

This is a concept we will see throughout scripture – blessing and responsibility go hand in hand (there are even five digits on each hand, to remind us that we have both blessing and responsibility to receive and perform). To the degree that we fulfill our responsibility we will also be blessed[1]. The parameter given in the exercising of this blessing was the responsibility to reproduce only according to kind. Birds will not produce fish, and fish will not produce birds. This will come up again many times, but there can be no ignoring the fact that God puts great importance on keeping different kinds separate. Life did not evolve from one kind into another kind. Attempts made to cross breed different kinds in nature generally fail, or result in sterile offspring.

THE FIFTH AGE OF TIME: THE DAY OF THE FISH AND THE EAGLE

Day Five of the Ages of Time (Fifth Millennia of Time or History) covers the years from about 33A.D.-1033A.D. (or about 4000-5000 years from Adam in the timeline). When Jesus rode triumphantly into Jerusalem, being proclaimed the King of Israel by the adoring crowd[2], it marked a pivotal moment in time. We do not know what might have happened had His own people received Him at that time, but we do know that within a week, the Jews, spurred on by their religious leaders, rejected Jesus as their king and called for His crucifixion[3]. When He was rejected by the Jews, and then mocked and proclaimed King of the Jews by Rome[4], it became a conspiracy to crucify the Son of God of which the whole world became guilty[5]. What has come to be known as the Passion Week of Christ marked the end of the time of Kings, and the beginning of a new Day on the Kingdom calendar. This fifth age of time encompasses the betrayal and crucifixion of Christ, His resurrection and the early Church Age.

---

[1]   Deut. 11:26-27
[2]   John 12:12-19
[3]   Mark 15:13-20
[4]   Mat. 27:29; Mark 15:18; Luke 23:38; John 19:3, 19
[5]   John 19:4-6; Matt.26:59-62

Remember, seas are prophetic symbols of nations[6], and in this Age, we see a shift from a focus on the nation of Israel to the Gentile nations of the earth. Gentiles are any people or nations who are not Jewish. Eagles are prophetic symbols of spiritual powers. So we see that the Fifth Age of time focuses largely on the battle for supremacy between global spiritual ruling powers.

Just as the fifth day of creation was dominated by fish and birds, the fifth age of time would be defined and dominated by the rise of two global powers: the Roman Empire, and the Christian Church. The symbol of the Roman empire was the eagle. The symbol of the early church was the fish.

The Times of the Gentiles

Although, we see a shift from a focus on the nation of Israel to the Gentile nations, in actuality, it is a continuation of the relationship between God and His people.

"Then Paul and Barnabas grew bold and said,
"It was necessary that the word of God should
be spoken to you (the Jews) first;
but since you reject it, and judge yourselves unworthy of everlasting life,
behold, we turn to the Gentiles.
For so the Lord has commanded us: 'I have set you as a light to the Gentiles,
That you should be for salvation to the ends of
the earth.'"" – Acts 13:46-47 NKJV

"that the blessing of Abraham might come upon the Gentiles in Christ Jesus,
that we might receive the promise of the Spirit through faith." – Gal. 3:14

"that the Gentiles should be fellow heirs, of the same body,
and partakers of His promise in Christ through the gospel," - Eph. 3:6

Before the nation of Israel, God had a people. Adam, Seth, Enoch and Noah; none of them were Jews. Not even Abraham was Jewish. He,

---

[6]   Rev. 17:15

in fact, was the father of "many nations"[7]. It was not until Jacob's name was changed to Israel that Israel became a people, and not until the time of Moses and the Exodus did they become a nation. At the time when the nation of Israel was dispersed (around 70 A.D. with the destruction of Jerusalem and the Temple), God still had a people. God's people are not determined by their earthly birth or nationality, but by their spiritual rebirth.

Paul said, "*For he is not a Jew which is one outwardly, neither is that circumcision which is outward in the flesh. But he is a Jew which is one inwardly, and circumcision is that of the heart, in the spirit, and not in the letter...*"-Rom.2:28-29

The eleventh chapter of Hebrews, sometimes called the Faith Chapter, lists biblical heroes of the faith, many of which predate the nation of Israel. The third through the fifth chapters of Romans goes into this doctrine in more detail, if you are inclined to look into it further. My point here is to draw attention to the fact that there is a continuity and flow to all that God does, and has done since creation. He had a plan and purpose in the beginning, and He scoped it all out for us in the very opening chapters of Genesis.

This Fifth Age of Time is the beginning of the Times of the Gentiles[8], but these times will extend through the Sixth Age as well. Although the New Testament church was born on the Day of Pentecost, just a few weeks after Christ's resurrection, it was not until the end of the first century or so that Christianity really took off in the Gentile nations. For the first three centuries after Christ, Christianity was considered a Jewish sect[9]. After that, it became almost exclusively associated with the Gentiles and all but invisible in the Jewish nation.

These two most prominent groups that emerged during this millennium: the Roman Empire and The Christian Church, would both grow to dominate the world in different ways. Though this Age begins with these two forces opposing one another, by the end of the Age they would become virtually one and the same thing.

---

7   Gen. 17:4-5.

8   Luke 21:24

9   Acts 24:5,14; 28:21-31

The Symbol of the Early Christian Church – The Fish

"Among the symbols employed by the early Christians, that of the fish seems to have ranked first in importance. Its popularity among Christians was due principally to the famous acrostic consisting of the initial letters of five Greek words forming the word for fish (Ichthus), which words briefly but clearly described the character of Christ and the claim to worship of believers: ... This explanation is given among others by Augustine in his Civitate Dei."[10]

"Basically, the fish represents the phrase of 'Jesus Christ God's Son is Savior'... During the times of persecution by the Romans in the first centuries, the fish symbol was used among Christians in hiding to display meeting places for everyone to meet and worship."[11]

As persecution from Rome increased, early Christians adopted the fish symbol not only to determine meeting places, but also to identify themselves to one another. The story goes that when meeting strangers, an early Christian might draw one arch of the fish symbol in the sand. If the stranger then drew the other arch, it would indicate that they too were Christian.

The reason for the fish becoming a Christian symbol are likely at least two fold. The Greek letters ΙΧΘΥΣ can be read as an acrostic for "Jesus Christ, God's son, savior." Additionally, Jesus used the analogy of fish when speaking to his disciples about the souls of mankind. Jesus told them;

"Follow Me, and I will make you fishers of men" – Matt. 4:19

Feeding the Multitudes with Bread and Fish

Fish figured prominently in a number of Jesus' teachings, and in His miracles: He fed the five thousand with five loves and two fish, and four thousand with seven loaves and a few small fish[12].

---

[10]   Maurice Hassett. *Symbolism of the Fish.* Catholic Encyclopedia. (New York: Robert Appleton Company, 1913)

[11]   Blair Parke. Ichthys, The Christian Fish Symbol: 5 Origin and History Facts. Biblestudytools.com. 2022

[12]   Mat. 14:17-22; Mat. 15:33-38

Bread is prophetically symbolic of the Word of God[13]; fish are symbolic of those who belong to God. In the Old Testament, God spoke to the nation of Israel through Moses and Aaron (two "fish"). In the New Testament, at the end times, He will speak to them through the 2 witnesses of Revelation[14]. Through Moses, He fed Israel with the five books of the Pentateuch, also known as the Torah (first five books of the Old Testament). The New Testament believers are fed through the Word and the Spirit.

"God, who at sundry times and in divers manners
Spoke in time past unto the fathers by the prophets,
Has in these last days spoken unto us by His Son,,,," – Heb. 1:1

Seven is the number of perfection or completion, and seven is always associated with Christ and His work on earth. He is the stone with the seven eyes (spirit of knowledge and wisdom) in Zechariah 3, and the lamb with seven horns and seven eyes in Revelation 5. He is the seven-armed menorah in Zechariah 4 and Revelation 1. He is the One who holds the seven stars and walks among the seven churches in Revelation 1. Feeding the four thousand with the seven loaves was symbolic of feeding His church, made up of people from every nation, with His spirit and commissioning the churches to distribute the Gospel.

There are eight who penned the New Testament (Matthew, Mark, Luke, John, Paul, James, Peter, and Jude). These "few small fish" penned the gospels and epistles that make up the New Testament.

Fish of the Sea

Jesus also said the kingdom of heaven was like a net that is cast into the sea and brings in many different kinds of fish[15]. Fish represent the souls of men, which the church is to captivate with the gospel of Christ. As fish are life in the seas (which symbolically are the nations), so men are lives or souls in the nations.

---

[13]   Mat.4:4
[14]   Rev. 3:3
[15]   Mat.13:47-50

To those who asked Jesus for a sign that He was the Messiah, He said that no sign would be given them except the sign of Jonah, who spent three days and three nights in the belly of the fish[16]. These are just a few examples of how fish were referred to in Jesus' teaching, so we see that fish are closely associated with Christ and His followers.

There is another beautiful symbolic fact to be found here. Though seas represent the nations; prophetically, water represents life and the Holy Spirit. Specifically, the life that comes through the Word of God and receiving the Spirit. As all life on earth rises out of water, and is sustained by water, so spiritual water gives and sustains spiritual life.

As God spoke, and life arose out of the water, so we are made new through the "washing of the water of the Word"[17], and the "washing of regeneration and renewing of the Holy Ghost"[18]. Fish do not only live in the seas, but they do only live in water. Fish, therefore, are symbolic of the souls of men who receive life from the Word and Spirit. The apostles are sent out as fishermen to catch these souls of men for God. It was on this Day of Time that the Holy Spirit was first poured out on all flesh.

In another amazing and beautiful symbology, the Holy Spirit is sometimes depicted as a Dove! So this age of time will be a spiritual conflict between the Eagle and the Dove.

The Symbol of the Roman Empire - The Eagle

"The eagle with its keen eyes symbolized perspicacity, courage, strength and immortality, but is also considered "king of the skies" and messenger of the highest Gods". With these attributed qualities the eagle became a symbol of power and strength in Ancient Rome. The eagle as a "heraldic animal" of the Roman Republic was introduced in 102 BC by consul Gaius Marius. An aquila, or eagle, was a prominent symbol used in ancient Rome, especially as the standard of a Roman legion. A legionary known as an aquilifer, or eagle-bearer, carried this standard. Each legion carried one eagle. The eagle was extremely important to the Roman military,

---

16   Mat.12:40
17   Eph. 5:26
18   Titus 3:5

*beyond merely being a symbol of a legion. A lost standard was considered
an extremely grave occurrence, and the Roman military often went to great
lengths to both protect a standard and to recover it if lost; for example, see
the aftermath of the Battle of the Teutoburg Forest, where the Romans
spent decades attempting to recover the lost standards of three legions."[19]*

Just as eagles are powerful birds of prey that dominate the air; prophetically, eagles represent mighty spiritual powers that rule over the earth. They may be good, or evil.

The four creatures that surround the throne of God in heaven have as one of their faces the face of an eagle[20], and the Lord is depicted as an eagle that rises with "healing in His wings"[21].

But the Bible also likens satanic forces and wicked kings to eagles.

> *"Your terribleness has deceived you,
> And the pride of your heart, O you that dwells in the clefts of the rock,
> That holds the height of the hill,
> Though you should make your nest as high as the eagle,
> I will bring you down from there, says the Lord." – Jer. 49:16*

The Bible indicates that the affairs of men on earth are controlled by spiritual beings, and that when we resist evil, we are not primarily resisting other humans, but spiritual hierarchies.

> *"For we wrestle not against flesh and blood,
> But against principalities, against powers,
> Against the rulers of the darkness of this world,
> Against spiritual wickedness in high places." – Eph. 6:12*

As fish represent souls for Christ, the eagles represent world powers that rule over the earth and that prey on the fish.

---

[19] James Yates, in the public domain, *A Dictionary of Greek and Roman Antiquities* (pp,1044-1046).

[20] Eze. 1:10; Rev. 4:7

[21] Mal. 4:2

"Where in time past you walked according to the course of this world,
According to the prince of the power of the air,
The spirit that now works in the children of disobedience." – Eph. 2:2

The power that most persecuted the early church was the Roman empire: The Eagle. In the first few centuries of this Age, Roman rulers such as Claudius, Nero, Domitian, Trajan and Diocletian persecuted and tried to suppress the growing Christian faith. Dr. Philip Irving Mitchell in his work, *Ancient Christian Martyrdom* writes:

"In the first few centuries, Christianity grew quickly. By AD100, it had become mostly Gentile and had begun to break from its Jewish origins. By 200, the faith had permeated most regions of the Roman Empire, though Christians were mostly in the larger urban areas (Gaul, Lyons, Carthage, Rome). By 325, an estimated 7 million were Christians with as many as 2 million killed for the faith."[22]

According to *Fox's Book of Martyrs*, there were many thousands executed by Rome for their Christian faith[23]. Although some scholars have argued against that number, John Fox heavily documents his claims with names, dates, and exacting detail. To me, the arguments of the doubters seem to miss the point. What number of innocents slain is acceptable? Whatever the number of people who have been martyred for their faith (and who continue to be killed to this day), the intent of their persecutors remains the same: the extermination of the Christian faith. The first half of this Age was marked by pressure and persecution of Rome against the growing threat to its power that the Christian church posed.

Why was Christianity, in particular, such a threat to the Roman empire? Emperor worship was mandatory in the empire, and this was necessary to maintain the absolute power the empire wielded over its subjects. When Rome conquered a new territory, the people were allowed to retain their own cultures and worship, as long as they paid homage to Rome as supreme. Christians were expected to perform a pagan religious

---

[22] Dr. Philip Irving Mitchell. *Ancient Christian Martyrdom. (www.3dbu.edu. mitchell)* 2001, Dallas Baptist University.

[23] John Fox. Fox's Book of Martyrs. (first published 1563, England) Edited by William Byron Forbush, D.D. (The John C. Winston Company. Philadelphia, Chicago.1926).

observance in which offerings were made and lip service was rendered to Rome.

> *"When undertaken, Christians would receive a Certificate of Sacrifice from the local Sacrificial Commission, and so be cleared of suspicion of undermining the religious unity of the Empire."*[24] – *Mark Galli, Christianity Today*

Many people complied rather than suffer persecution or death. To pagan faiths who already worshipped multiple gods, adding one more was not a problem. But for Christians, who confess only One God, compliance was out of the question. As a result, these few small fish set themselves up to become a particular target of the mighty Roman Eagle.

This time came to be known as the Era of the Martyrs, and many of the early bishops of the church gave their lives in spreading the gospel. *Fox's Book of Martyrs* chronicles many of their stories. If you have never read it, you would do well to acquaint yourself with the great men and women of faith who went before us.

One particular martyr I would like to tell you about is St. George.

> *"During the Diocletian persecutions, St. George went boldly to the senate house and avowed his being a Christian, taking occasion at the same time to remonstrate against paganism, and point out the absurdity of worshipping idols. This freedom so greatly provoked the senate that St. George was ordered to be tortured, and by the emperor's orders was dragged through the streets, and beheaded the next day.*
> *The legend of the dragon, which is associated with this martyr, is usually illustrated by representing St. George seated upon a charging horse and transfixing the monster with his spear. This fiery dragon symbolized the devil, who was vanquished by St. George's steadfast faith in Christ, which remained unshaken in spite of torture and death."*[25]

I wanted to share his story because, like many other true heroes of the faith, his story has been relegated to the status of myth and legend.

---

[24]   Mark Galli. *Christian History* Issue #23. Christianity Today, 1990.
[25]   (Fox, 1926 (first publishedn1563)). P. 33

In doing so, his testimony has become overshadowed by foolish fairy tales, and we lose the fact that he was a real flesh and blood person who heroically suffered painfully for the faith we all share. We owe it to those who have gone before us not to allow their sacrifices to be trivialized and dismissed as myth.

There were ten major persecutions during this time by the Roman empire, starting with Nero and ending with Diocletian. It is estimated that Christians only made up about 1.9 % of the Roman population in 250 A.D. The young faith continued to grow and flourish, despite persecution and threats from the mighty empire. By the middle of the fourth century, it is estimated that Christians comprised nearly one half of the Roman population![26]

About this time, in 313 A.D., the emperor Constantine converted to Christianity, and the tide began to shift in this epic conflict. Although that may seem to be a victory for Christianity, the sad truth is that by the end of this age, the church and Rome would merge into one entity. This united force then became the single greatest persecutor not only of the true disciples of Christ, but of Jews and Muslims as well as anyone who did not bow to their authority. The Crusades, which lasted well into the next Age, had begun.

Oddly enough, when the Church stopped being persecuted, and started getting organized and consolidating its power, it fell into many of the same abuses Rome did before them. The old saying "power corrupts and absolute power corrupts absolutely" proved to be true. As Rome could not tolerate any threats to its power, neither could the newly organized Roman Church. One of the first things Constantine instructed to be done after officially recognizing Christianity was for the church to consolidate power and doctrine. Up until that time, Christianity was largely made up of individual churches who mostly governed themselves. Constantine's edict resulted in the First Council of Nicaea in 325 A.D.[27] It was this council that codified and consolidated much early Christian doctrine and established authority in a central church in Rome.

---

[26] Rodney Stark. *The Rise of Christianity. Princeton University Press, Harper, San Francisco. 1996.* (Stark, 1996)

[27] The Encyclopedia Britannica. *First Council of Nicaea.* Updated Jan 2024. (britannica.com)

"The formation of the Holy Roman Empire was initiated by Charlemagne's coronation as 'Emperor of the Romans' in 800 A.D., and consolidated by Otto I when he was crowned emperor in 962 by Pope John XII." [28]

Thus was born the Holy Roman Catholic church, official religion of the Holy Roman Empire. And thus began a new kind of state sanctioned persecution against fellow Christians who did not fall into obedience to the Catholic Church.

Instead of being People of The Book (as the Jews represented themselves to be), those of the Roman Catholic tradition became people of The Church. One of the main dogmas of the Catholic Church is that there is no salvation outside of "the church". The catechism of the Catholic church states:

"Outside the Church There is No Salvation".
How do we understand this saying from the Church Fathers? All salvation comes from Christ through his Body, the Church which is necessary for salvation because Christ is present in his Church. Jesus said, "The man who believes and accepts Baptism will be saved; the man who refuses to believe in it will be condemned" (Mk 16:16). By these words Jesus also affirmed the necessity of the Church, because Baptism is its door to the Church." [29]

The King James Bible renders Mark 16:16 as:

"He that believeth and is baptized shall be saved;
But he that believeth not shall be damned."- Mark 16:16

Of the seventeen most prominent English versions of the Bible, none of them inserts the words "in it". Doing so changes the meaning, and the Catholic church does so in order to claim that they (the church) are the "it" that one must believe in in order to be saved.

This is not a treatise on Catholicism, but my point is that by the end of the first millennia A.D., the church, which was to be the body of Christ

---

[28] World Civilizations I (HIS101) – Biel. The Middle Ages in Europe. *The Holy Roman Empire.* (https://courses.lumenlearning.com)

[29] From the Catechism of the Catholic Church, Simplified (MaryFoundation@ catholicity.com)

on earth, stopped being a living, spiritual organism, and became instead a manmade organization. This organized, institutionalized church began usurping for themselves the same powers that Rome had claimed. Worse, they also claimed for themselves the power that only belongs to God. The pope became the king maker, and the Church became the state. And, like Rome, they persecuted severely any who did not fall into line.

We will look much more at this Day in Part II, but for now, we see that the two most dominate groups of the Fifth Day of History (Rome and the Christian Church), can be symbolized by birds and fish – just as the fifth day of Creation.

Day 5 - The Day of Fish & Birds

Years of Time from Adam

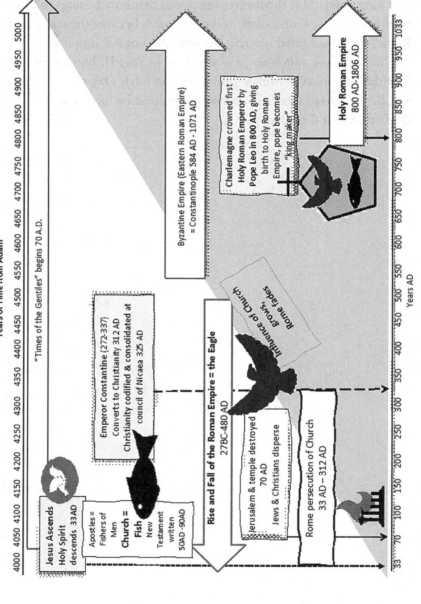

"Times of the Gentiles" begins 70 A.D.

Jesus Ascends
Holy Spirit
descends 33 AD

Apostles =
Fishers of
Men
**Church =
Fish**
New
Testament
written
50AD - 90AD

Emperor Constantine (272-337)
Converts to Christianity 312 AD
Christianity codified & consolidated at
council of Nicaea 325 AD

Rise and Fall of the Roman Empire = the Eagle
27BC-480 AD

Influence of Church
grows,
Rome fades.

Byzantine Empire (Eastern Roman Empire)
= Constantinople 584 AD - 1071 AD

Jerusalem & temple destroyed
70 AD
Jews & Christians disperse

Rome persecution of Church
33 AD – 312 AD

Charlemagne crowned first
Holy Roman Emperor by
Pope Leo in 800 AD, giving
birth to Holy Roman
Empire, pope becomes
"king maker"

Holy Roman Empire
800 AD-1806 AD

Years AD

CHAPTER 7

DAY SIX – Day of Beasts, Man & Bride

"Then God said, "Let the earth bring forth the
living creature according to its kind:
cattle and creeping thing and beast of the earth,
each according to its kind"; and it was so....
And God saw that it was good.
Then God said, "Let Us make man in Our
image, according to Our likeness..."
So God created man in His own image; ...
male and female He created them.
Then God blessed them, and God said to them,
"Be fruitful and multiply; fill the earth and subdue it;
have dominion over the fish of the sea, over the birds of the air,
and over every living thing that moves on the earth."
...Then God saw everything that He had
made, and indeed it was very good.
So the evening and the morning were the sixth day." – Gen. 1:24-31

On Day 6 the concepts of blessing, responsibility and authority are all mentioned again. The command to reproduce according to kind is given to all living things; plants, animals and man. Of all living creatures, only the man and woman were created in the image and likeness of God. The word "image" is the Hebrew word "selem" and it means "a shade, a shadow, a resemblance"[1].

---

[1]   James Strong, *The New Strong's Exhaustive Concordance of the Bible* (Nashville: T. Nelson, 1990), H6754.

Both the man and the woman were to be reflections of God on earth. Both the man and the woman were to exercise dominion and care over the earth and animals. Both were blessed.

But to each was also given some specific, unique abilities and responsibilities.

> *"And the Lord God said, "It is not good that man should be alone;*
> *I will make him a helper comparable to him." ...*
> *Then the rib which the Lord God had taken*
> *from man He made into a woman,*
> *and He brought her to the man. And Adam said:*
> *"This is now bone of my bones And flesh of my flesh;*
> *She shall be called Woman,*
> *Because she was taken out of Man." – Genesis 2:18, 22-23 NKJV*

Men and Women – Equal But Different

God is the author of marriage – it is not a product of man's invention, but a gift to mankind's need. Even in the beginning of creation, when everything was pronounced very good by God, the one thing that was not good was for man to be alone. God's solution to man's aloneness was to create woman. She would be a mate comparable to him, but also different from him. Adam called her "woman", which literally means "the other", or "the one who is other"[2]. She was part of him, but she was also altogether "other" than him.

In God's design, men and women were meant to compliment and complete each other, not compete with one another. Both were created in the image of God and without both, the reflection of God is incomplete. Paul writes:

> *Nevertheless, neither is man independent of woman,*
> *nor woman independent of man, in the Lord.*
> *For as woman came from man, even so man also comes through woman;*
> *but all things are from God." – 1 Corinthians 11:11-12 NLT[3]*

---

[2]   James Strong, *The New Strong's Exhaustive Concordance of the Bible* (Nashville: T. Nelson, 1990), H802.

[3]   Holy Bible, New Living Translation (NLT) (Tyndale House Publishers, 1996) Used by permission.

There are things about God that can only be reflected by a man. There are also things about God that only a woman reflects. It takes both together to make mankind, who reflects the image and glory of God.

In Genesis 2, God said He would create a "help comparable to" man. The Hebrew word used was *'ezer*, and it means "helper, comforter, reliever, rescuer, consoler"[4]. It is one who rescues by surrounding (as a shield) or embracing. The only other place in scripture the word is used is in reference to God, as in the Psalms when we are told the Lord is "our Help and our Shield"[5].

God created men and women to be side by side, united in joint responsibility over the earth and animals. In the Fall, as described in Genesis 3, there was a complete breakdown of the divine order. Everything was turned upside down.

After they had sinned, it was to Adam the Lord addressed His first question because, as the elder created being, he bore the greater responsibility. God addressed each one according to their rightful responsibility: Adam first, then Eve, and lastly the serpent.

Godly authority was established with the man carrying the greater responsibility to lead well right from the beginning. The fall was not what gave man the headship of the family. Rather, what the fall bestowed was abuse of that power, and resentment of his headship. The Angels in heaven, all of whom are greater in might and wisdom than humans, willingly submit to the headship of Christ and God. Authority is not a curse. It is part of an ordered and orderly society. Without leadership, chaos and confusion ensue. God is not the author of confusion. Where ever confusion reigns, you can be sure satanic forces are at work, it is one of his hallmarks.

"For God is not the author of confusion,
But of peace, as in all churches of the saints." – 1 Cor. 14:33

"For where envying and strife is,
There is confusion and every evil work." – James 3:16

---

[4]   James Strong, *The New Strong's Exhaustive Concordance of the Bible* (Nashville: T. Nelson, 1990), H5828.
[5]   Psalm 33:20; 115:9-11; 121:2.

This confusion of roles in many ways was the original sin, or at least the state that led to original sin. Dominion over the animals and earth was given to humans, and the man was given the responsibility to lead and protect his wife. In the fall, we see the woman being led by a beast, and the man being led by the woman. The whole order of things is confused.

THE SIXTH AGE OF TIME: THE DAY OF BEASTS, MAN & BRIDE

Following the pattern established in the sixth day of creation, the sixth age of time is characterized by the rise of the beasts of the earth, which represent the different nations. It will culminate with the appearance of the Son of God and Man returning for His Bride, the church.

Beasts and Men

A significant characteristic of this sixth age of beasts and men is the blurring of the lines between what is beast and what is man. The Theory of Evolution, which gained prominence in the latter part of this Day, and is now taught as absolute fact, teaches that man is nothing more than an evolved animal. Just as in the days of Noah (which preceded the last global extinction event), this millennia of time experiments with the mixing of different kinds of animal, plant and human DNA. Genetically modified plants and animals are so commonplace that pure specimens are considered heirloom or specialty. This has not been limited to plants and animals.

This state of confusion is not limited to the mixing of man and beast, but also extends to confusion of gender. Just as in the account of the fall of man in Genesis, the confusion that resulted when Eve usurped the place of Adam, is a dominating characteristic of our modern culture. We now have not merely confusion concerning the roles of the different genders, but of what gender even means. We live in an age in which a supreme court nominated judge does not feel qualified to judge what the definition of a woman is.

*"In the 13th hour of Judge Ketanji Brown Jackson's confirmation
hearing Tuesday, Sen. Marsha Blackburn, R-Tenn., asked the Supreme
Court nominee: "Can you provide a definition for the word 'woman'?'
Jackson, appearing confused, responded, "I'm not a biologist.""*[6]

It would be laughable were it not so tragic.

The sixth Day of Time, which is next to the last millennium of the
Seven Ages, is our present time. It encompasses the years 5000-6000
from Adam, or about 1033 A.D. to 2033 A.D. Remember these times are
approximate – we cannot know the exact day and hour, however, we can
certainly observe the times and seasons! In fact, Jesus strongly reprimanded
the Pharisees of His day because they failed to understand the times in
which they lived.

*"He answered and said unto them,
'When it is evening, you say, It will be fair weather, for the sky is red.
And in the morning, It will be foul weather
today, for the sky is read and lowering.
O you hypocrites. You can discern the face of the sky,
But can you not discern the signs of the times?" – Matt. 16:2-3*

Although we cannot know the exact day and hour that this age will
end and Christ will return, we certainly have a responsibility to discern
the prophetic times in which we live. The things that the Bible reveals are
meant for us to study and understand.

The Rise of The Beasts of the Earth

In the fifth millennia, the mighty Roman empire and the emerging
Christian church slowly fused into one entity: the Holy Roman Empire.
This mighty global power encompassed most of the known western world,
and even the new lands which were discovered. But in the course of this
thousand years, the empire would break up into many individual nations.
New religions in the east such as Islam, as well as the Protestant movement

---

[6]   Alia E. Dastagir, USA Today. March 24, 2022.

in the west became major influences in the world. As Europeans began to expand into the New World, new people groups, with their own religious traditions were discovered. The Age of Exploration and Discovery soon became the Age of Colonization, Industrialization, and World Wars.

From the end of the first millennia A.D. to the present, history has been dominated by the rise of the various kingdoms and nations of the earth. Some have attempted world domination, but invariably the would-be conquerors were defeated, and more nations fractured into sovereign states. In the book of Daniel, as well as the book of Revelation, we see these kingdoms are depicted as beasts that rise and dominate the world.

"Those great beasts, which are four,
are four kings *which* arise out of the earth." – Daniel 7:7

"Thus he said: 'The fourth beast shall be a fourth kingdom on earth,
Which shall be different from all other kingdoms, And shall devour
the whole earth, Trample it and break it in pieces. – Daniel 7:23

"So he carried me away in the Spirit into the wilderness. And I saw a
woman sitting on a scarlet beast which was full of names of blasphemy,
having seven heads and ten horns. ...
But the angel said to me, "Why did you marvel?
I will tell you the mystery of the woman and of the beast that carries her, ...
The ten horns which you saw are ten kings who have received no kingdom
as yet, but they receive authority for one hour as kings with the beast."
- Revelation 17:3,7,12

Even today we are familiar with the concept of kingdoms and nations representing themselves by various beasts and birds. We have the American bald eagle, the Russian bear, and the English lion.

In the Bible, Christ is represented as the Lion of Judah as well as the Lamb of God. The Anti-Christ is referred to as The Beast, and Satan is represented as a Dragon and a serpent.

From the standpoint of prophecy, one of the most significant occurrences during this sixth age of time is the re-emergence of the nation of Israel and their return to their homeland (in 1948 A.D., or year 5708 on the Jewish calendar). In the book of Micah, the Gentile nations are referred to as "beasts of the forest" and Israel as "a lion among flocks of sheep".

"And the remnant of Jacob Shall be among the Gentiles,
In the midst of many peoples,
Like a lion among the beasts of the forest,
Like a young lion among flocks of sheep,..."– Micah 5:8

The Times of the Gentiles

This Sixth Day of Time, together with the Fifth Age of Time, is also referred to as the Times of the Gentiles. The Times of the Gentiles began with two major events that shifted the Times: The first event was the day of Pentecost, when the Holy Spirit was given, and the Church Age was ushered in. That would be around 33 A.D. The second event was the destruction of Jerusalem and the temple, scattering the nation of Israel throughout the world in 70 A.D. The result of both of these events is a shift from God dealing with the world through the nation of Israel, to His working through His church, which is made up of people of all nations. The reemergence of the nation of Israel after nearly two thousand years of being without a homeland marks the beginning of the next shift in time.

The Church Age (which is another name for the Times of the Gentiles) will continue until Christ raptures His church – returning the focus again primarily on the nation of Israel. Some believe the rebuilding of the temple in Jerusalem and the resumption of the daily sacrifices will be what ushers in the end of the Times of the Gentiles. Others believe that it will be the rapture of the church. What is certain is that Jerusalem itself plays a key role in these prophetic times, as does the church. Until the temple in Jerusalem rises, or the church does, The Time of the Gentiles will continue.

Jesus said;

"And Jerusalem will be trampled by Gentiles
until the times of the Gentiles are fulfilled." – Luke 21:24

The Old Testament prophet Micah also testified of this time:

"And the remnant of Jacob Shall be among the Gentiles,
In the midst of many peoples, ..." – Micah 5:8

Note that Jesus uses the plural word "times" and not "time". Since this study is focusing on the measure of time, it seems worthy of note that the Times of the Gentiles encompasses two days of time or ages, ... hence "times".

Jesus said in numerous places,

"Destroy this temple, and in three days I will raise it up." – John 2:19

He was speaking of His resurrection from the dead, which was accomplished the third day after His death and burial. But I believe there could be an even broader application. Christ was cut off or killed in the fourth millennia of time, or in the middle of the Week of Time. He will certainly return after Three Days as well.

The 7th day of time, which corresponds with the Sabbath of the week, is the thousand-year reign of Christ on earth. This would be after His 2nd coming and the tribulation. Therefore, He must be returning sometime in THIS sixth day!

Bookends of History

There are several sets of events that bookend the Times of the Gentiles. The first set of events are the ascension of Christ into Heaven at the beginning of the times of the Gentiles, and the return of Christ from heaven at the conclusion of those times. The second set of bookended events is the coming of the Holy Spirit on Pentecost, and the taking up of the Holy Spirit at the rapture. And third is the destruction of the temple at Jerusalem (which ended temple worship); and the rebuilding of the temple which would result in the resumption of worship there. All of these have had their initial event occur, and all are now awaiting the culminating event of the age.

By any calculation, we are presently in the Times of the Gentiles. But the rebirth of the nation of Israel has great significance and signals the beginning of another shift in Time.

"For the day is near,
Even the day of the LORD is near;
It will be a day of clouds, the time of the Gentiles." – Ezek. 30:3

"And they will fall by the edge of the sword,
and be led away captive into all nations.
And Jerusalem will be trampled by Gentiles
until the times of the Gentiles are fulfilled." – Luke 21:24

Luke indicates that the regathering of Israel, and her repossession of Jerusalem, will indicate that the times of the Gentiles are nearly over.

The End of The Day

Much of the prophetic events which the Bible foretells concerning this Week of Creation have already played out. Historically speaking, we are living in the Sixth Day and it is nearly midnight!

The Sixth Day of History, as we have discussed, sees the rise of the beasts (or nations) of the earth. At the end of this Day, a new world leader will rise, and with him a new world order. He is known in the book of Revelation as The Beast[7]. He comes to his ultimate power during a period of time known as the Seven Year Tribulation, in which God judges the nations of the world through global wars and natural disasters. It will culminate with the return of The Son of Man. The Beast will be defeated by the Lamb of God, the Lion of the Tribe of Judah.

"Now I saw heaven opened, and behold, a white horse.
And He who sat on him was called Faithful and True,
and in righteousness He judges and makes war.

---

[7]   Revelation 13.

... And the armies in heaven, clothed in fine linen, white and clean,
followed Him on white horses.
...And I saw the beast, the kings of the earth, and their
armies, gathered together to make war against Him
who sat on the horse and against His army."
– Rev. 19:11,14,19

Just as in Noah's day when there was a one world government headed by a despotic ruler (Nimrod), whose kingdom was Babylon; so these things will all be again at the end of this Age. The book of Revelation refers to both the city and the kingdom of the Antichrist as Babylon[8].

We will look at the events of this time in greater detail in Part II of this book, but for now we see that the Sixth Age of Time, like the sixth day of creation, begins with the beasts, and ends with the Bride!

---

[8]   Rev.14:8; 18:10,21.

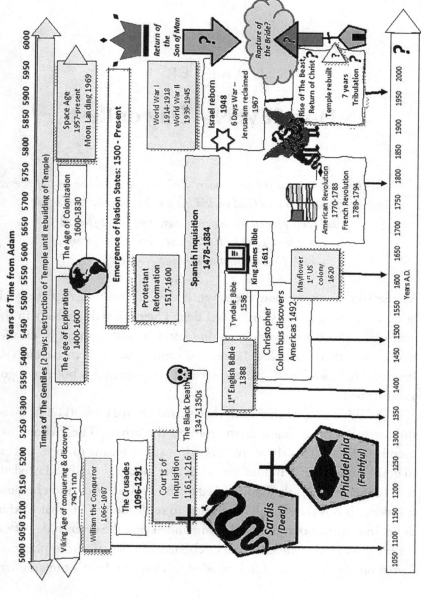

Day 6 - The Day of Beasts, Man & Bride

Years of Time from Adam

Times of The Gentiles (2 Days: Destruction of Temple until rebuilding of Temple)

5000 5050 5100 5150 5200 5250 5300 5350 5400 5450 5500 5550 5600 5650 5700 5750 5800 5850 5900 5950 6000

Space Age
1957-present
Moon Landing 1969

The Age of Colonization
1600-1830

The Age of Exploration
1400-1600

Viking Age of conquering & discovery
790-1100

William the Conqueror
1066-1087

The Crusades
1096-1291

Courts of Inquisition
1161-1216

The Black Death
1347-1350s

1st English Bible
1388

Tyndale Bible
1536

King James Bible
1611

Christopher Columbus discovers Americas 1492

Mayflower
1st US colony
1620

Protestant Reformation
1517-1600

Spanish Inquisition
1478-1834

Emergence of Nation States: 1500 - Present

World War I
1914-1918
World War II
1939-1945

Israel reborn
1948
6 Days War –
Jerusalem reclaimed
1967

American Revolution
1770-1783
French Revolution
1789-1794

Return of the Son of Man

Rapture of the Bride?

Rise of The Beast,
Return of Christ
Temple rebuilt
7 years
Tribulation

Sardis
(Dead)

Phiadelphia
(Faithful)

1050 1100 1150 1200 1250 1300 1350 1400 1450 1500 1550 1600 1650 1700 1750 1800 1850 1900 1950 2000

Years A.D.

CHAPTER 8

DAY SEVEN – Day of Rest

"Thus the heavens and the earth were finished, and all the host of them.
And on the seventh day God ended his work which he had made; ...
And God blessed the seventh day, and sanctified it:
because that in it he had rested from all his work
which God created and made." – Gen 2:1-3

As the sun dawned upon the seventh day of creation, Adam and his bride were living in the Garden of Eden. They enjoyed harmony in their relationship with the Lord, with one another, and with all of creation. Unlike the other days, God did no new creative work on the seventh day. Instead, He looked at all He had created and declared it both very good and finished.

The Bible tells us that God then rested from His work, and blessed the seventh day, setting it apart from all the others. The Hebrew word used here for "rest" is the word Sabbath – and it means to "rest, to cease, to desist from labor"[1]. It does not mean that God was tired and needed to rest. Rather it means that God ceased from His work of creation because it was done. It was time for all of creation to revel and rest in what God had done. In commemoration, God commanded that the seventh day of each week would be remembered and celebrated as a day of rest in perpetuity. Two thousand years later, God encoded this into the Ten Commandments.

---

[1]   James Strong, *The New Strong's Exhaustive Concordance of the Bible* (Nashville: T. Nelson, 1990), H7673.

Six days you shall labor and do all your work,
but the seventh day is the Sabbath of the Lord your God.
In it you shall do no work: ….
For in six days the Lord made the heavens and the earth,
the sea, and all that is in them,
and rested the seventh day. Therefore the Lord blessed the Sabbath day
and hallowed it." – Exodus 20:9-11

The Sabbath

The weekly observance of the Sabbath serves as both a memorial of what God has done in creation, and as a promise of what He will do in the future. It reminds us of where we came from, and of where we are going.

Contrary to what many believe, the concept of the Sabbath was not established with the Law which God gave to Moses on the mountain. In fact, all of the moral laws contained in the Ten Commandments were known to mankind long before God gave the Law to Moses. In Cain and Abel's day, man knew murder was wrong. God judged the world before the flood because of their wickedness[2], showing that there was an understanding of what was morally right and wrong. In Abraham's day even the pagan king Abimelech knew it was wrong to take another man's wife[3]. Jacob knew stealing was wrong[4].

The Law God gave Moses only encoded the moral law that was already known, and established a system for judging infractions of the law. It established ceremonial laws of sacrifice and worship. This ceremonial law is what Christ's sacrificial death did away with. He fully satisfied the righteous demands of the Law for dealing with sin[5]. He did not do away with the moral law, which is as eternal as creation.

The Sabbath was established in the Garden of Eden, in the first week of creation. God blessed the Sabbath day and sanctified it, meaning He set it apart. It was meant to be observed by rest from the very beginning.

---

2   Gen. 6:5-7.

3   Gen. 20:3-11.

4   Gen. 31:36-39.

5   Romans 10:4; Mat. 5:17.

Although the concept of the Sabbath did not start with Moses, the Laws about how the Sabbath was to be observed were given in the Law to Moses. These Laws were given specifically to the people of Israel, and they went into great detail about how the Sabbath was to be observed. Israel was to become a sign to all nations, revealing the Word and nature of God to every people. Through them the Law and the Prophets would testify to the whole world of salvation and the Messiah.

"Therefore the children of Israel shall keep the Sabbath,
to observe the Sabbath throughout their generations as a perpetual covenant."
— Exodus 31:16

A Day of Rest

The most significant observance of the Sabbath is that it was to be a day of rest and a day where no one was to bear burdens. Man has six days to do his work, but the seventh belongs to the Lord. Not only were God's people not to bear burdens, they were not to put burdens on anyone else either (not even animals). It was a time to release heavy burdens and to be free from the weight of toil.[6]

A Day Dedicated to the Lord

It was also to be a day that was wholly dedicated to the Lord – thinking His thoughts, doing His will. In the New Testament, it is even referred to as "The Lord's Day".[7]

God was to be utterly the Lord of the Sabbath. His will was to be considered above all else. It was not to be a burden, it was to be a blessing.

"If you turn away your foot from the Sabbath,
From doing your pleasure on My holy day,
And call the Sabbath a delight, The holy day of the Lord honorable,

---

[6]   Jeremiah 17:21-22; Isaiah 58:6-7.
[7]   Rev. 1:10

And shall honor Him, not doing your own ways,
Nor finding your own pleasure,
Nor speaking your own words,
Then you shall delight yourself in the Lord;
And I will cause you to ride on the high hills of the earth,
And feed you with the heritage of Jacob your father.
The mouth of the Lord has spoken." — Isaiah 58:13-14

Christ and the Sabbath

No one taught us more completely what it was to observe the Sabbath than Jesus Christ. He taught us that it is lawful to do good on the Sabbath, even if it meant going out of our way.[8] That it was to be a day dedicated to the Lord and His work – not to our own work. It was a rest, above everything else, from ourselves.

The Future Sabbath

The prophetic events of the first five Days of Time have already been completed in past history. The events of the Sixth Day of Time are still unfolding and will very soon come to a close. The events of the Seventh Day of Time are yet to come, although scripture gives us many glimpses of what they will be like. Paul tells us that there is a future Day of Rest yet to come for the Lord's people[9]. Clearly the Sabbath was not only a sign to Old Testament believers, but it was also to point toward a future Day of Rest for all who believe God. What day would that be?

THE SEVENTH AGE OF TIME: THE DAY OF THE LORD

The Seventh Day of Time begins when Christ returns to earth with His Bride to set up His earthly kingdom. The Beast and those who follow

---

8   Matt. 12:10-13; Luke 13:10-17.
9   Heb. 4:4-6, 9-10.

him are cast into the Lake of Fire, along with Satan, for a period of a thousand years.

"Then I saw an angel coming down from heaven,
having the key to the bottomless pit and a great chain in his hand.
He laid hold of the dragon, that serpent of old, who is the Devil and Satan,
and shut him up, and set a seal on him,
so that he should deceive the nations no more
till the thousand years were finished. ...
And I saw thrones, and they sat on them, and
judgment was committed to them...
And they lived and reigned with Christ for a
thousand years." – Revelation 20:1-4

During this time, Christ will sit on His throne and rule the nations. The earth will be restored to its rest, and conditions in nature will be like the Garden of Eden.[10] It is a time of world-wide peace, rest from the endless wars that have marked every other dispensation.[11] It is a time of healing and restoration. Those that have died in the Lord come to life again.[12] For those who live on the earth, death is rolled back (so that a person who dies at the age of 100 will be considered to have died as a child). Burdens are loosened, and good prevails. Consider these scriptures:

"... Because the former troubles are forgotten,...
The voice of weeping shall no longer be heard in her, Nor the voice of crying.
"No more shall an infant from there live but a few days,
Nor an old man who has not fulfilled his days;
For the child shall die one hundred years old, ...
For as the days of a tree, so shall be the days of My people,
And My elect shall long enjoy the work of their hands.
They shall not labor in vain, Nor bring forth children for trouble;
For they shall be the descendants of the blessed of the Lord,
And their offspring with them...

---

[10] Isaiah 51:3-5
[11] Isaiah 2:2-4.
[12] Rev. 20:6

The wolf and the lamb shall feed together. The
lion shall eat straw like the ox,
And dust shall be the serpent's food.
They shall not hurt nor destroy in all My holy mountain,"
Says the Lord." – Isaiah 65:20, 22-23, 25 NKJV

"So the ransomed of the Lord shall return,
And come to Zion with singing,
With everlasting joy on their heads.
They shall obtain joy and gladness;
Sorrow and sighing shall flee away." – Isaiah 51:11 NKJV

The Beginning, and The End

The Seventh Day of Time dawns much like the seventh day of creation did. It dawns with Christ (the second Adam) living with His Bride (the church) in a creation which has been restored to conditions it enjoyed in the Garden of Eden. It covers the thousand years reign of Christ, and ends with the final great battle for mankind. Just as the serpent entered Eden at the end of the seventh day of creation, Satan makes his entrance at the end of the thousand years. He is released from the Pit and gathers forces, once again, to challenge Christ's right to rule. It is almost as though mankind is given a second chance at the Garden of Eden – and again fails. We like to blame Adam and Eve for the fall, but this proves that even if we are returned to the Garden of Eden, we too would make the same choices they did.

"And when the thousand years are expired, Satan shall be loosed out of
his prison, and shall go out to deceive the nations which are in the four
quarters of the earth, Gog and Magog, to gather them together to battle:
the number of whom is as the sand of the sea." -Rev. 20:7-8

The Seventh Day of Time culminates with total destruction of Satan, Death, Hell, ... and Creation as we know it.

"But the day of the Lord will come as a thief in the night
And the elements shall melt with fervent heat,
The earth also and the words that are therein
shall be burned up." – 2 Peter 3:10

"…and fire came down from God out of heaven, and devoured them.
And the devil that deceived them was cast into the lake of fire
and brimstone, where the beast and the false prophet are,
and shall be tormented day and night for ever and ever.
And I saw a great white throne, and Him that sat on it,
from whose face the earth and the heaven fled away,
and there was found no place for them…
and death and hell were cast into the lake of fire…- Rev. 20:9-14

Jesus said, "Heaven and earth shall pass away,
But My words shall not pass away." – Matthew 24:35

The end of the Seventh Day of Time sees the end of this present creation, which was created in seven days. But it is not the end of the story!

The Day After the Seventh Day

So what happens after the Seventh "Day"?

"Now I saw a new heaven and a new earth,
for the first heaven and the first earth had passed away.
Also there was no more sea.
Then I, John, saw the holy city, New Jerusalem,
coming down out of heaven from God,
… And I heard a loud voice from heaven saying,
"Behold, the tabernacle of God is with men, and He will
dwell with them, and they shall be His people.
God Himself will be with them and be their God.
And God will wipe away every tear from their eyes;
there shall be no more death, nor sorrow, nor crying.

There shall be no more pain, for the former things have passed away."
Then He who sat on the throne said, "Behold, I make all
things new." And He said to me, "Write, for these words
are true and faithful." – Rev. 21:1-5 NKJV

"And he showed me a pure river of water of life,
clear as crystal, proceeding from the throne of God and of the Lamb.
In the middle of its street, and on either side of the river, was the tree of life,
which bore twelve fruits, each tree yielding its fruit every month.
The leaves of the tree were for the healing of the nations.
And there shall be no more curse, but the throne of God and of the Lamb
shall be in it, and His servants shall serve Him. They shall see His face,
and His name shall be on their foreheads. There shall be no night there:
They need no lamp nor light of the sun, for the Lord God gives them light.
And they shall reign forever and ever." – Rev. 22:1-5 NKJV

Day 7 - The Day of Rest

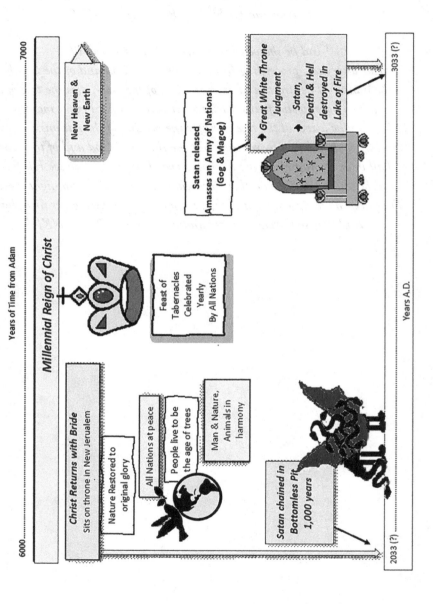

Years of Time from Adam

7000

6000

Millennial Reign of Christ

New Heaven & New Earth

Christ Returns with Bride
Sits on throne in New Jerualem

Nature Restored to original glory

All Nations at peace

People live to be the age of trees

Man & Nature, Animals in harmony

Feast of Tabernacles Celebrated Yearly By All Nations

Satan released
Amasses an Army of Nations
(Gog & Magog)

Great White Throne Judgment

Satan, Death & Hell destroyed in Lake of Fire

Satan chained in Bottomless Pit 1,000 years

2033 (?)

Years A.D.

3033 (?)

CHAPTER 9

What Time is It?

It's Later Than You Think!

As we study the Chart of the Seven Days of Time, the thing that strikes even a casual observer most forcefully is the fact that we are truly out of time. Whether we are telling time by the Jewish Calendar or the Years of Time – we are at the end of the 6th day. In fact, we are fully due for the events of Revelation to take place! The first thing I thought after completing the chart was, "Why are we still here?"!

The 7th Day is the 1000 years Reign of Christ – and before that happens, the Great Tribulation with its trumpet judgments and plagues, as well as the 2nd Coming of Christ must occur… BEFORE the 7th Day!

John was told:

> *"Behold, I am coming quickly!*
> *Blessed is he who keeps the words of the prophecy of this book"* …
> *And he said to me, "Do not seal the words of the prophecy of this book,*
> *for the time is at hand….*
> *He who testifies to these things says, "Surely I am coming quickly."*
> *Amen. Even so, come, Lord Jesus!"* – Rev. 22:7, 10, 20 NKJV

Daniel was told in Daniel 8:26 (NKJV):

> *"And the vision of the evenings and mornings which was told is true;*
> *Therefore, seal up the vision, For it refers to many days in the future."*

And again in Daniel 12:4 and 9:

*"But you, O Daniel, shut up the words, and seal the book, even to the time
of the end: many shall run to and fro, and knowledge shall be increased...
And he said, 'Go your way, Daniel,
for the words are closed up and sealed till the time of the end.'"*

Here is a mystery to consider: Daniel was told on the 4th Day (606-
526 B.C. approx.) to seal up his prophecy about the end times because it
pertained to things that were not to be until many days in the future. Yet
John was told on Day 5 (about 90 A.D. – about 700 years later) NOT to
seal up his prophecy of the end times because the time was at hand. That
was nearly 2 thousand years ago! The reason both these statements are true
becomes clear when we begin to study the book of Revelation (which is a
study for another book, which I'm working on!).

The book of Revelation tells us about a book in the hand of God
which is sealed with seven seals. In John's vision, he sees Christ entering
heaven after His resurrection and taking the book from the hand of His
Father. He then proceeds to break open the seals, one by one. As each seal
is opened, prophetic and increasingly more catastrophic events begin to
unfold on earth. When does this take place? Some teach that these events
will take place after the rapture of the church. However, it is clear from
the vision, that they begin to unfold shortly after Christ returns to heaven
after His resurrection.

Consider these evidences: In chapter four of Revelation, we see many
angels before the throne in heaven, and 24 elders sitting on thrones around
the throne of God. No mention of Christ or the church. In chapter 5, we
see John weeping because no one – not in heaven, in earth, nor under the
earth, is found worthy to take the book from the Hand of God and open
the seals. How can that be said of Christ after His resurrection and return
to Heaven? The only explanation is that at the time of this vision, Christ
had not yet completed His redemptive work.

What happens next? There is a sudden shift. Wait! Something has just
happened! Where a moment before the declaration in heaven is that there
is no one in heaven or earth who is worthy, now, a new announcement is
made. An angel tells John not to weep because "the Lion of the tribe of

Judah has prevailed to open the book".[1] And when John turns to look, he sees, not a lion, but a lamb! Christ appears as a "Lamb as it had been slain". If this event happens as Christ returns to haven with His bride, He would not appear as a slain Lamb, but as a conquering Lord. This clearly is Christ's first appearance in heaven after His resurrection.

Further, this Lamb is said to have seven horns and seven eyes "which are the seven Spirits of God sent forth into all the earth". [2] The verb tense of the original Hebrew word used here for "sent forth" indicates that this act is one that is completed at this moment, not needing to ever be repeated. As when Christ said from the cross, "It is finished!".

Jesus told His followers that He must return to the Father, because unless and until He does, the Spirit cannot be sent to them. [3] Revelation chapter five documents when that event happened. There are other evidences that Christ took the book and began to open the seals shortly after His ascension into Heaven, and not after He raptures the church.

In chapter 6, when the 5th seal is opened, the souls of those who have been killed for their faith cry out to God and ask how long it will be until He begins to judge the earth. If judgment had already begun, this would make no sense. And what are they answered? They are told to wait a little longer until their number is fulfilled. When the church is raptured, there will be great rejoicing in heaven, the bride being prepared for her wedding. But we do not see that happening in the seals.

I believe from the text, the seals describe this interval between when Christ returned to heaven and when He returns from Heaven for the church, His Bride. He is preparing a place for us. Step one: clean up the heavens, where Satan has had some access up until this time.

Consider the book of Job. We are told that Satan came before the throne of God to accuse believers. But Jesus said, shortly before the cross, that due to what was about to happened, "Now is Satan cast out".[4] Because Christ returned to heaven, having proving Himself alone as worthy to open the seals, He begins judgment with driving Satan out. No longer can he come boldly before the throne, accusing believers before God.

---

[1]   Revelation 5:5
[2]   Revelation 5:6
[3]   John 16:7
[4]   John 12:31

From the moment Christ entered Heaven at His resurrection, he took ownership of heaven and earth, and began preparing a place for us. From the moment He took the book out of the Father's hand and began opening the seals, we have been in the last days. That is why John was told not to seal up the words of his prophecy. Because the time when they would begin to unfold was at hand, even in his days.

Even in the time of Christ and the writing of the New Testament, we are told that the beginning of the end (the birth pangs as Christ referred to them), had already begun. In God's timetable, there are but two days between the cross and the second coming. On the third day after His death (on the fourth Day of time), Christ will rise again, and it is already nearing midnight of the sixth day! We are clearly at the end of days.

There have always been those who shrug off revelation and God's warnings, believing that the world will somehow go on just as it always has and rolling their eyes at end time gloom and doom warnings.

"Knowing this first, that there shall come in the last days scoffers,
walking after their own lusts,
And saying, 'Where is the promise of his coming? for since the fathers fell
asleep, all things continue as they were from the beginning of the creation.'

For this they willingly are ignorant of,
that by the word of God the heavens were of old,
and the earth standing out of the water and in the water:
Whereby the world that then was, being overflowed with water, perished:
But the heavens and the earth, which are now,
by the same word are kept in store,
reserved unto fire against the day of judgment ...

But, beloved, be not ignorant of this one thing,
that one day is with the Lord as a thousand years,
and a thousand years as one day.

The Lord is not slack concerning his promise, as some men count slackness;
but is longsuffering to us-ward, not willing that any should perish,
but that all should come to repentance.

But the day of the Lord will come as a thief in the night;
in which the heavens shall pass away with a great noise,
and the elements shall melt with fervent heat…"
-2 Peter 3:3-10

There is nothing new under the sun. There are some who will realize Time is up, and will do whatever they can to make sure they, and their loved ones, are ready – like Noah did. And there are those who think it won't happen to them – not in their lifetime – and maybe not at all.

"And as it was in the days of Noah,
so shall it be also in the days of the Son of man….
Likewise also as it was in the days of Lot; they did eat, they drank,
they bought, they sold, they planted, they builded; But the same
day that Lot went out of Sodom it rained fire and brimstone
from heaven, and destroyed them all. Even thus shall it be in the
day when the Son of man is revealed." – Luke 17:26-30

As In The Days of Noah

Jesus said that the end times, before His return would be as in the days of Noah. What happened in Noah's day? We will look at this in more detail in Part II, but it would be a good idea to take a glance at the highlights of Noah's day, for they will help reveal what time it is now.

Wickedness and Deception Abound

Genesis 6 tells us that in Noah's day, the whole earth was full of wickedness and that every imagination and thought of mankind was only evil continually. This means that above the evil actions people did, they had the desire and imagination to do even more. This was not ignorance. This was purposefully choosing to reject God's Truth and replace it with their own so-called truth.

"For the wrath of God is revealed from heaven against all ungodliness
And unrighteousness of men, who hold the truth in unrighteousness.
…Because that, when they knew God,
They glorified Him not as God,
Neither were thankful, but became vain in their imaginations,
And their foolish heart was darkened.
Professing themselves to be wise, they became fools, …
Wherefore God also gave them up to uncleanness
through the lusts of their own hearts…
And even as they did not like to retain God in their knowledge,
God gave them over to a reprobate mind, …
Being filled with all unrighteousness, fornication, wickedness, covetousness,
Maliciousness, full of envy, murder, debate, deceit, malignity,
Whisperers, backbiters, haters of God,
Despiteful, proud, boasters, inventors of evil things,
Disobedient to parents, without understanding, covenant breakers,
Without natural affection, implacable, unmerciful.
Who knowing the judgment of God,
that they which commit such things are worthy of death,
Not only do the same, but have pleasure in them that do them."
— Romans 1:18, 21-22, 24, 28-32

I do not think it is possible to read thorough those verses and fail to recognize our present culture in them. People like to think that the world pretty much goes on as it always has, but according to scripture that is not true. Culture is not stagnant. A culture that dislikes the idea of God and goes about to remove Him from the public mind and conversation will go from bad to worse. The great failure of our age is not a failure to know the truth, but a failure to embrace the truth.

There is no shortage of knowledge of God or of His Word. It is not because people don't know the truth, but because what they know of it, they reject and even outright hate. Deception abounds, not because the truth is not known, but because people are self-deceived, inventing their own truth and their own gods. It was so in the days of Noah, and it is so now.

The Just Live By Faith

In the midst of this crooked generation, Noah "found grace in the eyes of the Lord"[5].

Noah, whose family was the only one to escape the global judgement, is described by the Bible as a just man who was perfect in his generations, and one who walked with God[6].

First, he found grace. He did not work for it. He found it. Grace is defined as "favor, grace, charm, acceptance"[7]. Grace is not earned; it is a gift bestowed.[8] These were found "in the eyes of the Lord".

"Behold, the eye of the Lord is upon them that fear Him,
Upon them that hope in His mercy." – Psalm 33:18

"The eyes of the Lord are upon the righteous,
And His ears are open unto their cry." – Psalm 34:15

These are just a few of many verses in the Bible that tell us that the Lord's eyes are on all people. To find favor in His eyes is to know that you are looked on with grace and acceptance. Upon whom does the Lord look with favor? Upon those that fear (have a sense of awe and reverence for) Him. Upon those who like to retain Him in their knowledge; unlike the unrighteous, who do not like to.

To be righteous is not necessarily to never sin or trespass. If that were true, no human could ever be called righteous. According to the Bible, believing God (not just believing in God, but actually believing Him and what His word says) makes one righteous.

"For what says the scripture?
Abraham believed God, and it was counted unto him for righteousness.
…His faith is counted for righteousness." – Romans 4:3-5

---

5   Gen. 6:8.

6   Gen. 6:9.

7   James Strong, *The New Strong's Exhaustive Concordance of the Bible* (Nashville: T. Nelson, 1990), H2580.

8   Eph. 2:8.

Noah was righteous (or just) because he had a righteous fear of God and believed what God said. His actions proved his faith.

Perfect in His Generations

The second thing we are told about Noah is that he was perfect in his generations, in other words, there was something about his birth that made him acceptable. We have discussed this some detail in chapter three, and we will look into it more in Part II, but the similarity to our day is that it is also our birth that determines our acceptance (or lack of it) to God.

"Jesus answered and said unto him,
'Verily, verily I say unto you, Except a man be born again,
Her cannot see the kingdom of God...
That which is born of the flesh is flesh,
And that which is born of the Spirit is spirit.
Marvel not that I said unto you,
You must be born again." – John 3:5-7

"For to be carnally minded is death,
But to be spiritually minded is life and peace.
Because the carnal mind is enmity against God,
For it is not subject to the law of God, neither indeed can be.
So then they that are in the flesh cannot please God.
But you are not in the flesh, but in the Spirit,
If so be that the Spirit of God dwell in you.
Now if any man have not he Spirit of Christ,
he is none of His." – Romans 8:6-9

So how does one get "born again"? The same thing that made Noah acceptable will make us so as well.

"But without faith it is impossible to please Him (God),
For he that comes to God must believe that He is,
And that He is a rewarder of them that diligently seek Him.
By faith Noah, being warned of God of things not seen as yet,

Moved with fear, prepared an ark to the saving of his house,
By the which he condemned the world,
And became heir of the righteousness which is by faith." – Heb.11:6-7

"For by grace are you saved, through faith,
And that not of yourselves, it is the gift of God
Not of works, lest any man should boast." – Eph. 2:8-10

Noah was accepted by grace through faith, and so are we all. In Noah's time, what distinguished him from his fellow human beings, were his birth, his faith, and his walk. He walked with God. In other words, his faith and relationship to God were lived out in his day-to-day life. His faith informed all his decisions, conduct and life. So will it be for those who are walking with God in our generation.

In Noah's day, God sent Noah to preach to the world, warning them of imminent destruction of the earth. But in all the hundred and twenty years that Noah built and preached, no one except his own family were saved when doomsday came. There were doubtless others who had a faith of sorts, and whose physical pedigree was pure. The Bible tells us that Noah had brothers and sisters. But looking at our Days of Noah Chart, we can see that many people died just before the flood. Methuselah, famous for being the oldest person to have ever lived, attaining the age of 969 years, actually died the same year as the flood!

The Mystery of The Ark

When the appointed time came, Noah and his family entered the ark (the place that God instructed to be prepared for them) and the door was shut. For seven days Noah and his family and all the animals with him waited for the rain to begin. We do not know what people thought during this time, but there is no indication that any of their minds changed… until it began to rain.

When the rain began, the ark was lifted up with those who had found salvation in it. At the end of time, those who have put their trust and obedience in God will also be lifted up and taken to a place that Christ has prepared for them. Then will come a period of seven years, in which the world will be judged and cleansed.

The ark is a picture of Christ, in whom the righteous find salvation. His Name is the safe place the righteous run into and find safety[9]. In the Holiest place of the temple, there was the golden Ark of the Covenant. It contained a pot of manna (the bread from heaven the Lord fed Israel with during their wilderness wonderings). Jesus said, *"I Am that Bread from Heaven"*[10].

The Ark also contained the tablets of stone on which were written the 10 commandments, the Word of God. John said of Jesus;

> *"And the Word was made flesh,*
> *And dwelt among us, And we beheld His glory,*
> *The glory as of the only begotten of the Father,*
> *full of grace and truth." – John 1:14*

The word "Ark" comes from the Hebrew word for "chest, box of coffin"[11]. The Ark was covered with the Mercy Seat, which was guarded by 2 cherubim, which were holy angels[12]. When the blood of the sacrificial lamb was sprinkled on the mercy seat, atonement was made for sin[13].

This was all a foreshadowing of what Mary Magdalene saw on that first Easter morning when she looked in the empty tomb[14]. There was the slab where Christ's body had lain, and sitting at either end of it were two angels. Christ Himself had become the Lamb of God which takes away the sins of the earth. His tomb became the Ark and Mercy Seat where all may come to find atonement and salvation.

Paul sums up the Gospel (which means "good news") like this in the book of Romans:

---

9   Prov. 18:10.

10 John 6:33, 35, 41.

11 James Strong, *The New Strong's Exhaustive Concordance of the Bible* (Nashville: T. Nelson, 1990), H8392.(Brown-Driver-Briggs Lexicon).

12 Exodus 25:17-22.

13 Leviticus 16:14-16.

14 John 20:11-12.

"But now God has shown us a way to be made right with him without keeping the requirements of the law, as was promised in the writings of Moses and the prophets long ago. We are made right with God by placing our faith in Jesus Christ. And this is true for everyone who believes, no matter who we are. For everyone has sinned; we all fall short of God's glorious standard. Yet God, with underserved kindness, declares that we are righteous. He did this through Christ Jesus when he freed us from the penalty of our sins. For God presented Jesus as the sacrifice for sin. People are made right with God when they believe that Jesus sacrificed his life, shedding his blood." – Romans 3:21-25 NLT[15]

"If you confess with your mouth that Jesus is Lord and believe in your heart that God raised him from the dead, you will be saved. For it is by believing in your heart that you are made right with God, and it is by confessing with your mouth that you are saved… Everyone who calls on the name of the Lord will be saved." – Romans 10:9-10, 13 NLT[16]

Just as Noah, Abraham, and Moses had to trust in the Lord to save them, so must we. We hear God's word, and obey it, as they did. There ever was only one way to the Father. The work was always His, but it is for us to choose to believe and obey. The act of faith is not producing mountains of good works (although those who love God will certainly live godly lives). The act of faith is simply believing God, and saying so. It is choosing to speak with your mouth what you choose to believe in your heart. If we do so, God promises to make a new creation out of us. And He promises to return for us one day!

The prophecy of the second coming of Christ is not news to the world. The topic of doomsday and the end of the world are very popular in today's culture. It figures largely in movies, documentaries and media of all kinds. As in Noah's day, although His return will catch people unprepared, it will not take people entirely by surprise. According the Revelation 6, when the people of the earth see Christ return in the sky, they will recognize exactly Who it is, and what is happening. They may later choose to believe a lie, and whatever spin the world will put on it, but in that moment, they will

---

[15] New Living Translation (Tyndale House, 1996).
[16] Ibid.

know. In the Day Christ returns, just as in Noah's day, those who find refuge in the Ark of God will escape the coming storm.

Reading The Signs

Jesus tells us that there is no one who knows the exact day or hour that these things will take place...

"But of that day and hour knows no man,
no, not the angels of heaven, but my Father only.
But as the days of Noah were, so shall also the coming of the Son of man be.
For as in the days that were before the flood they were eating
and drinking, marrying and giving in marriage, until the
day that Noe entered into the ark," – Matt. 4:24-23

Though we cannot know the day or hour, He does tell us that when we begin to see these things happen, we are to look up! We are supposed to be awake and alert to what is happening around us, and to always be on the watch for His return. Some say, "We aren't supposed to be looking for signs, but for the Son.", and to that I say, "Amen!", but the POINT is that we are supposed to be watching and looking – not walking around with our eyes closed or asleep.

"Watch therefore:
for ye know not what hour your Lord doth come." – Matt. 24:42

"Now when these things begin to happen, look up and lift up your heads,
because your redemption draws near." – Luke 21:28

"Watch therefore, and pray always
that you may be counted worthy to escape all these things
that will come to pass, and to stand before the Son of Man." – Luke 21:36

"For yourselves know perfectly
that the day of the Lord so comes as a thief in the night...
But you, brethren, are not in darkness,

that that day should overtake you as a thief.
You are all the children of light and the children of the day.
We are not of the night nor of darkness.
Therefore let us not sleep, as others do,
but let us watch and be sober." – I Thess. 5:2,4-6

"So likewise... when ye shall see all these things,
know that it is near, even at the doors." – Matt. 24:33

If God did not want us to notice the signs, then why did He take the trouble to list them in such a detailed fashion in His word? When the disciples asked what would be the sign of His coming, Jesus did not rebuke them, He answered them – in some detail[17]. And that does not even bring into account the numerous prophecies given about the signs of the end times given in the Old Testament and elsewhere in the New Testament.

It is not a lack of faith to watch the signs that God gives – in fact He commands us to be watchful, and warns those who will not watch:

"Be watchful, and strengthen the things which remain, ...
Therefore if you will not watch, I will come upon you as a thief,
and you will not know what hour I will come upon you." – Rev. 3:2-4

It is a sign of faith to heed God's warnings, and to pass them on to others when God has shown you something. It is a mark of faith that we actually believe and expect that God would reward our seeking Him. He will reward our diligence.

"But without faith it is impossible to please Him:
for he that comes to God must believe that He is,
and that He is a rewarder of them that diligently seek Him.
By faith Noah, being warned of God of things not seen as yet, moved with
fear, prepared an ark to the saving of his house; by the which he condemned
the world, and became heir of the righteousness which is by faith."
– Heb. 11:6-7

---

[17]   Matt. 24; Mark 13; Luke 21.

God not only invites, He commands that we seek Him for knowledge and insight. He is willing to show us "great and mighty things which we do not know" – if only we ask[18].

> *"Blessed be the name of God forever and ever,*
> *For wisdom and might are His. And He changes the times and the seasons;*
> *… He gives wisdom to the wise*
> *And knowledge to those who have understanding.*
> *He reveals deep and secret things; He knows what is in the darkness,*
> *And light dwells with Him." – Daniel 2:20-22 NKJV*

Why have I not been taught this before?

Since I first saw these things, I have learned that this is not after all such a new concept. Surprisingly, ancient Jewish teaching also taught the "thousand years as a day" principle. But I think perhaps ours is the first generation to whom this knowledge about time could really be seen so clearly. There several reasons for this.

Accessibility to God's Word

Not until the last couple of hundred years has it been possible for the average person to have the ability to read, and to have access to God's Word in their own language (though many even in our time still do not).

Not until the computer age has knowledge, and our ability to sift quickly through large amounts of data, been so easily accessible. We can study now in an afternoon what would have taken us months and years just a few generations ago – if we even had access to the material at all. Even when I was in college, if I could not get a hard copy of a book in my hands for research, for all intents and purposes that knowledge did not exist for me. Even then, I had to sort and sift the information through a long, laborious process.

---

[18] Jer. 33:3

Lack of An Observable Pattern

Secondly, not until recent generations would the pattern have been so obvious. On Day Five of Time for instance, it would not have been as obvious to those living at the time that their Day could be represented by fish and fowl. They would have recognized the symbols, but not the pattern.

Not until our present place in time (the 6th day), knowing what we know about the rebirth of Israel and the rise of nations, could we have seen so clearly how History lines up with the Creation account. Even as I began to study this, it was not until I reached Day Four that I really began to think this was more than coincidence, that this was indeed what God had unfolded in the very beginning. The further I got in my study, the more convinced I became, and the clearer the pattern was revealed.

It Wasn't Time

God told Daniel that prophecy would not be understood by people until the time came for that prophecy to be fulfilled. Despite Daniel being the one to whom some of this prophecy was given, it was not given to him to understand what it meant. God told him:

"For the words are closed up and sealed till the time of the end.
Many shall be purified, and made white, and tried;
But the wicked shall do wickedly, and none of the wicked shall understand,
But the wise shall understand."- Daniel 12:9-10

Seven times[19] the Gospels tell us that the apostles of Christ did not understand the prophecies and words He spoke to them until they saw them fulfilled:

"These things understood not His disciples at the first:
But when Jesus was glorified,
then remembered they that these things were written of Him,
And that they had done these things unto Him." – John 10:6

---

[19] Matt. 16:12; Mark 9:32; Luke 2:50; Luke 9:45; John 8:27; John 10:6; John 12:16

The Word of God was often not clear to even the prophets themselves, though they were the ones giving the prophecy. They understood that the words were meant for people of another time, yet they faithfully recorded the Word given to them.

"How that by revelation He made known unto me the mystery…
Which in other ages was not made known unto the sons of men,
As it is now revealed unto His holy apostles and prophets by the Spirit,
That the Gentiles should be fellow heirs and of the same body,
And partakers of His promise in Christ by the gospel." – Eph. 3:3,5-6

"Unto whom it was revealed that not unto themselves,
But unto us they did minister the things,
which are now reported unto you
by them that have preached the gospel unto you
with the Holy Ghost sent down from heaven,
Which things the angels desire to look unto." – 1 Peter 1:12

There are things that cannot be understood until their time. I submit that as these things become clear to us in this time, it is a good indication that the time of their fulfillment is at hand. The time is short and the Day is drawing to an end.

The Lord never intended us to stop growing in wisdom and knowledge. He never planned that knowledge of Him should become stagnant, but that His children should hear His voice and continue to grow in all things, until the Day He returns.

"Then said He unto them,
'Therefore every scribe which is instructed
Unto the kingdom of heaven
Is like unto a man that is an householder,
Which brings forth out of his treasure
Things new and old." – Matt. 13:52

People who stop growing in their knowledge and understanding of God and scripture, are in real danger of becoming like the Pharisees of Christ's day. They were so sure they knew everything there was to know about God's word, that they became blind to it when He was standing right in front of them. I believe that God intended that we should be wowed and amazed every day when we go to His Word. There is so much more for us to discover, if only we have the eyes and ears to see and hear it, and the heart to search it out.

God Is In Control

The thing that impresses me the most about all this is the fact that God has always been in such complete control of history – telling the "end from the beginning". It shows that everything is unfolding exactly on time. God is neither early nor late in His acts. Everything has happened, and will happen, exactly on schedule and at its appointed time.

"And he said, "Look, I am making known to you what shall happen in the latter time of the indignation; for at the appointed time the end shall be." – Daniel 8:19 NKJV

"...the end shall be at the appointed time." – Daniel 11:27

Whether the reader finds any merit in the research presented in this work or not, I hope that I have at least given you food for serious thought. Hopefully, I have encouraged and energized my fellow believers to keep looking up. The time for all those promises really is at hand!

"And then shall they see the Son of man coming in a cloud with power and great glory. And when these things begin to come to pass, then look up, and lift up your heads; for your redemption draws nigh.– Luke 21:27-31

Does the Pattern Hold?

One of the most important Bible study principles I have been taught is to let scripture interpret scripture, whenever possible. One must also take the whole counsel of God into consideration when studying any topic. The pattern must hold. God will not say one thing here, and something contradictory over there. If what He seems to be saying in one place is not supported in other scripture, I should probably take a closer look at my interpretation.

So, if what I think God seems to be saying about seven days in Genesis were true, there should be proof of it in the other places where He specifically calls our attention to "seven". There is!

PART II
SEVEN CHURCHES

CHAPTER 1

The Book of Revelation

As I mentioned before, the two portions of Scripture where the number seven seems to be the most central and prevalent are the creation story in Genesis, and the book of Revelation. Seven is all over the book of Revelation. There are 7 lampstands, 7 Spirits of God, and 7 angels just in the first chapter! Throughout the book, there are 7 churches, 7 seals, 7 trumpets, and 7 bowls just to name a few.

As I began to dig deeper into the book of Revelation, coming off of my study of the days of creation, I could not help but notice that the first book of the Bible, and the last book had many things in common. The greatest parallel was in the seven messages to the seven churches. I realized that in these churches were many similarities to the events of the seven days of creation, and the seven ages of time. The Creation week of Genesis is a prophetic revelation of what God will do in every age of time. It is a roadmap of history, proving God's complete sovereignty through every moment of time. In the messages to the churches, the revelation is of Jesus Christ Himself in each of those ages. Let's take a look together.

The Message of Revelation is a Message for You!

*"The Revelation of Jesus Christ, which God gave Him to
show His servants..."I am the Alpha and the Omega, the
First and the Last," and, "What you see, write in a book
and send it to the seven churches." – Rev. 1:1, 11*

The book of Revelation was given by God, to Christ, who then gave it to His Angel to give to John, who was then to share it with the churches. He very specifically stated that these things (like the parables He spoke) were not for the world nor unbelievers, but for those who believed already.

The only message the Bible has for unbelievers is "Repent and receive Christ". It is what John the Baptist preached in the wilderness, and it is what Christ also preached to the world[1]. But, to those who have been born again, Christ has many things to say. The mysteries of Heaven belong to believers, not to unbelievers. These things will be meaningless and foolish to unbelievers. Neither will anyone be made a believer by hearing these things. If a person will not admit to the most basic message of the Bible (which is that God created the world and therefore everyone and everything in it is His and is answerable to Him), they will certainly not be willing to accept these messages.

Once someone has accepted the message of Genesis 1-3, they are open to the message of salvation. Once they have received salvation, they are open to greater mysteries. If they reject those, they will certainly not accept these deeper revelations of our responsibility before God and coming rewards and judgment. Those who struggle to believe the truth of Christ's first coming will certainly not be able to receive the message about His second coming.

"For whoever has, to him more will be given, and he will have abundance; but whoever does not have, even what he has will be taken away from him. Therefore I speak to them in parables, because seeing they do not see, and hearing they do not hear, nor do they understand." – Matt. 13:12-13

He Who Has Ears, Let Him Hear

One phrase that is found in both the messages to the churches and Christ's parables, is the exhortation, "He that has ears, let him hear"[2]. So believers today can know that these messages are for us as well. They are

---

[1] Matt. 3:2; Matt. 4:17; Mark 1:14-15.
[2] Matthew 13:9,43; Rev. 2:7,11,17,29; Rev. 3:6,13,22; Rev. 13:9, 22:17.

for anyone who is willing to hear the words of Christ and be obedient to Him. He says that to those who do not wish to hear or who do not believe, they will make no sense - just obscure stories. But to those who believe it is given to understand the mysteries of the kingdom of Heaven, and He desires for us to hear, listen, understand, and obey.

The parables were given to explain the mysteries of the kingdom of Heaven. And Revelation chapter one tells us that this is the revelation that God gave Him to reveal to his servants. There are some things we cannot know, but the things that are revealed belong to us and to our children[3]. The whole purpose of the book of Revelation is to reveal things to us, not hide them from us. These things are not beyond us. If you will receive it, the message is for you.

John's Introduction

Before John begins sharing the messages that Christ gave him to share with the churches, he first introduces himself: giving his bona fides, and showing the authority he has received to deliver these messages. He wants the churches to know that this prophecy did not originate with himself, but that he is only the messenger.[4]

According to John, what we are about to study is a message specifically for Christ's servants. The book of Revelation is not only a revelation of things to come, though it will certainly speak of "things which must shortly come to pass". It also speaks of things that have been and that are. As we understand its message more fully, we will more fully understand the true nature of everything that has ever happened! Revelation is a message that comes with a specific blessing for those who read, hear, and heed the things written there.

We are told that the time when these things are going to come to pass is at hand. The word used here is *"eggus" and it means "pressing, imminent, soon to come to pass"*. So, this is not a message for some far in the future, remote date. It is a pressing, immediate message. There is urgency to it.

---

3   Deut. 29:29
4   Revelation 1:1-3

The Revelation of Jesus Christ

The true unveiling of the Book of Revelation is the revelation of Jesus Christ Himself! As we read, the messages began to unveil Christ as He has appeared through every Age of Time. In His messages to each of the churches, He in essence begins by saying, "Remember when this happened? That was Me! I've been with you all along, every step of the way. And in case you didn't recognize Me, allow me to explain Who I Am."

After giving us a full accounting of the authority and knowledge with which he is about to speak, John then delivers the introduction of Jesus Christ. First, he only hears a voice saying:

> *"I am the Alpha and the Omega', says the Lord God,'*
> *who is, and who was, and who is to come, the Almighty.'" – Rev. 1:8*

Added to the former introduction, we are now told that Christ is the Alpha (first), the Omega (the last), and the Almighty. These are names by which He was also known to His people in the Old Testament times. This ties into what we saw in Part One regarding the week of creation. Everything was made by "et", the Aleph-Tav; the Alpha and Omega.

John turns towards the Voice and sees a vision of Christ:

> *"I turned around to see the voice that was speaking to me.*
> *And when I turned I saw seven golden lampstands,*
> *and among the lampstands was someone like a son of man,*
> *dressed in a robe reaching down to his feet*
> *and with a golden sash around his chest.*
> *The hair on his head was white like wool,*
> *as white as snow,*
> *and his eyes were like blazing fire.*
> *His feet were like bronze glowing in a furnace,*
> *and his voice was like the sound of rushing waters.*
> *In his right hand he held seven stars,*
> *and coming out of his mouth was a sharp, double-edged sword.*
> *His face was like the sun shining in all its brilliance." – Rev. 1:12-16 NIV*

Jesus in the Midst - The Menorah

There is a wealth of knowledge revealed here if we just take a moment to really take it all in. When he first turns to see who was speaking, John sees someone like a son of man standing among 7 lampstands.

In Hebrew translations of the New Testament, the word translated here "lampstand" is "menorah". Remember, the menorah was the lampstand that illuminated the first tabernacle and the temple. Jesus, who is the Light of the World[5], has sent His Spirit, and now all who have the Spirit of Christ shine as "lights" in the world[6].

John sees Jesus standing among the seven lampstands. The word "among" means "in the midst of", or "in the middle of". We are told in verse 20 of this chapter that the 7 lampstands represent the 7 churches, and the 7 stars in His hand represent the 7 angels or messengers of the churches. So John sees One who is like the son of man walking in the midst of the lampstands (fire). Notice the similar picture found in theses verses in Daniel:

"Then King Nebuchadnezzar was astonished;
and he rose in haste and spoke,
saying to his counselors,
"Did we not cast three men bound into the midst of the fire?
They answered and said to the king, "True, O king."
"Look!" he answered, 'I see four men loose, walking in the midst of the fire;
and they are not hurt,
and the form of the fourth is like the Son of God.'" – Daniel 3:24-25

And in Acts:

"And when the day of Pentecost was fully come,
they were all with one accord in one place.
And suddenly there came a sound from heaven as of a rushing mighty wind,
and it filled all the house where they were sitting.
And there appeared unto them cloven tongues like as of fire,
and it sat upon each of them." – Acts 2:1-3

---

[5] John 8:12.
[6] Matt. 5:14; Phil. 2:15.

Both of these describe Christ being in the midst of His people, manifested in the fire. What King Nebuchadnezzar saw was a foreshadowing of Pentecost!

Pentecost, the Menorah (or lampstand) of the Tabernacle, and the lampstands of Revelation are all pictures of the same thing – Christ in the midst. This is one of the most precious truths about Christ that can bless, comfort and strengthen us today. Christ is always to be found in the midst of His people.

If you are searching for the Lord and are not sure where to find Him, find where His people are gathering and go there!

When Joseph and Mary were looking for the boy Jesus, they found Him after three days sitting in the temple in the midst of those who were searching the scriptures[7].

Jesus promises, *"Where two or three are gathered in My name, there I will be in the midst of them."*[8]

In the Old Testament tabernacle, and in the temple, the lampstand (menorah), was one of the key items in the Holy of Holies. As one faced the Holiest Place (which contained the ark of God and was hidden behind the veil), the menorah was on the left, and the table of showbread, with its twelve loaves of bread, was on the right. Remembering that in Hebrew, things are read from right to left (not left to right as in English), the 12 loaves come first, then the Holiest place with the Ark, then the menorah.

The table with the twelve loaves represents the children of Israel, to whom the Word of God (symbolized by the bread) first came. The Holiest Place and Ark represent Christ (the One whose death made a way behind the veil, giving us access to the presence of God[9]). The menorah with its seven lights, is shown in Revelation to be a picture of Christ among His people!

If one is facing the Holy of Holies, about to enter behind the veil, the table of showbread would be in the right-hand position; the position of power and favor. But, if one is coming out of the Holies of Holies (which we now have access to through Christ), the menorah is in the right-hand position!

---

[7]   Luke 2:46.

[8]   Matthew 18:20.

[9]   Mark 15:37-38; Hebrews 10:19-22.

But Jesus Himself is in the midst of both congregations – the Old Testament and New. He, Himself, is the Bread from Heaven, which gave life to His people. And He is the Light of the World. He is not just with His people, but in them.

In the Genesis, He was the One who walked in the midst of the garden of Eden with Adam and Eve. In the wilderness, He was the One who walked in the midst of the camp with His people[10]. He traveled with Israel, always in their midst. In the New Testament, Jesus could always be found in the midst of the crowds, because He had compassion on them and loved them. Jesus is always the One in the Midst.

Write What You See

John is specifically instructed in verse 11 to write what he sees. Revelation is a very visual message, and one must use one's mind's eye to picture the scenes as they unfold. The Lord gave us our imaginations, and He wants us to worship Him with all our minds. This is the pure, holy use of imagination. Christ will engage our minds like never before in the words of the book of Revelation.

John was also told;

> *"Write the things which you have seen,*
> *And the things which are,*
> *And the things which shall be hereafter."- Rev. 1:19*

Everything from this point on (Chapter 1) will fall into one of these three categories.

At the time John had his vision and wrote the book of Revelation, the churches were both the things he had seen, and the things which are. By 70 AD, the believers were dispersed from Jerusalem, and the temple destroyed. By 90 AD, which is commonly believed to be the date Revelation was written, John was exiled on the Isle of Patmos and was the sole survivor of twelve apostles. Paul too had been martyred, but the many churches he established remained.

---

[10]   Deut. 23:14.

The messages to the churches were current, now messages to the believers then. They remain current now messages to believers and churches today. In that sense, they were also "things which shall be". In fact, every message to the churches has a past revelation, a future blessing, and an immediate call to action.

Seven Churches, Seven Ages

In Revelation 2-3, Jesus has specific messages to the 7 churches in Asia. These are seven literal churches, but they are also representational. Seven is the number of completion and so the seven churches can also be understood to be representational of all the churches. No one who seriously studies Scripture would imagine that at the time Revelation was written (nor at the future time when all these things will be fulfilled), there were only seven churches!

Understanding the Biblical meanings of numbers and symbols is important when reading Revelation (or any Scripture, for that matter, but especially any of the books of prophecy).

In addition to being literal and symbolic messages, I believe they are also prophetic. In the messages to the churches, there is a parallel with each of the seven ages or dispensations (thousand years) of time which the creation week alludes to. They refer to true believers and followers of God who live, and have lived at the different times of history. In each age of Time, God has had a witness to the world, both through His revelation, and through His witnesses, His church.

Who Is "The Church"?

Referring to these believers as churches, including those of the Old Testament times, is completely Biblical. The word church in the New Testament is the Greek word "ekklesia". It means "a called-out assembly". In Greek translations of the Old Testament, this word is used in place of the Hebrew word "qahal" found in the Old Testament. This Hebrew word means "assembly or congregation", and is translated as such. In Deut.

9:12, and Deut. 18:16, it is translated "assembly". In Deut. 31:30 and I Ch. 29:20, it is translated "the congregation", just to name a few examples.

In the New Testament, Ephesians 3:21 tells us: *"Unto Him be glory in the churches by Christ Jesus throughout All ages, world without end."* This clearly indicating that they are called churches in all ages.

The New Testament book of Hebrews, quoting the Old Testament book of Psalm, says: *"Saying I will declare thy name unto my brethren, in the midst of the CHURCH (ekklesia) will I sing praise to Thee."*[11]

Psalm 22:22 reads, *"I will declare your name unto my brethren, in the midst of the CONGREGATION (qahal) will I praise Thee."*

This clearly shows that the word church can be used of Old Testament believers.

Additionally, Acts 7:38 says,

> *"This is He, that was in the CHURCH in the wilderness,*
> *with the angel which spoke to him in the mount Sinai,*
> *with our fathers, who received the lively oracles to give unto us."*

Here, Paul clearly refers to Old Testament believers in Israel as "the church in the wilderness".

Of course, we must be careful not to make the Bible so symbolic that we fail to receive its primary application, which is always meant to be personal. Although these were messages written to literal, historic churches, they are very specifically intended to be heard, received and applied to anyone with ears to hear. We are to take these messages literally, historically, prophetically, and personally.

Universal Church vs. Local Church

There are a couple of important things to note about these messages to the churches. First note that they are addressed to specific and different local churches that actually existed in physical, real locations. The message was not addressed to the universal Church, or the "Body of Christ". Christ recognized that although they were all part of the body of Christ, they were

---

[11] Hebrews 2:12; Psalm 22:22.

also unique, individual, and literal churches. Christ's messages, though open for all to read, were addressed to specific local churches at specific locations.

This would refute those who do not believe in the Local church but think Christ only deals with the larger universal church. One day, the whole body of Christ will be assembled in one place at one location (Heaven), but until all things are made one, we each inhabit physical bodies that exist in particular locations on earth – and that is how the Church of Christ is to function. We are all meant to be part of that.

To further support this point, note that the churches are represented as lampstands or candlesticks, depending on the translation. We see this symbology on the day of Pentecost in which the Holy Spirit was seen in flames of fire that rested on the heads of all the believers present, showing many "lights"[12]. Jesus said that no one lights a lamp to hide it under a bushel or put it under a bed, but it is lit to be put on a candlestick or lampstand[13]. This is also the word menorah, and the same word used for the churches in Revelation.

The teaching is clear – we are not lit in order to remain alone and in secret. We are saved and filled with the Holy Spirit in order to take our place in the Church. Together, we give light to the world. A Christian who is not a part of a local Church is not fulfilling his purpose. Scripture specifically warns us that we are not to forsake the assembling of ourselves together[14], as some were in the habit of doing even then. True followers of Christ will always be drawn to, and seek out, fellowship with other true believers.

Secondly, these messages were to churches that were in the Gentile world and comprised of predominately Gentile believers. Revelation has been called a Jewish book, and in a sense it is. It was written by a Hebrew man and uses many Hebraic symbols. You cannot fully understand any of the Bible if you forget this: all of it was written by Hebrew men! It is through the nation of Israel that God has chosen to reveal Himself and His message to the world. But this particular message was not written to the nation of Israel, but to the New Testament churches, which comprised both Jewish and Gentile believers.

---

[12]   Act 2:1-4.

[13]   Matt. 5:15; Mark 4:21; Luke 8:16; 11:33.

[14]   Hebrews 10:25.

Church Defined

So, going forward, the working definition of church that we will use is:

- Those who are called of God, and who worship the One true God.
- Those who are awaiting the coming of the Messiah.
- Those to whom Christ reveals Himself.
- Those to whom the Word of God is given.
- Those who bear His name and are led by His Spirit.

In every generation or Age of Time, there were those who fit these stipulations. And they were often a mixed multitude. For instance, Cain fit these criteria. Almost. He was a worshipper of the one true God. He knew of the coming Messiah. God spoke to Him. Yet for all of this, the Bible calls him a "profane" person, because he, knowing the truth, chose to worship God in his own way rather than God's way. He refused to be led by God's Spirit. Shockingly, even Judas fits much of these criteria! He was called and chosen by Christ. He walked with Jesus and heard His words. Yet, he preferred the riches and approval of the world over Christ. This is why many of the messages to the churches contain both commendations and rebukes.

Seven Components of the Seven Messages

Each of the Seven Messages to the Churches in Revelation had Seven specific components.

1. A Specific revelation of Jesus Christ that was unique to that church.

Just as Christ reveals Himself to each of us in a unique way, depending on our need and on the work He is doing through us. Similarly, we see the way He reveals Himself to each church speaks to the unique trials and assignments of that age. The book of Hebrews speaks to this truth.

> "God, who at sundry times and in divers manners
> spoke in time past unto the fathers by the prophets,

Hath in these last days spoken unto us by his Son,
whom he hath appointed heir of all things,
by whom also he made the worlds." - Hebrews 1:1-2

We see this in the Old Testament especially: to those who were sick, He was the God who heals. To the lost and lonely, He was the God who sees. Jesus said He must be about His Father's business, so how Christ reveals and identifies Himself to each of the churches is key to what He is "about" in them. The same will be true of us individually. Although no one goes to the Father but through Christ, we each first encountered Christ in different ways. Peter, James and John met Him while they were going about their business as fishermen. The Samaritan woman met Him at a well as she was doing her daily chores. The blind man met him as he sat begging by the road. I met Him as a little child in a Sunday school class. Where and when did you first meet Him?

2. An Acknowledgement.

Jesus begins each message revealing Who He is. He then identifies who they are. He starts each address with these words, "I know your works". He saw each of them and knew not only what their works and efforts were, but also the true condition of their heart. He knew their reputation or "name", and also what they thought and said about themselves. But, it was His evaluation of them that was true, just as it is for us.

3. A Rebuke

Like the commendation, not all the churches had a rebuke. However, for most of them, what was going on in their church was a mixed bag of good and bad.

Most churches have those in them who are true followers of Christ, and those who are not. Wherever you find a flock of sheep, you will invariably also find wolves stalking them. This is not a mark of a false church, rather it is proof that real believers are present. Wolves don't hang around where there is no prey.

Jesus held the angel of the church (or the "messenger", or some versions say "pastor"- in any case, the one who was in position of leadership and accountability) responsible for what went on in the church. Some churches tolerated those with wrong doctrine to merely remain in the church, unrebuked. Some went so far as to allow those with false teaching to actually teach and lead in the church. And other churches were so permeated with wrong teaching that there were only a few true followers of Christ in the church.

The purpose of the rebuke was to identify in a specific way exactly what was wrong and appeal to them to repent. It is never God's will to condemn, but for all to come to repentance[15]. It is important that the appeal to repent is not directed only at the false teachers, but at the whole church. The false teachers needed to repent of their false and worldly teaching, but the leaders in the church needed to repent of allowing this on their watch. It was not to the false teachers that Jesus said He had something against, but to the angel, or pastor, of the church. The problem is never "them", the problem is "us". 2 Chron. 7:14 tells us that if God's people, called by His name, repent and seek His face, He will respond. God's judgment was against these churches not because of the sin of the world, but because of the unrepentance of those who are called by His name.

4. A Command

Christ did not simply stop with a rebuke - that would be hopeless. His purpose in rebuking was for them to turn around and repent. So, with each rebuke, there is a command telling them specifically what they needed to do in order to avoid evil consequences and to partake of the blessing He wanted to give them. The command was the way out. Judgment was not (and is not) inevitable.

5. A Warning to the Wayward

To those churches who received a rebuke, there was always a warning of the consequences their rebellion would bring on themselves. No one could say "we didn't know". He said to those who were unrepentant and disobedient, His coming would be sudden, like a thief - but that was not the way He preferred to come. He wanted them to be alert, watching and

---

[15]   2 Peter 3:9.

waiting eagerly for Him. The choice was up to them - He would not force it on them, and they may choose not to believe Him, but the warnings are as clear and certain as the rebuke.

6. An Encouragement to the Righteous

Because most of the churches were a mixed bag, He also had words of encouragement to the rest of those in the church who either were not participating in the wrong that was going on, or who had repented and made it right. The day will come when Christ will judge His people, but each one will be judged according to their own works. He will not condemn the righteous with the wicked - neither will the wicked escape because they are hidden in amongst the righteous. He sees each of them, and He has words of encouragement for those who are in the difficult position of trying to hold on to their faith in the midst of a very carnal, rebellious world... or church. Some of these are similar to the promises to overcomers, but these words of encouragement are specific to these people who are holding on to their faith in these specific challenges.

7. A Promise to Overcomers

Just as Christ reveals Himself in a unique way to each age, He also extends specific promises to those believers who hold true during their generation. These are promises of affirmation, and restoration of whatever the enemy tries to take away. Although these promises are spoken with specific meaning to each age, these are not just to these specific churches, but to anyone to has an ear to hear. To anyone, anywhere, who reads and heeds the words written to these churches, and who overcomes the enemy, these promises are given.

The Messages to the Seven Churches

Just as the book of Genesis tells us the beginning of all things, Revelation speaks of the end of all things. But it is not meant to be a revelation of end times events. It is meant to be a revelation of Jesus Christ throughout all of time. It begins in chapter one by revealing Jesus as the

One Who Walks Among the Churches. Jesus, throughout all of earth's history, throughout all the ages of time, has always been the One in the Midst. Revelation does not just reveal the end, it reveals the work of Christ that was, and is and is to come.

Comparing what I learned about the days of creation and the ages of time to the messages to the seven churches gave me a new insight to Revelation and of Christ.

Seven Candelsticks & Stars of Seven Churches = Seven Days & Ages

Center
"Servant Light" is Lifted Up and used to light all other lights, then replaced in highest, center position

1
Ephesus
*Day of Adam

2
Smyrna
*Day of Noah

3
Pergamos
*Day of Abraham, Moses & Judges

4
Thyatira
*Day of Kings & Prophets

Jesus Christ in Midst

7 Churches
7 Days

Candles are placed Right to Left

Candles are Lit Left to Right

5
Sardis
*Day of Fish & Birds

6
Philadelphia
*Day of Beasts, Man & Bride

7
Laodicea
*Day of Rest

CHAPTER 2

EPHUSUS – Lost Love

"To the angel of the church of Ephesus write,
'These things says He who holds the seven stars in His right hand,
who walks in the midst of the seven golden lampstands:
"I know your works, your labor, your patience, and that you cannot
bear those who are evil. And you have tested those who say they are
apostles and are not, and have found them liars; and you have persevered
and have patience, and have labored for My name's sake and have
not become weary. Nevertheless I have this against you, that you have
left your first love. Remember therefore from where you have fallen;
repent and do the first works, or else I will come to you quickly and
remove your lampstand from its place—unless you repent. But this you
have, that you hate the deeds of the Nicolaitans, which I also hate.
"He who has an ear, let him hear what the Spirit says to the
churches. To him who overcomes I will give to eat from the tree of
life, which is in the midst of the Paradise of God."' – Rev. 2:1-7

Revelation of Christ: The One in the Midst

Jesus reveals Himself to this first church, Ephesus, as "He who holds the seven stars in His right hand and who walks in the midst of the seven golden lampstands." Here again, we see a visual of the Menorah! Chapter one of Revelation tells us that the stars are the angels (or messengers) of the churches, and that the lampstands are the churches.

Holding the stars in His right hand is symbolic of His sovereignty and control. But Jesus is not standing above them, looking down from a distance, but as the One who walks among them. In each age of time, we will find Jesus among His people. In the opening pages of the Bible, in the first age of time, we see God walking with Adam and Eve in the midst of the garden.

Acknowledgement: I Know You, I See You

Jesus said He was aware of the works, labor, and patience of this first church. His relationship with His people is very personal. He calls each church by name. He knows the name of every star in the sky and of every person who has ever lived. To Him, we are not grains of sand, but individual children that He knows and loves. He sees us. He knows what we do and say. He even knows what we only think. Psalm 139 contains some of the most beautiful reassurances of His specific love for each of us.

Jesus was aware of all the deeds and efforts of the church at Ephesus. He saw that they were very concerned about truth and very eager to expose lies. He also knew their heart, that they were motivated by loyalty to His name and were tireless in their efforts. The Lord sees and knows all that we do and say, and more than this, He knows why we do what we do.

Rebuke: You Have Left Your First Love

Nevertheless. Chilling word. You cannot hide from the Lord. He sees what is hidden in the closet. The rebuke Christ gives reveals what He truly values, His true heart. You can learn a lot about a person by what upsets them. Jesus said that, although He saw they were very zealous about truth, He had something against them because they had left their first love. The church (or congregation) of Ephesus was more concerned with being correct in their doctrine than they were about being right in their spirit. The great failure of Ephesus, and of Adam and Eve, is that they prized knowledge over love. Ephesus became more known for what they hated than for what they loved.

This church was very zealous about correct doctrine and authority – they knew the Word of God and did not tolerate those who tried to teach something different. And they seemed to be a unified church in that, unlike the messages to the other churches, there doesn't seem to be a schism of those who believed or spoke one thing and those who believed or spoke another. That would not have been tolerated in this church. They were not going to be fooled or deceived. They made it their mission to sniff out, expose and condemn false teaching. They especially concerned themselves with exposing false apostles. An apostle is one who claims to be sent by God with a message. Satan, since the garden of Eden, is especially adept at pretending to be an angel of light, offering enlightenment, but always at the cost of true worship.

Shepherds of the church need to be very careful that they do not leave off watching over the sheep in their zealousness to watch out for wolves. We aren't to be so focused on making sure people obey The Law that we forget the purpose and greatest of those commands;

"The purpose of the commandment is love, from a pure heart, a good conscience and from a sincere faith." -I Tim. 1:5

Jesus said, *"'You shall love the LORD your God with all your heart, with all your soul, and with all your mind.' This is the first and great commandment. And the second is like it: 'You shall love your neighbor as yourself.' On these two commandments hang all the Law and the Prophets."* -Matt. 22:37-40

Paul said in I Cor. 13 that if he had all knowledge to understand all mysteries and all wisdom, yet lacked love, it would profit him nothing. God's people are to be conspicuous for their love - so much so that Jesus said it was the true litmus test of His disciples[1]. We are to speak the Truth in Love.[2]

Command: Remember, Repent, Do First Works

Jesus' command to this church, (as are all His commands to us) is not to condemn them, but to save them. He does not rebuke and then leave us to wallow in remorse and shame. He always has a solution and is eager for reconciliation. One of the ways we can know what spirit is addressing us is by this: Satan condemns and leave us hopeless. He labels us with our sin (liar, thief, adulterer), but gives no real hope of redemption. He name is Accuser of the brethren[3]. The Holy Spirit of God rebukes us, but He

---

[1]   John 13:35.
[2]   Eph. 4:15
[3]   Rev. 12:10.

always then gives a way to be reconciled. And always, no matter what the sin is, the Way is the same: Repent.

Jesus commanded the church of Ephesus to remember from where they had fallen. Adam and Eve, the first family and congregation, famously fell from their first estate. Jesus told this church to repent and do the first works. What were the first works that Adam and Eve were commanded to do? They were to keep the garden, care for the earth, and be fruitful and multiply. But above this, they were to walk with God and have fellowship with Him. As they walked and talked with God, they would learn wisdom and how to discern between right and wrong. Godly wisdom comes from constant exposure to the word of God and fellowship with Him[4].

James tells us if anyone lacks wisdom, he should ask God for it.[5] Our Heavenly Father liberally gives wisdom without berating or shaming us for asking. Adam and Eve craved the knowledge of good and evil, but instead of asking God for it, they chose to eat from the forbidden tree. Knowledge without wisdom "puffs up" (causes undue pride), and leads to harshness and lack of love[6]. It ultimately condemns and leads to death.

I remember going through a particularly difficult, confusing time in my life and wanting desperately to know what the truth was. There was so much deception going on, I just didn't know what to believe anymore. I cried out to the Lord, "Father, I just wish you would just give me the discernment to know what is true and what is a lie without always having to ask. Then I would just know what to do."

So clearly the Spirit spoke to my heart, "I do not give fruit from that tree."

I was stunned! It took me a moment to realize both what the Spirit was saying, and what I had actually asked for. I realized that the Lord's way of giving wisdom is always connected with relationship. He never intended that we would get to the place where we don't need to ask. His way is always, "Ask, and it shall be given to you."[7] But just as the manna had to be gathered every morning for that day, so God intends that we come to Him each day for everything that we need. Why? Because He loves us and

---

[4]   Heb. 5:14.

[5]   James 1:5.

[6]   1 Cor. 8:1.

[7]   Matthew 7:7.

desires to walk with us. Knowledge and wisdom must always come out of His heart of Love, otherwise, it becomes cold and cruel.

Warning: I Will Come and Remove Your Place

Jesus warns the church at Ephesus that if they do not repent of their lack of love, He would come to them quickly and remove their candlestick out of its place. Just as the way Christ reveals Himself to each church is significant, so too is the position of Christ. To the church at Ephesus He warns that He will come to them quickly, and when He comes, He will remove them from their place unless they repent. We see in Genesis chapter three that the Lord came to Adam in the garden, calling for him. The result of that meeting was that Adam lost his place in the garden. The Lord also talked with Cain after his sacrifice was rejected. Cain did not repent, but rather killed his brother, and Cain too lost his place.

What does it mean to lose one's place? It means the loss of the position and blessings that were intended for us. Although one may still repent and even be reconciled to Christ, the loss of ones intended inheritance is real. The Prodigal was welcomed back into the Father's home and family, but the squandered inheritance was still lost. In His message to the church of Philadelphia, Jesus warns that we are to "take heed that no man takes your crown"[8]. There are real consequences for our lack of love. Again, according to 1 Corinthians 13, only what is done in love counts. Not even personal sacrifice will avail us any reward in Heaven if it was done from any other motivation than love.

We don't know how much time elapsed between when Adam and Eve ate the forbidden fruit to when God came walking in the garden, calling for them. But I do know that God usually grants a window of time for us to voluntarily repent. We know there was at least as much time as it took for them to come up with their own solution and try to fashion garments made of fig leaves. Their first instinct was to cover their sin with good works and failing that, to hide. Since they chose their own works over repentance, part of their curse was that work, which God had meant to give meaning and joy to life, now because burdensome. The good works God intended for them became toil and they would live "by the sweat of the brow".

---

[8]   Rev. 3:11.

The result is that Adam and Eve, after leaving their first love, also lost their first place. They were driven out of the garden, and never again allowed in. They would be reconciled to God through the covering He proved, but the loss of their first place was real.

But Adam and Eve were not the only ones to lose their first place in this first age of time.

The angels that fell during the time of Genesis also lost their first place when they left their first love of loyalty to God. Jude, verse 6, speaks of "angels who kept not their first estate, but left their own habitation". Cain, Adam's second son brought fruit of the ground, which his own sweat had harvested, rather than the blood of the lamb as a sacrifice, causing the Lord to reject his offering. This was the same error of Adam and Eve and it is certain their children were well acquainted with the story. When God rebuked Cain, rather than repenting, Cain chose instead to spill the blood of his brother, Abel. The result was that Cain was driven out, and he too lost his first place.

The story of the first church, as of the first generation of time, is the story of choosing knowledge over relationship and self-righteousness over love. The result was becoming a slave to works, and the loss of the first estate.

Encouragement: You Hate What I Hate

Even while He was rebuking the church at Ephesus, Jesus acknowledged that He knew they hated the deeds of the Nicolaitans, which Christ also hated. The great problem with Ephesus is that while they hated what Christ hates, they did not love what He loves. Jesus said, "by this shall all men know that you are My disciples, by the love that you have for one another."[9] The great characteristic of true believers is that we love.

The Nicolaitans

We don't know exactly who these Nicolaitans were, but we do know that they troubled more than one church (also Pergamos), and that Christ hated their deeds. The name "Nicolaitans" literally means "Victory or

---

[9]   John 13:35.

destruction over the people", leading some to surmise that at least part of their teaching led to the leaders of the church lording it over the people and taking advantage of them. This goes against the servant leadership Christ taught[10]. Jesus said that true leadership within His church would look more like serving than being served. He also warned that in the last days, there would be many who call Him "Lord", and even do miracles in His name, but who are not true followers[11]. The church must learn to discern truth from lies.

I believe another interpretation of these Nicolaitans it that they were symbolic of the fallen angels who harassed and corrupted the antediluvian world. They represented themselves to be gods, but were not. These fallen ones intermingled with God's people and corrupted them. We will look more at this group in the message to the church of Pergamos.

True believers of this first generation of time included Enoch, who walked with God. According to the book of Enoch, much of his teaching was rebuking the immorality of these so-called gods, and of warning mankind of coming judgment.

Promise to Overcomers: Access to The Tree of Life

Overcomers (those who got the victory over the temptations this church faced) would be granted to eat from the tree of life in the midst of the paradise of God.

What Adam and Eve lost in leaving the garden was specifically access to the Tree of Life in the Garden. God graciously restores all that we have lost when we repent and return to Him. Not even death can separate us from His love and promises.

Ephesus, Symbolic of the First Age: The Day of Light and Dark

I have included a chart paralleling the message to the church of Ephesus with the historic events of the first generation (thousand years) of time as recorded in Genesis.

---

10   Matt. 20:27; Matt. 23:11.
11   Matt. 7:22.

The first day of creation, God separates Light from Dark.

The first Day of time (1,000 years), saw the creation of Adam and Eve and the Garden of Eden. It was a time when God walked with man in the garden, but it also was a Day in which another one, who pretended to be from heaven (Satan) appeared in the garden in the form of a serpent. His seductive lies convinced Adam and Eve to choose the Tree of Knowledge of Good and Evil over the Tree of Life. This led to the Fall of Man in which he lost his first place and was sent out into the wild to toil and work. In leaving the Garden of Eden, man also lost access to the Tree of Life. The tragic result of choosing knowledge and self-righteous works over love, eventually led to the first murder wherein Cain killed his own brother Abel over worship issues.

In this first Day, the sons of God (angels), left their first estate, and intermingled with mankind, creating a race of mighty men who dominated the earth and filled it with evil[12].

Jesus represents Himself to the first church at Ephesus as the one who walks among the lampstands, symbolic of God walking with Adam in the garden. Ephesus was so much consumed with discerning good and evil that they left their first love of God and others. This is similar to Adam's choosing to eat the fruit from the Tree of knowledge of Good and Evil, even though he knew it would lead to death. That church was warned they would lose their place as Adam did, and as the fallen angels did.

Ephesus was harassed by a group of people pretending to be apostles (sent from God), and by a group called the Nicolaitans. The doctrine of these false apostles and Nicolaitans led to idol worship, and sexual immorality. The fallen Nephilim were accredited with pretending to be gods, and their influence led to sexual immorality.

The promise to the church in Ephesus was that overcomers would be restored access to the Tree of Life which is in the Paradise of God. The similarities are striking. The great struggle for those in Ephesus, as well as those who lived in the first Age of time was to discern good from evil, while remaining true to their first love. This is the great challenge for believers even today.

---

[12]   Gen. 6:1-4.

First Church: Ephesus - Lost Love

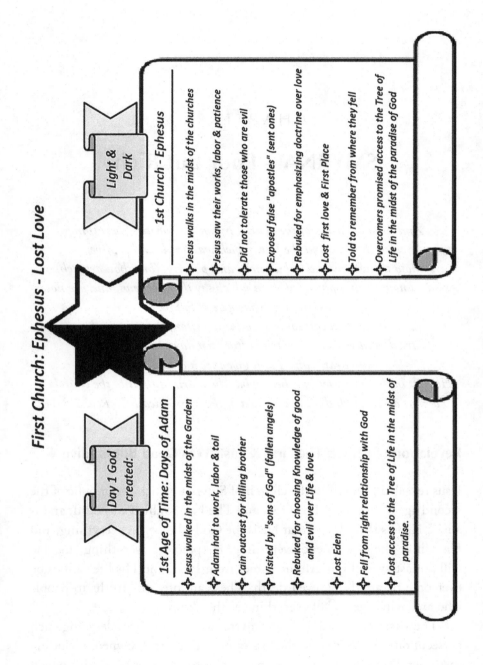

Light & Dark

1st Church - Ephesus

- ✧ Jesus walks in the midst of the churches
- ✧ Jesus saw their works, labor & patience
- ✧ Did not tolerate those who are evil
- ✧ Exposed false "apostles" (sent ones)
- ✧ Rebuked for emphasizing doctrine over love
- ✧ Lost first love & First Place
- ✧ Told to remember from where they fell
- ✧ Overcomers promised access to the Tree of Life in the midst of the paradise of God

Day 1 God created:

1st Age of Time: Days of Adam

- ✧ Jesus walked in the midst of the Garden
- ✧ Adam had to work, labor & toil
- ✧ Cain outcast for killing brother
- ✧ Visited by "sons of God" (fallen angels)
- ✧ Rebuked for choosing Knowledge of good and evil over Life & love
- ✧ Lost Eden
- ✧ Fell from right relationship with God
- ✧ Lost access to the Tree of Life in the midst of paradise.

CHAPTER 3

SMYRNA – Poor But Rich

"And unto the angel of the church in Smyrna write; These things
saith the first and the last, which was dead, and is alive;
I know thy works, and tribulation, and poverty, (but thou art rich)
and I know the blasphemy of them which say they are Jews, and are not,
but are the synagogue of Satan.
the devil shall cast some of you into prison, that ye may be
tried; and ye shall have tribulation ten days: be thou faithful
unto death, and I will give thee a crown of life.
He that hath an ear, let him hear what the Spirit saith unto the churches;
He that overcometh shall not be hurt of the second death." - Rev. 2:8-11

Revelation of Christ: The First & Last, Was Dead But Is Alive

Jesus revealed Himself to the church of Smyrna, which is symbolic of the
second age of time, as "The First, and The Last, Which was dead, and is
alive". He lets them know that He is the God who began everything, and
He will be the One to end everything. He predates everything, and He
will outlast everything. All life comes from Him, and His life cannot be
overcome by anything, even death. These are precious truths to people
who are facing the end of everything as they know it.

The first century church at Smyrna was a church undergoing such
persecution that they faced the loss of everything they owned, including
their own lives. The name "Smyrna" comes for the word "myrrh", which

means "bitter"[1]. Myrrh was a chief export of the city in early times. Myrrh is a tree resin with a bitter taste that was crushed and used in perfume, in incense, and as a preservative in burial[2]. It was an anointing perfume[3]. It is a symbol of death. It is interesting to note that it was one of the three gifts brought to Jesus by the Wise Men.[4] All three gifts pictured something about the Messiah, Jesus Christ, and His mission. Gold symbolized His royalty. Frankincense pointed to His deity, as offerings made to God in the Old Testament were often to be anointed with it. The myrrh symbolized His suffering and death on the cross.

As Christianity began to spread throughout the world, the pagan world did not always receive it with open arms. The idea of One God and One true King, was a threat to ideologies everywhere, but especially to Rome, which ruled the world at that time. They were tolerant of other religions, as long as people would acknowledge Caesar as the supreme king and ruler. People were free to worship their own gods, as long as they paid tribute to Caesar as God. For many pantheistic religions, adding another god to the list was not blasphemous. But to Christianity, which only acknowledged one God, this was not possible.

There were some who proposed doing what was expedient for the sake of government and commerce, and just keeping their religious beliefs private. They reasoned, "What would it matter if one paid tribute to Caesar and bowed to his likeness? It was just for the sake of business". This is a tension and temptation to compromise that believers still face today. But true believers could not reconcile their hearts to this. And thus persecution.

Acknowledgement: I See Your Tribulation and Poverty

To this church Jesus says He knows their works, tribulation and poverty. But He assures them that, though they lose everything in this

---

[1]   James Strong, *The New Strong's Exhaustive Concordance of the Bible* (Nashville: T. Nelson, 1990), G4666.

[2]   Thayer's Greek Lexicon, Electronic Database. 2011 by BibleSoft, Inc.

[3]   Joseph H. Thayer, *Thayer's Greek-English Lexicon of the New Testament* (Grand Rapids: Baker Book House, 1977), 4666.

[4]   Matthew 2:11.

world, they are in fact rich. They have laid up treasures in heaven which cannot be corrupted or stolen.

The first church, Ephesus, was troubled by those who said they were apostles and were not. This church was undergoing tribulation at the hands of those who say they are Jews and are not. In fact, Jesus said they were a synagogue of Satan!

It is important to note that according to Strong's definitions, the word translated "synagogue" means "an assemblage of persons, especially a Jewish synagogue; by analogy, a Christian church: assembly, congregation, synagogue."[5]. It refers to a congregation of believers. The true church of Christ here is being persecuted by a false church within it. Every church will have to be on the look out for people who pretend to be believers, but aren't. These so-called "Jews", were persecuting this church and Jesus warned them that there was more suffering to come at their hands.

Who are Jews? In the Old Testament, the term "Jew" was applied to the portion of the nation of Israel who remained loyal to God and the kingly line of David. It comes from the word "Judah", which means to praise God.

In the New Testament, those who identified as Jews were often the very ones who persecuted Christians and rejected Christ. Paul explains in the book of Romans that it is not outward keeping of the Law or circumcision that makes one a Jew, but what a person is inwardly. Those who claim they are the chosen people of God, and claim to be speaking and acting on God's behalf, but who in reality do not even know God, are like those who claim to be Jews but are not.

Jesus warns His disciples about those who claim to be Jews.

"These things have I spoken unto you, that you should not be offended.
They shall put out of the synagogues,
yes, the time comes that whosoever kills you will
think that he does God a service.
And these things will they do unto you,
because they have not known the Father, nor Me." – John 16:1-3

---

[5]   James Strong, *The New Strong's Exhaustive Concordance of the Bible* (Nashville: T. Nelson, 1990), G4864.

The church is to be made up of those who praise and glorify God alone – therefore, the church is symbolically, or spiritually, made up of Jews. This is not replacement theology, which teaches that God rejected the nation of Israel and replaced them with the church – Romans is very clear on that point as well. One does not cancel out the other, any more than a wife cancels out a sister – they are different, but both loved and of the same family. Parents need not reject their firstborn children in order to welcome new children into the family. Real love multiplies, not divides.

Synagogue of Satan

Who were these people who claimed to be Jews but were not? We will look at this term in more depth when we get to the message to the 6th church, but is should be noted that this is not an anti-Semitic term. The problem was not that they were Jews, but that they were not! The text says that this group "say they are Jews, but are not". They claim to be the people of God, but they are not. God reserves the right to decide who His people are.

It could be this group were the same ones who greatly troubled and persecuted Paul, and about whom he constantly warned new believers against. This group taught that those who wanted to come to God, would have to convert to Judaism, keep the law and be circumcised.

But the first counsel at Jerusalem[6] prayerfully sought the Lord on this matter and came to the conclusion that all - whether Jew or Gentile - are saved by grace through faith in Jesus Christ. They reminded new Gentile believers that, if they were true followers of Christ, there would be a life change resulting in purity (more on this in the message to Pergamos). But these actions would be evidences of salvation - not causes of salvation. Works cannot save. We are not saved by works, but by faith - and we are kept by faith as well.

Nevertheless, these so-called Jews continued to persecute Paul and the Gentile churches. Paul mentions them in all his letters, so it seems likely these are the same who are troubling and persecuting the church at Smyrna as well.

---

6   Acts 15:6-21.

No Rebuke:

This is one of only two churches for which Christ has no rebuke, and both of them were suffering persecution and hardships. Just as real gold is purified and refined by fire, real Christians are purified and revealed in suffering. People who are fake very quickly abandon ship when the going gets tough, but authentic people respond to suffering by become even more pure.

Command: Do Not Fear What You Will Suffer

Jesus' command to this church was to not fear any of the things which they were about to suffer. He encourages them to be faithful unto death, and He would reward them with life!

Warning: Suffering Is Coming

Jesus warned the church at Smyrna, not of coming judgment from Him, but of coming persecution from the devil. This is important, because when we go through hardships, we are prone to wonder if God is mad at us and if this is some sort of punishment or judgment from Him. Jesus encouraged the believers at Smyrna with the assurance that it was the devil who would be throwing some of them into prison. He also let them know that this situation would not last forever. It was about to come, but it would only last "10 days". And at the end of that time, there would be a crown waiting for them. He did not allow suffering and persecution to come on them without a warning. They were not to be unprepared for it.

He also told them why He was allowing it: "that you may be tested". This is an assaying term. It is what is done to gold to test its purity and value. Their true value would be evident to all through the way they endured suffering. Those who overcame would be given the crown of life and not hurt by the 2nd death.

Jesus said, "I know your poverty... but you are rich!"

Death and suffering are not able to keep us from the love and blessing of Christ. The same One who had passed from death to Life, promised them that they too would receive a crown of Life and not be hurt by death.

"What then shall we say to these things? If God
is for us, who can be against us?
He who did not spare His own Son, but delivered Him up for us all,
how shall He not with Him also freely give us all things? ···
Who shall separate us from the love of Christ?
Shall tribulation, or distress, or persecution, or famine,
or nakedness, or peril, or sword?
As it is written: "For Your sake we are killed all day long;
We are accounted as sheep for the slaughter."
Yet in all these things we are more than conquerors
through Him who loved us.
For I am persuaded that neither death nor life,
nor angels nor principalities, nor powers,
nor things present nor things to come,
nor height nor depth, nor any other created thing,
shall be able to separate us from the love of God
which is in Christ Jesus our Lord."- Rom. 8:31-39

Mystery of the 10 Days of Suffering

Jesus tells this church that they are going to go through "10 days" of suffering. This is a very interesting, and mysterious phrase. In the Western church, this phrase does not have a particular meaning, but to John and first century believers who had strong Jewish traditions, it had a very specific meaning.

The 10 days are a reference to the Ten Days of Awe, which Jews observe between the Feast of Trumpets and the Day of Atonement, in which they examine themselves and repent of sins[7].

---

[7]   John Klein & Adam Spears. Lost In Translation Vol.1, Rediscovering the Hebrew Roots of Our Faith (2007), p.165.

The first day of Rosh Hashanah begins this ten-day season, the entire focus of which is repentance. It is a time to heed the warning of God, to closely examine oneself and repent of anything that displeases God. The aim is to be prepared for coming judgment. These ten days conclude with the observance of the Day of Atonement.

The judgment of God is always preceded by a warning and a time given to repent. In Noah's day, there were one hundred and twenty years given for repentance before the flood. This does not even count the ministry of Enoch before Noah, who also warned of judgment to come.

> *"One of the ongoing themes of the Days of Awe is the concept that God has 'books' that He writes our names in, writing down who will live and who will die, who will have a good life, and who will have a bad life, for the next year. These names are written in the Book on Rosh Hashanah, but our actions during the Days of Awe can alter God's decree. The actions that change the decree are ... repentance, prayer, good deeds (usually charity). These books are sealed on Yom Kippur. This concept of writing in books is the source of the common greeting during this time as 'May you be inscribed and sealed for a good year.'"[8]*

Another tie in to the second day of creation, and the second age of time, in which the earth is covered in water (literally washing the sins away in a flood), is the observance of "Tashlikh" (literally, "cast off")[9]. This is a Jewish atonement ritual observed during these 10 Days of Awe in preparation for the Rosh Hashanna. It is performed, if possible, at a large, natural body of flowing water. The worshipper stands before the water and recites Biblical passages and prayers, and then they symbolically throw their sins into the water. This very much brings to mind Noah, the righteous man.

---

8   Judaism 101. *Judaism: Holidays & Festivals/ Rosh Hashanah*. (www. jewishvirtuallibrary.org)
9   Lesli Koppelman Ross. "Tashlich, the Symbolic Casting Off of Sins". Myjewishlearning.com, 2024.

Encouragement: You Are Rich!

Jesus' encouragement to the church at Smyrna was that, though they seemed to have lost everything, they were in fact rich. He encouraged them that, though suffering would come, it was not coming from Him.

Promise to Overcomers: Crown of Life

To those who overcame, Jesus promised a crown of Life. The Spirit promises that they will not be hurt by the second death. There was a saying that was popular back in my Bible college days that went: "Born once, die twice. Born twice, die once." Jesus promises that those who are "born again" (born of the Spirit), "though he were dead, yet shall he live. And he that lives and believes in Me shall never die."[10]

Smyrna, Symbolic of the Second Age: The Day of Sky and Seas

The second day of Creation, God separated the waters above the earth from the waters under the earth. Again, waters are symbolic of the nations of the earth.

The second Day of Time (1,000-2,000 years from creation), saw Noah and the great flood, in which all peoples and nations were destroyed. If one took a snapshot of the earth on the second day of creation, and also one in the second age of time, they would look the same.

This age of time also saw the rise of the tower of Babel, and the creation of nations. Seas or waters in prophetic language represent tribes, tongues, nations and peoples. With the rise of nations and different languages, we see the people being dispersed throughout the world.

Noah: Poor, but Rich

The second generation of Time was the time of Noah. Noah, like the believers at Smyrna, was both very poor, and very rich. He literally lost

---

[10]   John 11:25-26.

the whole world, but gained his own soul. He was the last man of the old world, and the first man of the new one. He saw the death of everything, but also the rebirth of everything. Noah saw the first great Death – the first global extinction, but he also saw the dawn of a new earth. The church at Smyrna would as well.

They endured great suffering, but they also were promised a crown of life. For many of them, they experienced persecution from the Jews as well as Rome. They lost everything to follow Christ. But they were rich spiritually, and promised eternal life.

According to Genesis 6, the earth had become so corrupted by the intermarrying of the sons of god with the daughters of men that God looked for a man who was "pure in his generation". In other words, Noah's genetic make up was not polluted by this intermarrying. He was of pure human blood. This intermarrying resulted in the earth being filled with violence and evil. It was also filled with blasphemous worship of gods, which also made Noah stand out as a man who walked with God.

The Bible does not go into great detail of what the days before the flood, as Noah was building the ark, were like, but we can imagine they were not smooth sailing (pun intended). The book of Jude, speaking of false teachers in the church, compares them to those in Enoch's time before the flood, saying:

"…these filthy dreamers defile the flesh, despise dominion,
and speak evil of dignities…
These are spots in your feasts of charity, when they feast with you,
feeding themselves without fear; clouds they are without water,
carried about by winds,
trees whose fruit withers without fruit, twice dead, plucked up thy the roots.
Raging waves of the sea, foaming out their own shame,
wandering stars, to whom is reserved the blackness of darkness forever.
And Enoch also, the seventh from Adam, prophesied of these saying,
'Behold the Lord comes with ten thousand of his saints.
To execute judgement upon all, and to convince all that are ungodly among
them of all their ungodly deeds which they have ungodly committed,
and of all their hard speeches which ungodly
sinners have spoken against him.

These are murmurers, complainers, walking after their own lusts,
and their mouth speaks great swelling words,
having men's persons in admiration because of advantage.
But, beloved, remember you the words which were spoken before
of the apostles of our Lord Jesus Christ.
How that they told you there should be mockers in the last time,
who should walk after their own ungodly lusts.
These be they who separate themselves, sensual, having not the Spirit."
— Jude 8, 12-19

The book of 2 Peter also speaks of this time:

"For if God spared not the angels that sinned, but cast them down to hell,
and delivered them into chains of darkness, to be reserved unto judgment,
and spared not the old world, but saved Noah, the eighth person, a preacher
of righteousness, bringing in the flood upon the world of the ungodly....
The Lord knows how to deliver the godly out of temptations,
and to reserve the unjust unto the day of judgment to be punished."
— 2 Peter 2:4-5, 9

"Knowing this first, that there shall come in the last days scoffers, walking
after their own lusts, and saying, "where is the promise of His coming?
For since the fathers fell asleep, all things continue as
they were from the beginning of the creation.'
For this they willingly are ignorant of,
that by the word of God the heavens were of old,
and the earth standing out of the water and in the water:
Whereby the world that then was, being overflowed with water, perished.
But the heavens and the earth, which are now,
by the same world are kept in store,
reserved unto fire against the day of judgment and perdition of ungodly men.
But beloved, be not ignorant of this one thing,
that one day with the Lord as a thousand years,
and a thousand years as one day." 2 Peter 3:3-8

We can be sure of one thing; if Noah was alone in preaching while he was preparing the ark, he was subject to ridicule and persecution. The world has never dealt kindly with those who don't fall in and lock step with them.

Noah, as the church in Smyrna, faced great persecution. But both chose to lose the whole world rather than their own souls. The first century church of Smyrna faced, imprisonment, the loss of material goods, and even the loss of their own lives. Noah was also imprisoned, in a sense, in the ark. And he saw the loss of his entire world and everyone in it, except just what was in the ark with him. He survived the first great extinction event! Precious indeed was the revelation of Christ as the one who is victorious over death.

The Days of Noah Will Return

Although the church of Smyrna is symbolic of believers in the second age of time, believers of the end times (which the Bible states we are in) should pay special attention to the message to this church. Jesus said that just before His return, civilization would once again be "as in the days of Noah". What were the days of Noah like?

The adjectives that are used in the Bible are violent, lawless, immoral, and the prevalent characteristic of the times will be deception. In Noah's day this deception rose from fallen sons of God who pretended to be gods. In the church of Smyrna, it rose from those who claim to be Jews, but were not. Meaning those who were in charge of religious establishments claim to be acting on the part of Christ, but in practice deny Him. These same religious and secular leaders will persecute true believers.

I've heard it taught that there would be a great revival at the end times, but I do not necessarily see that in scripture. The Bible does say that in the end times God would pour out His Spirit on all flesh, which happened at Pentecost, and continues to be available to all today. Revelation also tells us that the gospel of the kingdom would be preached in all the world before the end comes. But what the Bible does warn us about, repeatedly, is that there will be a great falling away from the faith[11]. So much so that Jesus

---

[11]   2 Thess. 2:3.

said, "Nevertheless when the Son of Man comes, shall He find faith on the earth?"[12] It's a rhetorical question, but the implied answer is maybe not. In Noah's day, only 8 were saved! Jesus warned that many would be offended because of Him and turn on even their own families.[13]

There is another interesting parallel with Noah's time and ours. According to the Book of Enoch, the Nephilim taught humans advanced technology. They stressed the accumulation of knowledge and science. Today much of what is called science is not actual science, but theory and philosophy. It masquerades as science, but it is not based on observed facts nor on provable scientific method, but on theoretical suppositions. They reason like this, "Since we KNOW there is no God, we then surmise…". There is tremendous pressure on people of faith to compromise their beliefs when it comes to science, and a prevalent supposition that true faith is not compatible with true science. This despite the fact that much of the traditional, provable science that we have was fathered by men and women of faith. It is not my purpose here to explore this further, my intention is merely to point out the worship of science and knowledge over Biblical faith, has been around since Adam chose Knowledge over God, and was a characteristic of both the days of Noah, and of this present age.

The Return of the Nephilim?

The Nephilim also "took" wives of all they wanted. The Hebrew word used is "Laqah"[14] and indicates they seized, snatched away, or carried them off. This puts a whole new spin on Jesus' words that in the days of Noah they were "marrying and giving in marriage"[15]. Marriage is an honorable institution, but there is clear indication that whatever was going on, it was neither good nor honorable.

For what purpose were they snatching away these women? To procreate and create a hybrid human race. The Bible refers to them as giants. Today, science is splicing genes together to create all sorts of hybrid plants and

---

12   Luke 18:8.

13   Matt. 2:10.

14   James Strong, *The New Strong's Exhaustive Concordance of the Bible* (Nashville: T. Nelson, 1990), H3946.

15   Matt. 24:38.

animals. There are even animal genes being spliced into humans, and vice versa. This is a direct violation of God's command that everything was to reproduce after its own kind.

Thirty years ago, anyone who claimed to have seen a UFO (or UAP = Unidentified Arial Phenomenon, as they are now called) was not only in the minority, they were generally believed to be quacks. Today, the proliferation of documentaries, book and podcasts on this subject is astounding. Not only do the majority of people believe that so called aliens exist, nearly half believe they have visited the planet at some point in history. The list of those who are now fully convinced includes scientists, politicians and military personal. It is no longer a fringe belief.

Every culture on earth has some sort of alien mythology wherein beings from another planet visit the earth and intermingle with the population. Genesis 6 alludes to this, while the book of Enoch outright teaches this. Except according to the Bible and the Book of Enoch, they are not aliens but fallen angels. Once again, deception is the key factor. Those who claim to be something they are not. It is possible this surge of interest, abduction accounts and sightings of alien aircraft could be yet another Biblical sign of the end times.

Second Church: Smyrna - Poor but Rich

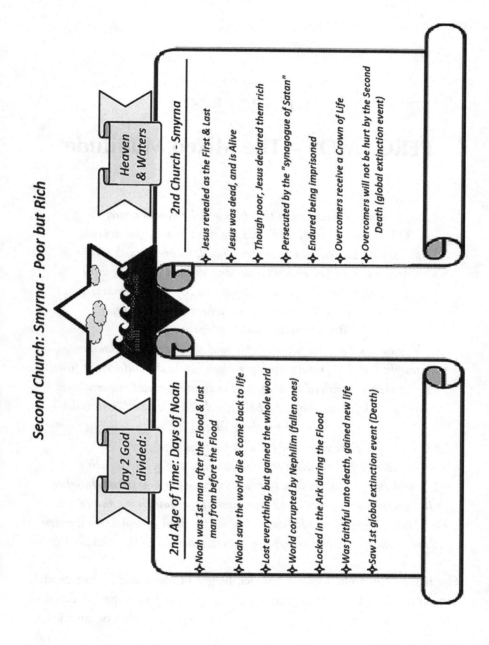

Day 2 God divided:

Heaven & Waters

2nd Age of Time: Days of Noah
- Noah was 1st man after the Flood & last man from before the Flood
- Noah saw the world die & come back to life
- Lost everything, but gained the whole world
- World corrupted by Nephilim (fallen ones)
- Locked in the Ark during the Flood
- Was faithful unto death, gained new life
- Saw 1st global extinction event (Death)

2nd Church - Smyrna
- Jesus revealed as the First & Last
- Jesus was dead, and is Alive
- Though poor, Jesus declared them rich
- Persecuted by the "synagogue of Satan"
- Endured being imprisoned
- Overcomers receive a Crown of Life
- Overcomers will not be hurt by the Second Death (global extinction event)

CHAPTER 4

PERGAMOS – The Mixed Multitude

"And to the angel of the church in Pergamos write,
'These things says He who has the sharp two-edged sword:
"I know your works, and where you dwell, where Satan's throne is.
And you hold fast to My name, and did not deny My faith
even in the days in which Antipas was My faithful martyr,
who was killed among you, where Satan dwells.
But I have a few things against you,
because you have there those who hold the doctrine of Balaam,
who taught Balak to put a stumbling block before the children of Israel,
to eat things sacrificed to idols, and to commit sexual immorality.
Thus you also have those who hold the doctrine of the Nicolaitans,
which thing I hate.
Repent, or else I will come to you quickly
and will fight against them with the sword of My mouth.
"He who has an ear, let him hear what the Spirit says to the churches.
To him who overcomes I will give some of the hidden manna to eat.
And I will give him a white stone, and on the stone a new name written
which no one knows except him who receives it."' - Rev. 2:12-17

The name "Pergamos" means "citadel, height or elevation."[1] Most citadels
were constructed on high ground, giving a better vantage for defense.
The feminine form means "the city of the serpent" or "to be married to

---

[1]   James Strong, *The New Strong's Exhaustive Concordance of the Bible* (Nashville:
    T. Nelson, 1990), G4010.

power". This is particularly appropriate for Pergamos because the temple of Aesculapius, depicted as a serpent god, was located there. Both forms can be revealing of the strengths and challenges that faced this congregation of believers.

Revelation of Christ: One With the Two-Edged Sword

Jesus revealed Himself to the church of Pergamos as "He who has the sharp two-edged sword." Always, we look to Jesus and how He reveals Himself to understand what is happening within the church. Christ repeatedly showed up to this age of believers as the One with the Sword.

We see in Rev. 1:16 that the two-edged sword came out of his mouth. The Word of God (which comes out of the mouth of God) is depicted as a sword in Hebrews 4:12:

> *"For the word of God is quick, and powerful, and sharper than any two-edged sword, piercing even to the dividing asunder of soul and spirit, and of the joints and marrow, and is a discerner of the thoughts and intents of the heart. "*

The fact that Jesus reveals Himself to this church as the One with the sharp two-edged sword tells us that they were in need of having the word of truth rightly divided among them. Error and deception had crept in and the people were tolerating people in their midst that they ought to have rebuked and exposed.

Acknowledgement: You Hold Fast To My Name & Faith

This church had much to be commended for. They were faithful, even when faced with persecutions, and even though they dwelled "where Satan's throne" is.

Jesus said that He knew those of this congregation had held fast to his name and not denied the faith even when faced with the death of Antipas. There are some revealing things about the name "Antipas" that are worth considering, and which we will see when we study how this church is symbolic of the Third Age of time.

Rebuke: Allow the Doctrine of Balaam & Nicolaitans

The church of Pergamos were steadfast in holding up the name of Christ, yet, they also allowed those among them who held doctrines that were hateful to God.

This congregation was also plagued by Nicolaitans, as was mentioned in the message to the church at Ephesus.

Command: Repent

Jesus' command to this church was for them to Repent. There are many ways of departing from God, but there is only one path back to Him. Repentance does not mean merely being sorry for sin. And it is far more than a desire to avoid punishment. Repentance involves agreeing with God about our sin, and turning from it to God. It is not just acknowledging our sin, but forsaking it.

Repentance is only possible because Jesus opened the way through His sacrificial death on the cross, becoming the "Lamb that was slain". The Law says, "the soul that sinneth, it shall die."[2], "The wages of sin is death"[3], and all have sinned, therefore all must die.[4]

We all are under the penalty of death, because we have all sinned. Efforts to earn our way back are futile, we could never pay the price required, because the price required is death. Even if you or I died for our sin, we are only paying what we owe. Our death could not ransom anyone else. Only One could pay the price and yet be victorious over death. Death has no power over Christ because He was sinless. Jesus owed no debt of sin, therefore His death could be offered as a ransom for us.

---

[2]   Eze. 18:4, 20.

[3]   Romans 6:23.

[4]   Romans 3:23.

All that remains to be done is for us to agree to this exchange, and swap our death for His life. No matter how far one goes away from God, the path back is short. Repent.

Warning: I Will Come & Fight With My Sword

Jesus' warning to this church was that if they did not repent, He would come to them quickly and will fight against them with the sword of His mouth. Not to trivialize His warning, but it does remind me of when my dad would tell us to behave or else he was going to "come in there and you won't like it".

The church is supposed to be eagerly awaiting the return of Christ, but Christ warned that when He came, He would deal with those who were abusing their fellow servants rather than watching, waiting, and occupying themselves with their Father's business.[5] The return of the King will be a joyous event for those who are faithful to him, but it will be a fearful event for the disobedient.

Jesus said that not everyone who calls Him Lord is truly His, but only those who actually do the will of His father.[6] Those who teach and practice that one may do whatever one wants, as long as they prayed a prayer to accept Christ, are both deceived and deceiving. We are not saved by good works, but obedience to Christ is as natural to those who are truly born of His Spirit as breathing. It doesn't make one a fish just because one lives in water; but if one is a fish, he most certainly will be in water. Biblical faith is not merely believing in Jesus Christ. According to James 2:19, even demons believe. Faith is when one puts action to that belief. I may believe a chair will support me, but sitting in the chair turns the belief into faith. James goes on to say in verse 20 that "faith without works is dead".

---

[5]   Luke 12:45-47.
[6]   Matt. 7:21-23.

Promise to Overcomers: Hidden Manna, White Stone, New Name

To the overcomers, Christ promises that He will give them hidden manna to eat, a white stone, and in the stone a new name. Perhaps more than any other message to the churches so far, this reward to overcomers revels the identity of the Age of Believers this message symbolizes.

Pergamos, Symbolic of the Third Age: The Day of the Land & the Seed

This third church represents the believers during the third millennium of time; the age that began with Abraham and goes through the time of the judges of Israel. It included Moses, Joshua, and Gideon, just to name a few.

The third day of creation saw the emergence of land from the waters, and of plants bearing seed after their own kind. The Third Millennium of Time (or Third Age) begins with the promise of a Land to be given to the Seed of Abraham, and ends with that seed (children of Israel) in the Promised Land. It covers the birth of the patriarchs, the days of captivity in Egypt, the sojourn in the wilderness, and the days of Moses and Joshua. It extends through the times of the Judges. Biblically, it extends from Genesis 12 through 1 Samuel.

Earlier, we noted that in His message to Pergamos, Jesus mentions Antipas as one who was martyred as His faithful witness. The name "Antipas" literally means, "before the father"[7]. Gen. 11:28 tells us that Abraham had a brother, Haran, who died "before his father". According to the book of Jasher (which is referred to in the Bible and was widely read and accepted in John's time[8]), Terah, Abram's father, betrayed his son Haran to Nimrod, the evil king. He was betrayed because he refused to worship Nimrod and held to the belief that there was only one true God, the creator of the universe[9]. As a result, he was put to death "before his father", or in the presence of his father, making him a martyr for his

---

[7]   James Strong, *The New Strong's Exhaustive Concordance of the Bible* (Nashville: T. Nelson, 1990), G494.

[8]   Joshua 10:13; 2 Sam. 1:18.

[9]   Jasher 12/

faith. Both Haran and Abraham belong to the Third Age of Time, which Pergamos represents.

When Abraham left home for the promised land, he didn't quite obey all that God commanded him. God had instructed him to "leave his father's house" and go where God would lead him[10]. Abraham did leave, but he took Lot with him. This decision led to such strife that they eventually had to part ways.

When the children of Israel left Egypt, they were a "mixed multitude".[11]This means intermingled with the children of Israel were others of different nationalities, and more importantly, of other faiths. There were some in their midst who worshipped the gods of Egypt, and whose hearts and loyalties were more aligned with Egypt than with some future promised land. In the same way as Abraham and Israel, there were those in the church at Pergamos whose loyalties and belief systems were more aligned with the world than with Christ.

Hidden Manna

Manna is what God fed the children of Israel during their wilderness wanderings. There was a hidden pot of manna which was placed in the ark of the covenant under the mercy seat as a memorial of God's goodness and provision. Jesus made the analogy that He was the bread from heaven, which if one receives, will result in real, eternal life[12]. Manna is uniquely associated with God's provision for His people

White Stone and New Name

The white stone with a new name written on it would have had meaning to this congregation, for their judges used black and white stones to deliver decisions – a white stone meaning that your case was won and you were exonerated. The priests also had gem stones upon their breastplate and shoulders that represented the 12 tribes, and were engraved with each

---

[10]   Gen. 12:1,4.

[11]   Exodus 12:38.

[12]   John 6:31-33.

of their names. Abram, Sarai and Jacob were all given new names when they followed God and believed His promises. Abram became Abraham, Sarai became Sarah, and Jacob became Israel. All these lived during this historic age.

The One With The Sword

We have proposed the hypothesis that Pergamos is symbolic of the believers of the Third Age of Time, but did Jesus come to believers of this Age, as He says He will do in His message to this church? He did. There were many instances of preincarnate appearances of Christ to Abraham, Moses, and Joshua to name a few. Jesus revels Himself to the church at Pergamos as the One with the sharp, two-edged sword, and He repeatedly showed up during this Age of Time as the One with The Sharp Sword.

The story of Balaam[13]

During this age, as Moses was leading the children of Israel to the Promised Land, Balaam was prevented from cursing Israel by the angel of the Lord with a sword in his hand. Since God would not allow Balaam to curse Israel, the wicked prophet instead taught Balak how to get Israel to curse themselves – by seducing them into immorality and idol worship. It is interesting that Jesus specifically mentions Balaam and Balak in His message to the church at Pergamos, which is symbolic of the Third Age of Time. Balak and Balaam lived during this Age!

Joshua just before the battle of Jericho

"And it came to pass, when Joshua was by Jericho, that he lifted up his eyes and looked and behold, there stood a man over against him with his sword drawn in his hand, and Joshua went unto him and said unto him, 'Art thou for us, or for our adversaries?' And he said, "Nay, but as captain of the host of the Lord am I now come. And Joshua fell

---

[13]   Numbers 22:23-31.

on his face to the earth, and did worship, and said unto him, 'What saith my lord unto his servant?' And the captain of the Lord's host said unto Joshua, 'Loose thy shoe from off thy foot, for the place whereon thou standest is holy." And Joshua did so." – Joshua 5:13-15

This is the same instruction the VOICE from the burning bush said to Moses in Ex. 3:5 – indicating it is the same ONE speaking.

Gideon

Joshua instructed the 300 men with whom he defeated the Midianites to declare that they fought by the sword of the Lord,

> *"When I blow with a trumpet, I and all that are with me, then blow ye the trumpets also on every side of all the camp, and say, 'The sword of the Lord and of Gideon!'" – Joshua 7:18*

Amazingly, though they declared "the sword of the Lord", not a man carried a sword! They had trumpets in one hand and torches hidden under jars of clay in the other – it was the Lord who fought for them and won the battle!

Psalm 149:6-9

> *"Let the high praises of God be in their mouth,*
> *And a two-edged sword in their hand.*
> *To execute vengeance upon the heathen, and punishments upon the people.*
> *To bind their kings with chains, and their nobles with fetters of iron.*
> *To execute upon them the judgment written:*
> *this honor have all His saints. Praise ye the Lord!"*

Nicolaitans and Nephilim Again!

As with the church at Ephesus, this congregation was also plagued by Nicolaitans. As we have seen, this group could be representative of the

Nephilim ("giants"), as was mentioned in more detail in the message to the Ephesians. During this Third Age of Time (of which the church at Pergamos was symbolic), Israel also struggled with this group.

Although the flood wiped out the race of giants (who were the offspring of fallen angels), Genesis 6 is clear that there were giants "also afterward". The Old Testament tells of several races of giants, whom the Israelites were to extinguish from the land. We are not given exact details of how they came to be, but the Bible leaves no doubt that when it says giants, it means giants, even giving dimensions so as to leave no doubt. This is not commonly taught, and I find it odd that the same people who claim to believe the Bible to be inerrant are often uncomfortable when confronted with what it actually says.

Genesis 15:18-21 lists the names of the nations whom the Israelites were to completely dispossess from the land. Among them were the Rephaim, which name is also translated "giants" seventeen times out of the twenty-five times it is used in the Old Testament.

In Deut. 2:10-11 mentions the Emims (whose name means "terrors"), and the Anakims (whose name means "long-necked"). Both are identified as races of unusually tall and fierce people, as were the Zamzummims, spoken of in Deut. 2:20-21. The Anakims were called the Anunnaki by the Assyrians, Sumerians and Babylonians. They were recognized as a race of giants, who were the offspring of gods who came from the heavens and intermarried with mankind.

When the spies were sent into the promised land by Moses to map it out, they came back with the report that the land was inhabited by a race of giants in whose eyes they were "as grasshoppers"[14]. And most are familiar with the story of the young shepherd David (before he was king), slaying the giant Goliath of Gath.[15]

Jesus reveals Himself to Abraham, as the One who brings judgment to Sodom and Gomorrah[16]. This same One gave Abraham and Sarah new names, and promised them a land and a "seed"[17]. He appeared to Jacob as

---

[14] Numbers 13:33.

[15] I Sam. 17.

[16] Gen. 18:16-22.

[17] Gen. 17:1-16.

the One with whom Jacob wrestled, and who then gives him a new name[18]. He appeared to Moses in the burning bush and gave him power to lead the promised seed into the promised land. He appeared to Joshua as the One with the sharp, two-edged sword, who fought as the commander of the Host of Heaven's Armies[19]. He appeared with a drawn sword to the wicked Balaam, preventing him from cursing what God had blessed[20]. Gideon and young David, before he was king, both conquered their enemies by "the sword of the Lord"[21]. The Lord let them know that it was not their own sword that got them the land, but His.

But the warning to this church and age was that they were a mixed multitude, having in their midst those who seduced the Lord's people into idol worship and immorality. Jesus specifically mentions Balaam and Balac in His rebuke to this church, and these two lived in the Third Age of Time, which Pergamos symbolizes.

Despite the wonderful miracles and heroic deeds done by this Age of Believers, Israel never could quite separate themselves from that mixed multitude who would seduce them back into idol worship. Throughout the times of the Judges we see God delivering the people, only to have them slip back into their old ways. The church at Pergamos had the same problem. They were not yet dominated by these subversive groups, but they tolerated them to remain among them, and their influence would grow.

In this Age of Time, as we have seen, Jesus repeatedly shows up as the One With The Sword, the Manna, and the One Who gives a New Name.

---

[18]   Gen. 32:24-30.
[19]   Joshua 5:13-15.
[20]   Num. 22:31.
[21]   Judges 7:18-20; 1 Sam. 17:45.

Third Church: Pergamos - Mixed Multitude

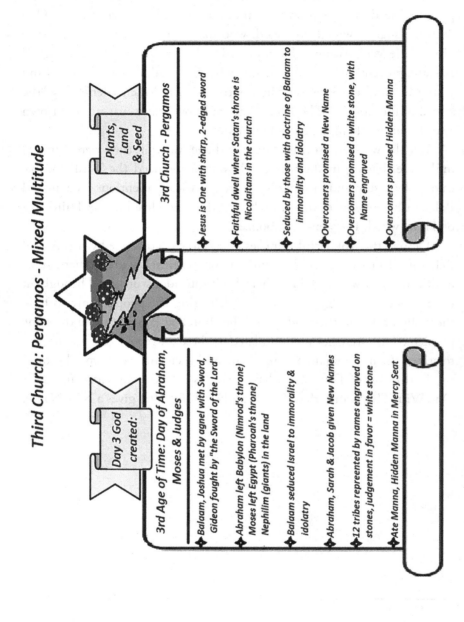

Plants, Land & Seed

3rd Church - Pergamos

- Jesus is One with sharp, 2-edged sword
- Faithful dwell where Satan's throne is Nicolaitans in the church
- Seduced by those with doctrine of Balaam to immorality and idolatry
- Overcomers promised a New Name
- Overcomers promised a white stone, with Name engraved
- Overcomers promised Hidden Manna

Day 3 God created:

3rd Age of Time: Day of Abraham, Moses & Judges

- Balaam, Joshua met by agnel with Sword, Gideon fought by "the Sword of the Lord"
- Abraham left Babylon (Nimrod's throne) Moses left Egypt (Pharoah's throne) Nephilim (giants) in the land
- Balaam seduced Israel to immorality & idolatry
- Abraham, Sarah & Jacob given New Names
- 12 tribes repreented by names engraved on stones, judgement in favor = white stone
- Ate Manna, Hidden Manna in Mercy Seat

CHAPTER 5

THYATIRA – Unequally Yoked

"And to the angel of the church in Thyatira write,
'These things says the Son of God, who has eyes like a flame of fire,
and His feet like fine brass:
'I know your works, love, service, faith, and your patience;
and as for your works, the last are more than the first.
Nevertheless, I have a few things against you, because you allow that woman
Jezebel, who calls herself a prophetess, to teach and seduce My servants
to commit sexual immorality and eat things sacrificed to idols.
And I gave her time to repent of her sexual
immorality, and she did not repent.
Indeed, I will cast her into a sickbed,
and those who commit adultery with her into great tribulation,
unless they repent of their deeds.
I will kill her children with death,
and all the churches shall know that I am He
who searches the minds and hearts.
And I will give to each one of you according to your works.
Now to you I say, and to the rest in Thyatira,
as many as do not have this doctrine,
who have not known the depths of Satan, as they say,
I will put on you no other burden.
But hold fast what you have till I come.
And he who overcomes, and keeps My works until the end,
to him I will give power over the nations...

as I also have received from My Father;
and I will give him the morning star.'
He who has an ear,
let him hear what the Spirit says to the churches." – Rev. 2:18-29 NKJV[1]

What began with allowing a fringe element with corrupt teaching to remain in the church in Pergamos, now becomes tolerating these wolves in sheep's clothing to actually teach and hold positions of leadership in the church at Thyatira. Not only did they allow those with immoral beliefs and practices to remain in the church, the church leadership actually embraced this immorality, teaching it as new doctrine. When deception and immorality are not dealt with and exposed, we allow its influence and power to grow.

The name "Thyatira" literally means "odor (or perfume) or sacrifice of labor.[2] Dyeing was one of the important industries of Thyatira, and it could be due to the odor that is produced by that industry that the city got its name. It is certain that what was happening in this church was not a pleasing aroma to the Lord.

The principal deity of the city was Apollo, but there was also a temple dedicated to Sambethe – a female deity who was served by a prophetess who would impart messages to those who worshipped at this shrine. Some suppose this is the woman "Jezebel" that is referred to in this letter. I am not inclined to this belief for one very simple reason: the message was to the church of Christ's – not to the city of Thyatira. The church would not have been condemned for what happened outside of it, but it would be held responsible for the teaching that went on inside.

Revelation of Christ: The Son of God

Jesus represents Himself to the church at Thyatira as "The Son of God, with eyes like a flame of fire and feet like burnished bronze."

The early church at the time John wrote this book would have recognized the title of "Son of God" from a Jewish perspective. The apostle

---

[1]   (1982)

[2]   James Strong, *The New Strong's Exhaustive Concordance of the Bible* (Nashville: T. Nelson, 1990), G2363.

Nathanael declared of Jesus, *"Rabbi, thou are the Son of God, thou art the King of Israel."* – John 1:49

At Jesus' birth, wise men from the east came to Jerusalem seeking the child who had been born to be "king of the Jews". The Angel, announcing the birth of Christ told Mary, *"...therefor also, that holy thing which shall be born of thee shall be called the Son of God."*[3]

When Satan was tempting Jesus during the 40 days in the wilderness, he began with, *"If you are the Son of God".*[4] In addition, when Christ cast out the unclean spirits, they cried out, *"Thou art the Son of God".*[5]

Jesus was even crucified under the banner, "The King of the Jews", because He had declared Himself to be the Son of God. The centurion, which stood at the cross and watched Jesus die said, *"Truly this man was the Son of God".*[6]

To the Jews (which at the time Revelation was written were still the dominate group in the church), the titles "Son of God" and "King" were synonymous. By announcing Himself under this title, Jesus is asserting His supreme sovereignty over not just the church, but nations (and thus the culture). This is particularly stressed because the woman Jezebel, who was corrupting the church, has the same name as a notoriously evil queen who ruled Israel in the Fourth Age of Time. Jesus is asserting His sovereignty over all other rulers and kings. If the powers that be, inside or outside of the church, place pressure and demands on God's people to act in ways that are contrary to His Word, Jesus is the supreme King Who should be obeyed.

We will look at the revelation of Christ to this church in more detail when we study it's significance to the Fourth Age of time, but what is significant for all those who have ears to hear is that Jesus is not only the Sovereign King and Son of God, He is also the one who sees and who weighs every thought and action with His eyes like flames. Nothing is hidden from Him.

---

[3]   Luke 1:35.
[4]   Matt. 4:3-6.
[5]   Matt. 8:29; Mark 3:11; Luke 4:4.
[6]   Mark 15:39.

Acknowledgement: Your Last Works Are More Than Your First

Jesus said He knows their works, love, service, faith and patience. He also says He knows their last works to be more than the first. That is something I would aspire to have said of me.

To be continually growing in our service and faith is the aim of all true disciples of Christ. Stagnant things die, all living things grow. However, it is clear that all the good works in the world cannot cancel out the wrong that we do.

The messages to the churches should be the definitive argument against the notion that when we stand before God, as long as our good works outweigh the bad, we'll be fine. From Jesus' words, that clearly is not the case. If it were, He would have said, "Your last works are more (greater) than the first, so Good Job!" We will not be measured by the quantity of our work, but whether they are done in purity of faith and love.

The fact that Thyatira permitted this "Jezebel" to perpetrate false and immoral teaching in the church shows that they had a lack of awe and godly fear for the holiness of God, as well as a lack of compassion for those young believers corrupted by her teaching.

Rebuke: You Allow Jezebel To Teach My People

Jesus rebukes the church at Thyatira for allowing a "Jezebel" to teach false and corrupting doctrines.

An interesting interpretation holds that this text could actually read, "I have a few things against you because you allow that *wife*, Jezebel, who calls herself a prophetess, to teach..." The word translated *woman* could also mean wife. The result of her teaching was that Christ's servants were seduced into committing sexual immorality and eating things sacrificed to idols. We'll see the significance of this when we look at Thyatira as the symbol of the fourth age.

What is meant by sexual immorality is probably fairly clear, but what the problem is with eating things sacrificed to idols may be less clear. To get clarity we need to go back to previous letters to the churches in the New Testament and see what was going on and what had already been instructed.

In I Corinthians chapters 8-10, Paul speaks quite a lot about eating things sacrificed to idols. He taught that eating these things which had been sacrificed to idols was the equivalent to sharing communion with idols. We will go into this in a lot more detail in the chapter dedicated to the ancient Hebrew wedding traditions, but practically, there was great pressure and incentive to eat things sacrificed to idols. Some believers in the early church would purchase meat in the market that had been sacrificed to idols because it was cheaper. In addition, those who were members of a professional guild were compelled to participate in token offerings to various gods and Caesar in order to practice their trade. Compromise was a lot easier than the persecution that would follow by resisting the powers that be.

But Christ said you cannot serve God and mammon (money)[7]. Believers are to have communion with Christ alone. For expediency's sake, probably involving both economic expediency as well as social, many believers in the early church were beguiled into compromising with the world in both moral and religious practices. In Acts 15, the first counsel of Jerusalem instructed Gentile believers that they should be careful not to engage in sexual immorality and not to eat things offered to idols.

It was no easier for first century Christians to stand up for their faith and draw a line against compromise than it is for us. In fact, it was much harder. Their livelihoods, relationships, and even very lives were on the line. If Christ required this level of purity from them, there can be no doubt that He will not turn a lenient eye towards compromise in the church today. We must always love all people, but we must always rebuke their sin, for their own soul's sake, and for ours.

It may not be vogue to hold on to old fashioned values of right and wrong, but God's Word does not change with the fashions of the day. There is a great effort to reframe good and evil in our culture today. Many in the church prefer not to engage in the debate, taking a less offensive and more inclusive stance. Jesus did not buy it in the church at Thyatira, and He will not buy the notion that tolerance of evil is compassionate and loving when we try to sell it either. It is not. It is lazy, self-serving and cowardly. In fact, to refuse to speak up when we see wrong, and know the

---

[7]   Matt. 6:24.

judgment it will bring, is in God's eyes, criminal and worthy of the same punishment the perpetrators earn.

"When I say unto the wicked,
'O wicked man, you shall surely die';
If you do not speak to warn the wicked from his way,
That wicked man shall die in his iniquity;
But his blood will I require at your hand." – Ezekiel 33:8

Command: Repent

The solution for this church was, as always, for them to repent. Repentance means to turn around and go back the way you came. It is not just a verbal agreement or confession of wrong doing. It is a change of direction and behavior. Jesus said "I gave her (Jezebel) space to repent of her fornication, and she repented not". Some translations read "she does not want to repent". It was not a lack of understanding or opportunity; it was a lack of will.

None who stand before God will be able to claim ignorance or lack of opportunity. No smoke screen will hide our complicity in either participating in immorality, or in tolerating its teaching. Especially when that teaching targets our young ones. We cannot afford to turn a blind, tolerant eye to what God's Word clearly spells out as immoral and wrong. To do so makes us complicit in what is destroying lives. Sin leads to death – physically and spiritually. To opt to turn a tolerant eye to the evils of the culture around us, especially when it permeates the church, makes us complicit in the evil and destruction of innocent souls.

Warning: I Will Cast Her Into Great Tribulation

Because those who were troubling this church (and who were in leadership there) chose not to repent, Jesus warns that when He comes, He will cast her (Jezebel) into a bed (of suffering), and those who commit adultery with her into great tribulation, unless they repent. We see once again that judgment is not inevitable. With His warning God is giving an opportunity to change the ending.

"As I live, says the Lord God,
I have no pleasure in the death of the wicked,
But that the wicked turn from his way and live.
Turn you, turn you from your evil ways!
For why will you die, O house of Israel?" – Ezekiel 33:11

"I call heaven and earth to record this day against you,
That I have set before you life and death,
Blessing and cursing.
Therefore, choose life
That both you and your seed may live." – Deut. 30:19

Encouragement: I Put No Other Burden On You

To the faithful of the church in Thyatira, Jesus said He would put no other burden upon them. In the Old Testament books of the prophets, a prophetic vision was often referred to as the "burden" from the Lord.[8]

In Acts 15:28-29, the early converts of the Apostles (who would be of this fourth age of time) were told that the Lord would put "no greater burden" (same phrase) upon them except to keep themselves from eating things sacrificed to idols, and to abstain from fornication. This exactly matches the message to this church.

In the chapter on Ancient Hebrew Marriage customs[9], we will look in greater detail as to why the two offenses mentioned most often in the messages to the churches were sexual immorality and eating things sacrificed to idols. Of all the sins Christ could have named, and which were undoubtedly occurring in every church, it is these two that most offend and which He views as the greatest threat to His church.

We are not made acceptable to God by our good works, but only through the work of Christ. However, as those who carry His Spirit and

---

[8]   Isa. 15:1, 17:1, 19:1, etc.
[9]   Part 2; Chapter 7 *Ancient Hebrew Wedding & Revelation*

bear His name, we now have an obligation to conduct ourselves as the people of God. Jesus said He put no other burden on believers than to remain morally and spiritually pure. He was pleased with "the rest" not because of their mountain of good works, but because they remained faithful and loyal to Him, even in the midst of an evil and immoral culture.

Promise to Overcomers: Power to Rule Over the Nations, Morning Star

Because they had overcome the temptation to compromise with the world, Jesus said the overcomers of this church would be given power over the nations and the right to rule with Christ. They did not bow to the pressures of their age and culture (even when it was within the church), so they are deemed worthy to rule.

People who do not stand up for what is right now will not be qualified to rule and reign with Christ later. This life is a testing ground, a school room, in a way. What we do here; the faith and spiritual muscle we build here and now, will be what determines what we will be entrusted with in the eternal kingdom of God.

"If therefore you have not been faithful in the unrighteous mammon, Who will commit to your trust the true riches?" – Luke 16:11

Let's now compare Jesus' message to this fourth church to the Fourth Age of Time.

Thyatira, Symbolic of the Fourth Age: The Day of Rule of the Sun, Moon & Stars

The fourth Age of Time, known as the Time of the Kings and Prophets, was represented by the church at Thyatira. This age included David, a man after God's own heart, and Solomon, who built the magnificent first temple in Jerusalem. It concluded with Christ riding into Jerusalem on a donkey and being declared the last King of Judah.

This age also included all the great Old Testament prophets, including the last great Old Testament prophet, John the Baptist. The last works of this age, would be the ministry of John the Baptist, of whom Jesus said,

"Verily I say unto you, Among them that are born of women,
there has not risen a greater than John the Baptist.
Notwithstanding, he that is least in the kingdom of
heaven is greater than he." – Matt. 11:11

This Day or generation of believers had many great deeds: the feats of David, Solomon and the righteous kings. Also the acts of the prophets, including Isaiah, Ezekiel, Elijah, and Daniel. They built the first and second temples, and the last works were indeed greater than the first, for it culminated with the ministry of John the Baptist and the proclaiming of Christ as king. No other age up to this time had witnessed the mighty acts and presence of God like this age did! This generation saw the fulfillment of the Old Testament prophets in the birth and early ministry of Jesus Christ.

Yet the Lord rebuked them because they also tolerated the woman Jezebel, who called herself a prophetess to teach and lead people astray. Queen Jezebel, who was married to King Ahab, lived and reigned over Judah during this Day (or thousand years) of time. She worshipped Baal, yet she married a king of Israel, which supposedly worshipped the one true God. Just as Ahab was unequally yoked with an pagan woman, Thyatira was the unequally yoked church. This was a phrase Paul used in 2 Cor. 6:14 when speaking to the church in Corinth:

"Be ye not unequally yoked together with unbelievers.
For what fellowship hath righteousness with unrighteousness?
And what communion hath light with darkness?"

Jesus Himself identified when this new Day on the kingdom calendar began, and ended. He said;

"From the days of John the Baptist until now
the kingdom of heaven suffers violence,
and the violent take it by force.
For all the prophets and the Law prophesied until John." – Matt. 11:12-13

"The Law and the prophets were until John: since that time, the kingdom of God is preached, and every man presses into it." – Luke 16:16

This was the Age of All the Prophets. This fourth day of time lasted until the death of John the Baptist, and the triumphal entry of Christ into Jerusalem.

This was also the last Age in which believers were predominately Jewish. The next two millennia after this one would, to a growing degree, be dominated by the Gentiles.

The Revelation of The Son of God

To those of this Age of time, Jesus revealed Himself to be the Son of God and the King of Kings. To Israel, the terms were interchangeable. When the high priest was questioning Jesus before His crucifixion, he asked, *"I adjure thee by the living God, that thou tell us whether thou be the Christ, the Son of God.' – Matt. 26:63*

Jesus, the 4th man in the fire

Interestingly, the first time in scripture this phrase "Son of God" is used of a person, is in Daniel 3:25. This portion of scripture tells the story of the 3 Hebrew children: Shadrach, Meshach, and Abednego in the fiery furnace.

"The Nebuchadnezzar the king was astonished and rose up in haste,
and spoke and said unto his counsellors,
'Did not we cast three men bound into the midst of the fire?'
and they answered and said unto the king, 'True, O king."
He answered and said, 'Lo, I see four men loose,
walking in the midst of the fire,
and they have no hurt,
and the form of the fourth is like the Son of God!' – Daniel 3:24-25

This also echoes His description as having "feet like burnished bronze" (in other words, fiery, molten metal). Jesus was the fourth man in the fire, walking about in the midst of the furnace. This event occurred in the Fourth Age of Time.

Daniel's vision of the Lord

Daniel was a prophet of the Old Testament who lived and served during the time of the Babylonian exile – about 500BC (also in the Fourth Age).

While serving in Babylon, Daniel sees a vision of the Lord, which exactly matches what John reports in Revelation.

"Then I lifted up my eyes, and looked and behold a certain man
clothed in linen, whose loins were girded with find gold of Uphaz,
His body also was like the beryl, and His face as the appearance of lightning,
and his eyes as lamps of fire,
and His arms and His feet like in color to polished brass,
and the voice of His words like the voice of multitude." – Daniel 10:5-6

Eyes like a flame of fire

Jesus is represented as the One who has eyes like a flame of fire, and feet like brass. The significance of this is that the Lord sees everything, and He judges everything He sees as either good or evil.

In the very first chapter of the Bible, after each day of creation it says "and the Lord saw that it was good". The eyes of the Lord are synonymous with judgment – either for or against – He sees all.

"For the eyes of the Lord run to and fro throughout the whole earth,
to show Himself strong
in the behalf of them whose heart is perfect toward Him…" – 2 Chron. 16:9

"The eyes of the Lord are in every place,
beholding the evil and the good." – Prov. 15:3

"For the eyes of the Lord are over the righteous,
and His ears are open unto their prayers.
But the face of the Lord is against them that do evil." – 1Peter 3:12

Who Was Jezebel?

Jesus specifically mentions Jezebel in His rebuke of this church at Thyatira. Jezebel historically lived during this fourth age of time, but who was she and why should Christ single her out in His rebuke?

I Kings 18- 2 Kings 9 chronicle the story of Jezebel and Ahab and how they slaughtered the prophets of God. Jesus said that the blood of all the prophets would be required of "this generation". Jezebel instigated the worship of Baal, replacing the priests of God with her false, idolatrous priests. Elijah and Elisha prophesied during this time and greatly opposed these evil rulers.

Speaking of, and to, the generation of Israel to which Jesus came during His ministry, Jesus said:

"Therefore, behold, I send unto you prophets, and wise men, and scribes.
And some of them you shall kill and crucify, and some of them you shall
scourge in your synagogues, and persecute them from city to city.
That upon you may come all the righteous blood shed upon the earth,
… Verily I say unto you, All these things shall come upon this generation.
O Jerusalem, Jerusalem, you that kills the prophets, and stones them which
are sent unto you, how often I would have gathered your children together,
even as a hen gathers her chickens under her wings, and you would not!
Behold, your house if left unto you desolate." – Matt. 23:34-38

Compare these verses with what Jesus said of the church of Thyatira:

"And I gave her space to repent of her fornication, and she repented not.
Behold, I will cast her into a bed (of suffering), and them that commit
adultery with her into great tribulation, except they repent of their deeds.
And I will kill her children with death, and all the churches shall
know that I am he which searches the reins and hearts,
and I will give unto every one of you according to your works."- Rev. 2:21-23

When asked by His disciples what the sign of His coming and the end of the age would be, Jesus began to tell of events that would follow His death, and He spoke of the destruction of Jerusalem. Some believe He was speaking of the events of the tribulation period which will precede His second coming. Others believe that He was speaking of the destruction of Jerusalem which occurred in 70 AD. It would be consistent with other prophecies of Christ's coming that this passage would have both a near and far future application.

> "And when you shall see Jerusalem surrounded by armies,
> then know that the desolation thereof is nigh. ... For these be the days
> of vengeance, that all things which are written may be fulfilled.
> But woe unto them that are with child, and to them
> that give suck in those days! For there shall be great
> distress in the land, and wrath upon this people.
> And they shall fall by the edge of the sword, and shall be led away captive
> into all nations, and Jerusalem shall be trodden down of the Gentiles,
> until the times of the Gentiles be fulfilled." – Luke 21:21-24

The word "tribulation" which Jesus used to describe these days in Matthew 24 and Mark13, is the Greek word "thlipsis" and is variously translated; "tribulation, affliction, trouble, anguish, persecution, burdened"[10]. It means a pressing together, oppression, affliction, distress, tribulation.

It is the same word used in John 16:33 when Jesus was talking with His disciples when He said, "*These things I have spoken unto you that in Me you might have peace. In the world you shall have tribulation, but be of good cheer, I have overcome the world.*"

This generation of believers saw the destruction of Israel by the Assyrians, and the destruction of the temple, Jerusalem and Judah by the Babylonians, which the Lord warned them would happen.

> "And if you will not for all this harken unto
> me, but walk contrary unto me....

---

[10]   James Strong, *The New Strong's Exhaustive Concordance of the Bible* (Nashville: T. Nelson, 1990), G2347.

I will bring the land into desolation,
and your enemies which dwell therein shall be astonished at it.
And I will scatter you among the heathen, and will draw
out a sword after you, and your land shall de desolate,
and your cities waste." – Lev. 26:27,32-33

"For thus saith the LORD, Behold, I will make thee a terror to thyself,
and to all they friends; and they shall fall by the sword of their enemies, and
thine eyes shall behold it: and I will give all Judah into the hand of the king
of Babylon,

and he shall carry them captive into Babylon,
and shall slay them with the sword." – Jer. 20:4

People who lived at the end of this Day also saw the second destruction of the temple and Jerusalem by Rome. This was a result of their continual refusal to acknowledge the kingship of Christ, the Son of God, and their continual persecution of the prophets and apostles the Lord sent to them. Jesus said this would happen in the very generation in which He spoke these words:

"And when you shall see Jerusalem compassed with armies,
then know that the desolation thereof is nigh...
for these be the days of vengeance,
that all things which are written may be fulfilled...
for there shall be great distress in the land, and wrath upon this people.
And they shall fall by the edge of the sword, and shall be led away captive
into all nations: and Jerusalem shall be trodden down of the Gentiles,
until the times of the Gentiles be fulfilled." – Luke 21:20,22-24

These words were fulfilled in 70 AD, less than forty years after Christ spoke them. The devastation of Israel and Jerusalem, and the dispersal of the people of Israel throughout the nations, lasted until 1949 AD, when the people began to be regathered in the Land once again. Of all the wonders we have seen, perhaps none points more surely to the imminent return of Christ than the regathering of Israel.

The term "great tribulation" is worthy of a closer look as well, as it is only used in two other places in scripture. The first was when Jesus was speaking of the destruction that would occur to the temple and Jerusalem after they had persecuted and killed many of His disciples:

"You shall hear of wars and rumors of wars,
See that you be not troubled, for all these things must come to pass,
But the end is not yet...
Then shall they deliver you up to be afflicted,
And shall kill you,
And you shall be hated of all nations for My name's sake...
Then let them which be in Judaea flee into the mountains,...
For then shall be great tribulation,
Such as was not since the beginning of the world to this time,
No, nor ever shall be." – Matt. 24:6,9,16,21

There are two fulfillments of this scripture. The first was in the very generation that was standing there when Christ spoke these words. Jerusalem was destroyed in 70 AD. Although this would technically not happen until the next Age began, the warning came first. Israel did not repent, but rather conspired to have Christ put to death as one of the first acts of the next Age of Time. There will also be a future fulfillment. We know this because He says in verse 29 that "immediately after the tribulation of those days" Christ will return.

This is echoed in Revelation 7:14, which is the only other place in scripture where this phrase is found. It is speaking of the events that occur at the opening of the sixth seal, and before the Trumpet judgements begin. When the fifth seal is opened (Rev. 6), many believers are martyred. At the opening of the sixth seal, the heavens are rolled up like a scroll and the people of earth see the Lord on His throne in heaven and are terrified. The scene then shifts to heaven, and John has a vision of a great multitude from every kindred, people, tongue and nation standing before the throne of God. When John asks an angel who they are he is told:

And have washed their robes,
And made them white in the blood of the Lamb." – Rev. 7:14

As was mentioned, Thyatira was the last Generation of Believers who were predominately Jewish. They lived in the final events of Daniel's 69th week. Daniel was told by an angel that there were "Seventy weeks" (or seventy, seven-year periods of time) determined for the people of Israel.[11] He was told that the Messiah would be "cut off" after 69 weeks, and the temple and Jerusalem destroyed.

When the temple was destroyed in 70 AD, it pushed pause on the prophetic countdown for Israel. It also began the Times of the Gentiles. Once the times of the Gentiles is fulfilled, the clock will again start ticking for Israel's 70 week.

What does all this have to do with our discussion? Well, the phrase "great tribulation" is only ever used in reference to a time of mortal peril for the nation of Israel. When the believers of the New Testament church are raptured out, God will then finish His work with Israel. The Great Tribulation is a time in which Israel has a final chance to embrace Christ as their messiah. The church of Thyatira received the warning before the first time of great tribulation for the Jews, and the Jews will also be targeted in the next Great Tribulation. The purpose will not be (nor was it ever) to destroy them, but to save them.

Overcomers Will Rule

Since this generation of time included the kings of Israel, it is appropriate that overcomers of this church will be given power over the nations and the right to rule with Christ. His promise to overcomers of Thyatira echoes the words of the Psalmist:

"Ask of Me, and I shall give you the heathen for your inheritance,
And the uttermost parts of the earth for your possession.
You shall break them with a rod of iron,
You shall dash them in pieces like a potter's vessel." – Psalm 2:8-9

"He that overcomes, and keeps My works unto the end,
To him will I give power over the nations.

---

[11] Daniel 9:24.

And he shall rule them with a rod of iron,
As the vessels of a potter shall they be broken to shivers,
Even as I received of My Father." – Rev. 2:26-27

Jesus says they will rule with a rod of iron and crush the wicked like a potter's vessel. This exactly matches the prophecy of Jeremiah concerning the destruction of Jerusalem which occurred in his lifetime at the time of the Babylonian captivity, but which was also prophesied by Jesus (which indicated a future destruction).

"I will make void the counsel of Judah and Jerusalem in this place,
and I will cause them to fall by the sword before their enemies,
and by the hands of them that seek their lives, and their carcasses will I
give to be meat for the fouls of heaven and for the beasts of the earth.
And I will make this city desolate, ... every one that passes by shall be
astonished and hiss because of all the plagues thereof. ... And thou shalt say
unto them, 'Thus says the Lord of hosts; Even so will I break this people and
this city, as one breaks a potter's vessel that cannot be made whole again, ...
And the houses of Jerusalem, and the houses of the kings of Judah
shall be defiled as the place of Tophet, because of all the houses upon
whose roofs they have burned incense unto all the host of heaven,
and have poured out drink offerings unto other gods." – Jer. 19:7-13

This prophecy very clearly states that this destruction would come because of their idolatry. Jesus said it would come as retribution for the blood of the prophets which was spilled in the city. The prophet's blood was spilled because they testified against the immorality and idolatry that was corrupting the nation. The church of Thyatira was told their desolation would come as a result of sexual immorality which had been taught by Jezebel, and because of their idolatry.

Jesus promises overcomers from this church the same authority He received from His father, which is what He promised to give to Peter and His disciples in Matt. 16:19, when He promised the keys of the kingdom. In fact, all the words Jesus spoke to this generation were received from His father, and given to them.[12]

---

[12]   John 14:10.

The Morning Star

They were also promised to receive the morning star. Rev. 22:16 tells us that Jesus is the Bright and Morning Star. Simeon blessed the baby Jesus saying He was *"a light to lighten the Gentiles, and the glory of thy people Israel"*.[13] Of His birth Matthew 4:16 says, *"The people which sat in darkness saw a great light, and to them which sat in the region and shadow of death, light is sprung up."* It was to this generation that the Morning Star came as a baby in the manger – illuminated by the Star of Bethlehem the wise men followed!

---

[13]   Luke 2:32.

Fourth Church: Thyatira - Unequally Yoked

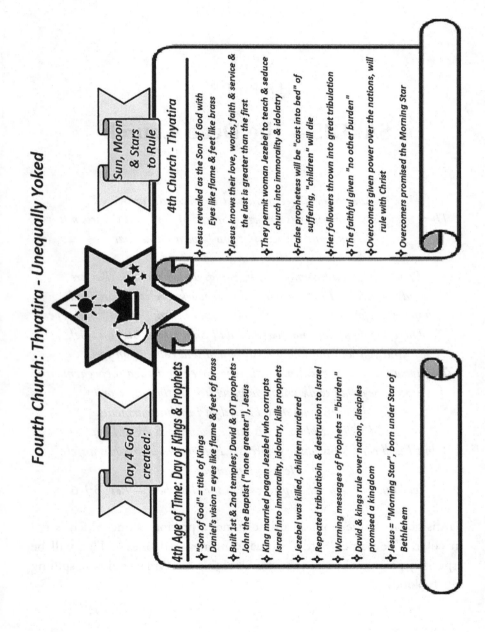

Sun, Moon & Stars to Rule

4th Church - Thyatira

- ✦ Jesus revealed as the Son of God with Eyes like flame & feet like brass
- ✦ Jesus knows their love, works, faith & service & the last is greater than the first
- ✦ They permit woman Jezebel to teach & seduce church into immorality & idolatry
- ✦ False prophetess will be "cast into bed" of suffering, "children" will die
- ✦ Her followers thrown into great tribulation
- ✦ The faithful given "no other burden"
- ✦ Overcomers given power over the nations, will rule with Christ
- ✦ Overcomers promised the Morning Star

Day 4 God created:

4th Age of Time: Day of Kings & Prophets

- ✦ "Son of God" = title of Kings
  Daniel's vision = eyes like flame & feet of brass
- ✦ Built 1st & 2nd temples; David & OT prophets - John the Baptist ("none greater"), Jesus
- ✦ King married pagan Jezebel who corrupts Israel into immorality, idolatry, kills prophets
- ✦ Jezebel was killed, children murdered
- ✦ Repeated tribulatioin & destruction to Israel
- ✦ Warning messages of Prophets = "burden"
- ✦ David & kings rule over nation, disciples promised a kingdom
- ✦ Jesus = "Morning Star", born under Star of Bethlehem

CHAPTER 6

SARDIS – The Dead Church

"And to the angel of the church in Sardis write,
'These things says He who has the seven Spirits of God and the seven stars:
'I know your works, that you have a name that
you are alive, but you are dead.
Be watchful, and strengthen the things which remain, that are
ready to die, for I have not found your works perfect before God.
Remember therefore how you have received and heard; hold fast and repent.
Therefore if you will not watch, I will come upon you as a thief,
and you will not know what hour I will come upon you.
You have a few names even in Sardis who have not defiled their garments;
and they shall walk with Me in white, for they are worthy.
He who overcomes shall be clothed in white garments,
and I will not blot out his name from the Book of Life;
but I will confess his name before My Father and before His angels.'
He who has an ear,
let him hear what the Spirit says to the churches." – Rev. 3:1-6

Sardis got its name from a sardine stone; a precious stone which is red in color. The name "Sardis" actually means "red ones"[1]. This will be especially poignant because the church of this Age will be guilty of spilling much blood.

---

[1]   James Strong, *The New Strong's Exhaustive Concordance of the Bible* (Nashville: T. Nelson, 1990), G4554.

The church of Sardis, unlike the other churches, was made up mostly of non-believers, self righteous Pharisees, false teachers and hypocrites. This is the only church which received no commendation or praise. The church had become completely corrupt in its leadership, and largely in its congregation. Despite making the claim to be alive, Jesus said they were actually dead. Everything about this church was a sham.

This is the state in which Jesus found the church, the chosen people of Israel and the religious organization at the time of His crucifixion. This is the Age of Time which Sardis represents.

Sardis, Symbolic of the Fifth Age of Time: The Day of Fish & Birds

On the fifth Day of Creation, God created the fish and birds. In the Fifth Age of time, the early Church was symbolized as the Fish, and the Holy Spirit was given, symbolized as the Dove. The symbol of the Roman Empire (who ruled the world in this Age) was the Eagle.

But when Jesus appeared to those in this Age of Time, those who were outwardly the church (people of God) were the Jews, whose religious leaders were the scribes and Pharisees. Though they were the "keepers of the Law", most were actually unbelievers. The true believers were "the few". This is what Christ was speaking about when He said the kingdom of God was like a tiny mustard seed, which though small, would grow into a great plant, filling the earth and providing a place for the fowls of the air to lodge.[2]

Historically, this Fifth Age of Time covers the ministry of Christ after John the Baptist's death, and extends through the days of the early church until around 1033 AD. The Fourth Age, which was the Age of Kings, could be considered to have ended with Jesus' triumphant entry into Jerusalem on the first Palm Sunday. On that day, the final king of Israel rode into Jerusalem being proclaimed as their Messiah, only to be crucified one week later under the banner, "The King of the Jews". Alternatively, it could be considered that the Fifth Age does not begin until the outpouring of the Holy Spirit on Pentecost. Without a doubt, that event occurs within

---

[2] Mark 4:30-32.

the Fifth Age of time. Many times, the events at the end of one Age overlap with those of the next. This happened during Samuel's ministry. He is identified in scripture as both the last of the Old Testament judges, and the first of the prophets[3].

Jesus seems to be indicating that a new Day on the kingdom calendar was marked by the ministry of John the Baptist, the last Old Testament prophet. He said;

> *"From the days of John the Baptist until now,*
> *the kingdom of heaven suffers violence, and the violent take it by force.*
> *For all the prophets and the Law prophesied until John." – Matt. 11:12-13*

Jesus not only identified when this new Day in the kingdom began, He also identified what the predominant characteristic of this age would be: violence against the kingdom of heaven. It was this Age that would take the Prince of Life, and with violent and wicked hands crucify Him.[4]

This was also the Day that saw Christianity spread and gain such force, that by the end of the millennia, the Roman Catholic church controlled much of the western world. The vast empire once ruled by Rome, now belonged to the Church. But as the church became more organized and its power centralized, it became as abusive as the worldly powers before them. Jesus warns this church that there are things "about to die", and to remember how they first heard. The Word of God, source of true, Biblical faith, was at first commonly available in the little home churches and congregations. But, by the end of this age, the church at Rome actively suppressed the Bible and even forbade it to be read by the common people. The church purported to be the sole distributer of truth and salvation. This is the exact same abuse of the Pharisees of Christ's day, and of Rome. By the next Age, the church would resort to violence in order to make her converts.[5]

---

[3]   1 Samuel 3:20, 7:15; Acts 13:20.

[4]   Acts 3:14-15.

[5]   (Fox, 1926 (first publishedn1563))

The Violent Take The Kingdom By Force

I have heard some teach that Matt. 11:11-12 is urging believers to take the kingdom by violence. That we must be loud, violent and aggressive in prayer to get what we need from heaven and to overcome and rebuke the work of the enemy. That is false teaching and is taking this verse out of context.

When Peter drew his sword to protect Christ (who is the King of the kingdom), Christ rebuked him.[6] When His disciples offered to call fire down from heaven to devour those who opposed Christ, Jesus rebuked them and said, "*You know not what manner of spirit you are of*".[7]

Those with the Holy Spirit are never characterized by violence. In fact, one of the reasons the Bible gives for the Flood was that:

> "*The earth also was corrupt before God,*
> *And the earth was filled with violence.*" – Gen. 6:11

Violence is always associated with the wicked in Scripture:

> "*The mouth of a righteous man is a well of life,*
> *But violence convers the mouth of the wicked.*" – Prov. 10:11

> "*And they covet fields,*
> *And take them by violence,*
> *And houses, and take them away,*
> *So they oppress a man and his house,*
> *Even a man and his heritage.*" – Mic. 2:2

Note in Micah how one of the characteristics of the wicked is that they take things by violence. If it is an abomination for men to take things from one another by violence, how much viler is it to teach people to take the kingdom of God by violence! We do not take the kingdom with violence, but by faith in the complete work of Christ.

---

6   John 18:10-11; Matt. 26:51-52.
7   Luke 9:55.

False Prophets Are Violent

It was the false prophets of Baal on Mt Carmel who screamed and cried aloud and carried on in long, demonstrative prayer.[8] Meanwhile, Elijah, the prophet of God prayed a two sentence prayer and fire fell from heaven. Jesus said,

> *"When you pray, use not vain repetitions, as the heathen do,*
> *for they think that they shall be heard for their much speaking.*
> *Be not you therefore like unto them. For your Father knows*
> *what things you have need of before you ask Him."*
> -Matt. 6:7-8

He encouraged his disciples; *"Fear not, little flock, for it is your Father's good pleasure to give you the kingdom." – Luke 12:32*

True disciples of Christ need not beg and shout to get Heaven's attention, for Heaven is attentive to them and is already on their side.

Neither do true disciples scream and shout at the enemy, thinking that they can somehow bully, force or frighten demons into submission to their will. That sort of thinking is nothing more than incantations and demonic. Jude warned true disciples of this false teaching when he said,

> *"Likewise also these filthy dreamers defile the flesh,*
> *despise dominion, and speak evil of dignities (supernatural beings).*
> *Yet Michael, the archangel,*
> *when contending with the devil he disputed about the body of Moses,*
> *durst not bring against him a railing accusation, but said,*
> *'The Lord rebuke thee.'" -Jude 1:8-9*

In Matthew 11:11-12, Jesus was not giving instruction to His disciples on how to advance the kingdom. He was prophesying what kind of death He would suffer at the hands of this generation. What Jesus was teaching is that during this Day, the age that immediately followed the ministry of John the Baptist, the kingdom of heaven would suffer violence. The word "suffer" means both to suffer pain, but it also means to "permit". As when

---

[8]   1 Kings 18.

Jesus said *"Suffer it to be so for now"*.[9] He was warning His disciples that in this world, they would have tribulation, and that those who would be His disciples must be willing to take up their cross and follow Him.

The kingdom of God is wherever the King is crowned Lord and wherever His Lordship reigns. It is made up of His people; those who pledge allegiance to Christ and His agenda alone. Those who do so will suffer the same persecution their king suffered. Jesus said if they reject and persecute Him, so will the world do to all those who follow Him.[10]

Remember, the definition of church we are using. It is those to whom Christ reveals Himself and to whom the Word of God (spiritually and physically) comes. They are the called (many are called, few are chosen), those who worship the One true God and who also await the Messiah. In this Age of Time, Israel as a nation (those who had the name of people of God), rejected Christ and persecuted His followers.

Because they feared the loss of prestige and power, these religious leaders betrayed Christ to the Romans and demanded His death. Jesus was crucified by a joint conspiracy (because both parties knew Him to be innocent), of Jews and Gentiles, so that all the world is guilty of this crime. By the next age, the powers that ruled the Holy Roman Catholic church would similarly persecute and kill those who held true to the Word of God and sought to see it prosper.

Is it any wonder that this church, symbolic of this Fifth Age of Time, would be characterized as having a name that they are alive, but are actually dead? Could one be more dead spiritually than to crucify the Prince of Life? By the next Age, the church held the power of life and death over much of the globe, and she chose to kill any who did not bow to her authority.

On the fifth day of creation, which foretells what this Age would be about, God created birds and fish. In the beginning of this age, the eagle ruled over the fish. By the end of the age, the fish and the eagle were the same thing. The church, initially persecuted by Rome, eventually became accepted by Rome, and ended up becoming Rome! Today, "Rome" and "the church" are synonymous.

---

9   Luke 22:51.
10   Matt. 10:22-25.

Revelation of Christ: The One with the 7 Spirits of God and 7 Stars

Jesus reveals Himself to the church at Sardis as "He who has the seven Spirits of God and the seven stars." We are told in chapter one of Revelation that the stars represent the angels (or ruling messengers) of the churches.

To this Dead Age not only came the Prince of Life, but also the Holy Spirit, who gives life.

"For the Law of the Spirit of Life in Christ Jesus,
Has made me free from the law of sin and death." – Romans 8:2

At Pentecost, the Holy Spirit was poured out on all believers and the New Testament church began to grow and "turn the world upside down".[11] In the early days of this Age, the Roman eagle ruled over most of the known world, while the early church (symbolized by the fish), was just beginning to fish for men.

John the Baptist, who would be the last of the Old Testament prophets and whose ministry it was to "prepare the way of the Lord" said,

"I saw the Spirit descending from heaven like
a dove, and it abode upon Him.
And I knew Him not, but He that sent me to baptize with water,
the same said unto me, 'Upon whom you shall see the Spirit descending,
and remaining on Him, the same is He which baptizes with the Holy Ghost.
And I saw and bare record that this is the Son of God." – John 1:32-34

A new Day had come with the anointing of Christ by the Holy Spirit. The Spirit, who had been given by measure before, would, through the work of Christ, be poured out on all people.

To the church of this age, Peter said on the day of Pentecost:

"You men of Judaea, and all you that dwell at Jerusalem,
be this knows unto you, and harken to my words;
…this is that which was spoken by the prophet Joel;

---

[11] Acts 17:6.

'And it shall come to pass in the last days, saith God,
'I will pour out of My Spirit upon all flesh.
And your sons and your daughters shall prophesy,
and your young men shall see visions, and your old men shall dream dreams.
And on My servants and on My handmaidens
I will pour out in those days of My Spirit,
and they shall prophesy… And it shall come to pass,
that whosoever shall call on the name of the Lord shall be saved.'
You men of Israel, hear these words:
Jesus of Nazareth, a man approved of God among you
by miracles and wonders and signs, which God
did by Him in the midst of you,
as you yourselves also know: Him, being delivered by the determinate
counsel and foreknowledge of God, you have taken,
and by wicked hands have crucified and slain." – Acts 2:14-23

Acknowledgement: A Few Are Worthy to Walk With Me

Though Jesus acknowledges this church, saying "I know your works", he had no words of commendation for the majority. This is the only church of whom this can be said!

It can be no surprise that when those who were supposed to be God's people start the Day (or Age), by betraying the Son of God in order to retain power and prestige for themselves, and end the Day by persecuting and executing any who don't bow to their authority, that the Lord would have no words of praise for them. What possible good thing could God have to say to those who committed such atrocities?

Jesus told a parable in Matthew 21 of husbandmen who were hired to keep a vineyard for their master. But they decided they wanted to keep the profits for themselves, and ended up killing the master's son and heir when he came to inspect the vineyard. He later said of the Pharisees:

"Woe unto you, scribes and Pharisees, hypocrites!
For you shut up the kingdom of heaven against men,
For you neither go in yourselves,
Neither suffer you them that are entering to go in." – Matt. 23:13

It was not enough that they reject the Lord and the truth, they actively put up blocks and persecutions against anyone else who would choose to believe.

At this time in history, the true church, made of true believers in Christ were The Few. That is actually true of every age in history. Jesus said these few were "worthy". What makes a person worthy in the eyes of the Lord? Jesus said if anyone truly wanted to follow Him, they must be willing to take up their cross and follow Him. He said anyone who refuses to do so "is not worthy of Me"[12]. The implication is clear: Sardis is unworthy because she is unwilling to suffer in any way for her Lord. She is ashamed of the gospel of Christ. The Few are worthy because they are faithful, regardless of the cost.

The official congregation of Sardis who claimed to be God's people were those who rejected Christ. To those Jesus said He knew their works and that they had a reputation for being alive, but they were dead. They were only pretending to be something they were not.

Of this generation Jesus said,

"This is an evil generation.
They seek a sign, and there shall no sign be given it,
but the sign of Jonah the prophet.
For as Jonah was a sign unto the Ninevites,
so shall also the Son of Man be to this generation." – Luke 11:29-30

To the generation of so-called believers to whom Christ in physical form revealed Himself, Jesus said,

"Woe unto you, scribes and Pharisees, hypocrites!
For you are like unto whited sepulchers, which
indeed appear beautiful outward,
but are within full of dead men's bones, and of all uncleanness.
Even so you also outwardly appear righteous unto men,
but within you are full of hypocrisy and iniquity." – Matt. 23:27-28

---

[12]   Matthew 10:38.

"Jesus said unto them, 'If God were your Father, you would love Me,
for I proceeded forth and came from God,
neither came I of myself, but He sent Me.
Why do you not understand My speech?
Even because you cannot hear My word.'" – John 8:42-43

Not Found Your Works "Perfect'

Jesus said to Sardis that He had not found their works perfect before God. What does this mean? Is He saying that only sinless perfection will be accepted? If so, we are all doomed.

Parable of the Sower

In Luke 8, Jesus gives the parable of the Sower who goes out to sow seed in his field. He later reveals that the seed is the Word of God. The Word of God came first to the nation of Israel through Moses and the prophets[13]. But when the Word came in the flesh, they rejected Him[14]. He then goes on to describe how the seed (or Word) is received by different soil, which represents the hearts of those who hear the word. Some reject or ignore it. Some receive it, but then fall away when persecution comes.

"And that which fell among thorns are they, which,
when they have heard, go forth and are choked with cares and riches and
pleasures of this life, and bring no fruit to perfection." – Luke 8:14

Jesus said those to whom the Word of God comes, but who prefer the riches and acclaim of this world over the kingdom of God are those whose fruit does not come to perfection. The word "perfection" here means to come to full maturity; to produce that for which the seed was sown. The Word of God did not prosper during these Dark Ages. Fox's Book of Martyrs lists many who died horrible deaths for the crime of holding true to the Word of God and wanting to put it in the hands of the people.

---

13   Hebrews 1:1-2.
14   John 1:10-14.

Parable of the Fig Tree

Jesus told another parable of the Jews in Luke 13:6-9:

"A certain man had a fig tree planted in his vineyard, and he came and sought fruit thereon, and found none. Then he said unto the dresser of his vineyard, 'Behold, these three years I come seeking fruit on this fig tree, and find none. Cut it down. Why should it cumber the ground?'

In prophetic language, the nation of Israel is the fig tree. In the Garden of Eden, Adam sought to cover his nakedness (the result of his sin) with fig leaves that he fashioned into an apron. Thus the fig tree symbolically came to represent those who seek to be righteous through their works and adherence to the Law. By the end of this Fifth Age of time, the official church of Rome was also teaching salvation through good works and penance.

Jesus' earthly ministry lasted three years, and He specifically said He came to the nation of Israel, but He found no "fruit".[15] John said, *"He came unto His own, and His own received Him not, but to as many as received Him to them gave He power to become the sons of God, even to them that believe on His name."*[16]

John further tells us in John 12:42-43, *"Nevertheless among the chief rulers also many believed on Him, but because of the Pharisees they did not confess him, lest they should be put out of the synagogue. For they loved the praise of men more than the praise of God."*

The Church of Judas

Sardis, in a sense, is the church of Judas. He was chosen and called of Christ. He walked with Christ, he heard the words of Christ and even participated in His ministry. But, his heart was never to worship, but for whatever benefit he could receive by his prominent position. When the tide turned against Christ, so did he.

---

[15]   Matt. 15:24.

[16]   John 1:11-12.

It is the church of the Pharisees, who loved the prominent position they had by being religious leaders. They loved lording it over the common people and thought their self-righteous rituals earned them favor with God. They equated gain with godliness. They loved being the guardians and interpreters of the truth, but when the Truth came in the flesh, they hated him. To them, the coming of the Lord was a threat to their whole system of worship and way of life.

It is also the church of the vast, religious organization which calls itself "The Church", but denies Christ. It rejects the authority of the Word of God while deflecting all authority to themselves. The official Christian Church of this Age very soon became Rome, and it shut away the Word of God from the vast majority of believers for centuries.

The Few

The early New Testament church was just a handful of Jewish believers. It would be hundreds of years before Christianity was thought of as anything other than a Jewish sect. But these few were those who went out into the world, and (by the admission of their own detractors) turned the world upside down[17]. They were persecuted by the religious establishment, the state, and the world; yet their message began to spread and take hold. They faced persecution from without, and false teachers and wolves from within. Much of the New Testament Epistles focus on warnings about those who will infiltrate the church and bring in heresies; denying Christ and encouraging people into immorality and idol worship.

The predominate influences in this Age of history are Rome and the early Christian Church, which by the end of the age were the same thing. But the influences of this church last well into the next Age.

The Mystery of the Two Days

Although the other churches to this point have represented believers of only one thousand years (Day), the influences of this church actually represent two days. The reason for this can be found in understanding

---

[17]   Acts 17:6.

that a Day not only represents a thousand years, it also refers to a period of time that is characterized by a unifying theme. We use it this way when we speak of someone doing something "in his day". It may cover any length of time. In effect, the church of Sardis represents the nation of Israel in their 69th week of the 70 weeks of Daniel 9:24-27. It marks the end of God dealing directly with the nation of Israel. He will not do so again until His return (after two "days"). When He returns, it will commence the final week, the 70th "week" (or seven-year period) of Daniel. It will be when the Lord completes His work through Israel.

The unifying theme of this Day is what Jesus referred to as the "Times of the Gentiles"[18]. Note it is plural, not singular. A "time" may cover one day, or a thousand years. But "times" indicates more than one. That this period of time would last two "days" has many prophetic pointers.

The prophecies that foretell that the lull in Daniel's 70 weeks, wherein Jesus deals with the nations rather than with Israel are several. Starting in the Old Testament, the prophet Hosea, speaking of a time after Jerusalem would be destroyed and Israel dispersed wrote:

"After two days will He revive us.
In the third day He will raise us up, and we
shall live in his sight." – Hos. 6:2

Nothing Jesus did was ever incidental or without purpose and meaning. In John 4, we are told that Jesus left Judaea because the Pharisees were stirring up trouble. The wording of the King James version is very interesting. It says in verse 4 He "must needs go through Samaria".

The people of Samaria were not Jewish believers. To devout Jews, they were worse than Gentile because they were of the tribes that intermarried with Gentiles and were assimilated after the Assyrian conquest of the northern tribes. The word translated "must needs" is the Greek work "dei". It means it is necessary, right, required, commanded. It carries the idea that it was Christ's duty to go there.

And what did Jesus do there? He went to a well and met a woman. She is Gentile, and she is immoral, without obedience to (and probably ignorant of) the Jewish Law. In prophetic symbolism, the woman at the

---

18   Luke 21:24.

well is the Bride. Rebecca was the woman at the well, and the soon to be bride.[19] Rachel was the woman at the well, and soon to be bride.[20] Hagar met "the God who sees" at a well.[21] Moses met Zipporah, his wife, at a well.[22] The Bride of Song of Solomon is depicted in chapter 4 as being a garden with a well. Another thing all these brides have in common is that they are not Jewish. So Jesus meets the Samaritan woman at the well and tells her of the Water He can give her that will become a well within her! She joyfully accepts Christ's offering, and out of her flows a testimony that brings many others to faith. This is the same symbology we see in the Song of Songs 4:15.

After this Samaritan woman went and evangelized the men of her town, many of them also came to Jesus and urged Him to stay with them. He did so for two days.

I believe the Times of the Gentiles, are represented all the way through by two churches: Sardis and Philadelphia. Sardis represents dead, worldly, institutionalized religion that is more concerned with having wealth and power, than being right with God. She suppresses the Word of God, and often persecutes genuine believers. Philadelphia represents the faithful church – those who are willing to take up their cross and follow Jesus. Neither of these is a particular denomination, but rather two types of believers which both claim to be Christian. Not all who call Him "Lord" are known by Him.

I have included an additional chart at the end of this chapter that illustrates the Times of the Gentiles so you can better visualize how these two churches both make up this time.

Rebuke: Alive, But Dead

The rebuke to the church at Sardis was that, though they had a reputation (or name) of being alive, they were actually dead! What does Jesus mean by this?

---

[19]   Gen. 24:15-16.
[20]   Gen. 29:9-10.
[21]   Gen. 16.
[22]   Exodus 2:16-21.

Paul said that, because sin brings death, we are all in a sense, born dead.

"And you hath he quickened, who were dead in trespasses and sins,....
But God, who is rich in mercy, for his great love wherewith he loved us,
Even when we were dead in sins,
hath quickened us together with Christ, (by
grace are you saved)." – Eph. 2:1,4-5

In John 3, Jesus said that He did not come to condemn anyone, but to save us. Mankind is condemned already because we are born with original sin, which has a penalty of death. Those who do not come to Christ to be born again, are both literally and figuratively dead. To the religious, but unbelieving Pharisees of His age, Jesus said;

"But you do not have His word abiding in you, because whom He sent,
Him you do not believe.
You search the Scriptures, for in them you think you have eternal life;
and these are they which testify of Me.
But you are not willing to come to Me that you
may have life." – John 5:38-40

Jesus warned, *"Not everyone that says unto Me, "Lord, Lord" shall enter into the kingdom of heaven; but he that does the will of My Father which is in Heaven." – Matt. 7:21*

In every other church to this point, the church had been troubled by those who said they were one thing, but were not: false apostles, false prophetesses, false teachers, false Jews. But here in Sardis, it was the church herself who was false. She appeared to be alive, but she was dead. In Smyrna, the church was pure. In Pergamum, they had some who held wrong teaching; in Thyatira, they were a split congregation. But here in Sardis, there were only a few names who had not defiled their garments. When Christ appeared to this church, only a few recognized Him. Only a few were actually disciples of Christ in the whole congregation.

To the Pharisees and religious leaders of His time Jesus said;

"You have not His word abiding in you,
for whom He hath sent, Him you believe not.
Search the scripture; for in them you think you have eternal life:
and they are they which testify of Me.
And you will not come to me, that you might have life." – John 5:38-39

Of this church age John the Baptist wrote:

"He was in the world, and the world was made by him,
and the world knew him not.
He came unto His own, and His own received Him not.
But as many as received Him, to them gave He
power to become the sons of God,
even to them that believe on His name." – John 1:10-12

Command: Strengthen What Remains and Is About To Die

The command to the church at Sardis was to be watchful and to strengthen the things which remain and are ready to die.

What are the things which remain? Paul, writing in what has come to be known as the "love chapter" said;

"And now abideth faith, hope, charity,
these three. But the greatest of these is charity."- 1 Cor. 13:13

The word translated here "adibeth" is the Greek word "meno"[23]. It means "to remain, abide, continue, survive". Of all that we can attain in this life, only three things will remain throughout all time: faith, hope and love. Over and over in New Testament writing, believers are encouraged to prioritize these three things, and to grow in them. They are the gold and precious stone which alone will survive the fire of judgment.

The first church at Ephesus lost their first place because they let go of love. This church is predominately dead, with only a few in it that still

---

[23]   James Strong, *The New Strong's Exhaustive Concordance of the Bible* (Nashville: T. Nelson, 1990), G3306.

hold on to the true faith, hope and love. The solution was to strengthen these things before they die.

In the other churches up until this time, the persecution came from without, or from those who had infiltrated the church. But in Sardis, the danger was the church herself. Those who claimed to be the people of God and who had the Word of God. These were the very ones who rejected and betrayed Christ when He came. These were the ones who martyred the true saints throughout this Age and the next.

What remained, yet was about to die in this Age of Time? In the beginning of the Age, Jerusalem and the nation of Israel were about to die! When Jesus came, it was a pivotal point in history for the nation of Israel. Jesus called it the "time of their visitation". Visitation of whom? The visitation of their Messiah! He came to His own, but they received Him not. The result was that the hour of destruction was upon them. Jesus' desire was for the things that are about to die, would instead be strengthened and live!

> *"And when He was come near,*
> *He beheld the city, and wept over it,*
> *Saying, 'If thou had known, even thou, at least in this thy day,*
> *The things which belong to thy peace!*
> *But now they are hid from thine eyes.*
> *For the days shall come upon thee,*
> *That thine enemies shall cast a trench about thee,*
> *And compass thee around,*
> *And keep thee on every side.*
> *And shall lay thee even with the ground,*
> *And thy children within thee,*
> *And they shall not leave in thee one stone upon another,*
> *Because thou knew not the time of thy visitation." – Luke 19:41-44*

By the end of this Age (circa 1033 A.D.), the thing that was about to die was the pure doctrine of the church. Soon after the church became an empire, it began to persecute those who remained faithful to the Word of God and the simple doctrine of Christ. The beginning of the church age saw many church leaders being martyred for their faith, but by this time in history, the church began to persecute, and even kill those who opposed her dictates.

When the Catholic church became the official church of the Roman empire, she began to incorporate many pagan practices into worship. This was the same method Rome had used to assimilate people of all cultures and faiths. Instead of myriad idols, the church instead offered prayers to the saints. The veneration of icons and relics, as well as the suppression of the Word of God led to a Christian church that differed little in practice from the worship the pagans were accustomed to before.

Remember How You Receive and Hear

Jesus further commands that the church remember how they had received and heard, and hold fast and repent. Since all the messages to the churches are for those who have an ear to hear, understanding how one hears and receives spiritually is vital to receiving the blessings promised.

How did the church first receive and hear?

"Faith comes by hearing
And hearing by the word of God." – Romans 10:17

In Luke 8, Jesus tells a parable of the Sower to warn those who claim to have the Word of God, and yet produce not "fruit". He ends by saying;

"Take heed therefore how you hear:
for whosoever hath, to him shall be given,
and whosoever hath not,
from him shall be taken even that which he seems to have." – Luke 8:18

Jesus is warning that how you hear determines whether or not you truly become His disciple. Those who filter the Word through their own lusts, or desire for worldly things, will not prosper spiritually. Though they receive the True Word, yet it has no power to transform them because they prefer the cares and blessings of this world.

The self-righteous Pharisees who persecuted Christ and resisted His teaching, did so mainly because they feared the loss of prestige, affluence and power that their position gave them. Later, the officials of the church at Rome also persecuted believers, and for the same reasons. To follow Christ, they would have to humble themselves, confess their sins (which they did not believe they had), and leave all to follow Him. Even in the church today, there are those who only use prayer and faith as a means of bettering their life here and now. Paul warned believers of these in 1 Timothy 6:5-12:

> *"Perverse disputings of men of corrupt minds, and destitute of the truth,*
> *supposing that gain is godliness,*
> *from such withdraw yourself.*
> *But godliness with contentment is great gain.*
> *For we brought nothing into this world, and it*
> *is certain we can carry nothing out.*
> *And having food and raiment, let us be content.*
> *But they that will be rich fall into temptation and a snare,*
> *and into many foolish and hurtful lusts,*
> *which drown men in destruction and perdition.*
> *For the love of money is the root of all evil;*
> *which while some coveted after, they have erred from the faith,*
> *and pierced themselves through with many sorrows.*
> *But you, O man of God, flees these things, and follow after righteousness,*
> *godliness, faith, love, patience, meekness.*
> *Fight the good fight of faith.*
> *Lay hold on eternal life, whereunto you are also called...."*

The Best Is Yet To Come

Any teaching that urges you to seek all your rewards and blessings NOW, and to focus on getting wealth and prestige in this world is heresy. While pursuing the will of God, we may certainly ask for whatever we have need of, but stirring up lust for things and claiming that this is your inheritance is blasphemy. It is selling your birthright for a mess of pottage, as Esau did. It is choosing temporary things and immediate gratification over eternal glory.

Paul arguing against this "best life now" heresy wrote:

*"For we know that the whole creation groans and travails in pain
together until now. and not only they, but we ourselves also, which have
the firstfruits of the Spirit, even we ourselves groan within ourselves,
waiting for the adoption, to wit, the redemption of our body. For
we are saved by hope. But hope that is seen is not hope. For what a
man sees, why does he yet hope for it? But if we hope for that we see
not, then do we with patience wait for it." – Romans 8:22-25*

To those who insist that we are to reign in this life, taking up our
inheritance now, before the return of the King, the Bible says:

*"Thou (God) has put all things in subjection under His (Christ's) feet.
For in that He put all in subjection under Him,
He left nothing that is not put under Him.
But now we see not yet all things put under Him.
But we see Jesus, who was made a little lower than the angels
for the suffering of death, crowned with glory and honor,
that He by the grace of God should taste death for every
man. For it became Him, for whom are all things,
and by whom are all things,
in bringing many sons unto glory,
to make the captain of their salvation
perfect through sufferings." – Hebrews 2:8-10*

Peter said,

*"Forasmuch then as Christ has suffered for us in the flesh,
Arm yourselves likewise with the same mind.
For he that has suffered in the flesh has ceased from sin." – 1 Peter 4:1*

True believers and disciples of Christ eagerly await the coming of
Christ, for they know that when He comes, we will enter into His kingdom
and receive all the rich inheritance which we were promised. But to a
disobedient apostate church, Jesus' return is viewed as a threat, rather than
a promise. His coming will stop the party. Just as the official religious
leaders of Israel viewed Christ as a threat to their power and position, His

return will be viewed as a threat to many who claim to be Christians, but are enjoying the riches and pleasures of this world.

Warning: Jesus Is Coming!

The warning to this church was, once again, that Jesus would come as a thief to those who were unrepentant (see message to Ephesus).

To those who are faithful, the coming of the Lord will not be as a thief, but as the bridegroom for whom they are waiting. The apostles and early disciples welcomed Christ's appearing and they hailed Him as their King at His triumphal entry into Jerusalem. But the religious leaders, the official church, rejected Him and were so outraged that they plotted to have Him killed.

From the moment He rose into Heaven, true believers have been anxiously awaiting His return. No one knows the day or the hour of His coming, but to His faithful servants who are watching and waiting for Him, it will not be a rude surprise, but a long awaited and much longed for day. It is the wicked who will be terrified and hide at His coming, as Adam hid from the Lord. The Bride will celebrate His coming to rescue and claim her.

"But concerning the times and the seasons, brethren, you have no need that I should write to you. For you yourselves know perfectly that the day of the Lord so comes as a thief in the night. For when they say, "Peace and safety!" then sudden destruction comes upon them, as labor pains upon a pregnant woman. And they shall not escape. But you, brethren, are not in darkness, so that this Day should overtake you as a thief. You are all sons of light and sons of the day. We are not of the night nor of darkness. Therefore let us not sleep, as others do, but let us watch and be sober. For those who sleep, sleep at night, and those who get drunk are drunk at night. But let us who are of the day be sober, putting on the breastplate of faith and love, and as a helmet the hope of salvation. For God did not appoint us to wrath, but to obtain salvation

through our Lord Jesus Christ, who died for us,
that whether we wake or sleep,
we should live together with Him." – I Thess. 5:1-10 NKJV

When Jesus came in physical form to the people of this Fifth Age of Time, they were mostly not prepared. He came into the temple suddenly and threw out the money changers. To the Pharisees, He came as a thief, threatening their power and prestige. Although they were the keepers of the Word, and teachers of the Law and Prophets, when the Word in flesh stood before them, they rejected Him.

Encouragement: The Worthy Walk With Jesus

But Jesus said that there were still a few names in Sardis who had not defiled their garments, and He said they would walk with Him in white, for they are worthy.

In the traditional Jewish wedding ceremony, all in attendance to the wedding wear white, not just the Bride and Groom.

Remembering that this Age of Time began in the later part of Christ's ministry, those who recognized Him as Messiah were the "few" of Israel. The apostles, who were few in number, walked with Him, because they recognized Him when He came. They walked with Him during His three years of teaching, and also for forty days after His resurrection. Once the Holy Spirit came, they continued to walk with Him and followed Him all the way to their own martyrdom. They would only be the first to lay down their lives for Christ, as the persecution of true believers continued. First by Rome, and later by the Church of Rome.

Promise to Overcomers: White Raiment

In Rev. 3:5, to those who overcome in Sardis, Jesus made three promises: They would be clothed in white; They would not have their names blotted out of the Book of Life; and Jesus would confess their name before His Father, and the angels.

In Matthew 22, Jesus tells a parable of the kingdom of Heaven in which He likens it to a certain king who made a marriage for his son. Servants were sent to call the wedding guests to come, but they refused. In the end, after the repeated refusal of these wicked guests, who ended up killing the servants sent to call them, the king "destroyed those murders and burned up their city.".

Matthew 22:8 then says,

> *"Then said he to his servants, 'The wedding is ready,*
> *but they which were bidden were not worthy."*

Then he sends his servants to go call anyone they could find, "both bad and good" to come.

In the Jewish concept "bad and good" is much like the Old Testament references to "clean and unclean". It doesn't necessarily mean morally good or bad, but what is kosher and what is not. In other words, Jewish or Gentile. Israel, the family of the Christ, and as such the friends and family of the groom, rejected Christ's invitation when He came. Jesus therefore sent His disciples into "all the world".

In the parable, when the king later comes in to see the guests, he sees one without wedding clothes on and confronts him. In traditional Jewish weddings of the time, the groom provides wedding clothes (white garments) to the entire wedding party (much as the bride and groom these days provide special garments for their wedding party to wear). To show up wanting to partake of the feast, but refusing to wear the clothing provided is the height of disrespect and insolence. This wicked person is cast out of the wedding.

In Heaven, we are told that the righteous, Christ, Angels, and the Bride all wear white. This is a promise of Heaven. But it is also a specific promise to those in this Fifth Age of Time. When Jesus came to this Age, there were a few who recognized and followed Him. They literally walked with Him. The promise is that they will do so again.

Note: in the parable, it is those who refused to acknowledge the wedding invitation who were deemed not worthy. In the message to the overcomers in Sardis, Jesus said these few would walk with Him in white for they are worthy.

In the traditional Jewish wedding, the friends of the groom walk with him for the entire week of the wedding, and all wear the wedding clothes he provides. These are not the bride, but friends of the groom. John the Baptist, speaking of the relationship between himself and Christ said,

"He that has the bride is the bridegroom;
but the friend of the bridegroom, which stands and hears him,
rejoices greatly because of the bridegroom's voice.
This my joy therefore is fulfilled." – John 3:29

When the Pharisees criticized the apostles of Christ for not fasting, Jesus said,

"Can the children of the bridechamber mourn,
as long as the bridegroom is with them?
But the days will come when the bridegroom shall be taken from them,
and then shall they fast." – Matt.9:15

Jesus also said to His disciples,

"Let your waist be girded and your lamps burning;
and you yourselves be like men who wait for their master,
when he will return from the wedding,
that when he comes and knocks they may open to him immediately.
Blessed are those servants whom the master,
when he comes, will find watching.
Assuredly, I say to you that he will gird himself
and have them sit down to eat,
and will come and serve them. And if he should come in the second watch,
or come in the third watch, and find them so, blessed are those servants.
But know this, that if the master of the house
had known what hour the thief would come,
he would have watched and not allowed his house to be broken into.
Therefore you also be ready,
for the Son of Man is coming at an hour you
do not expect." – Luke 12:35-40

Note: He is addressing His disciples as friends of the bridegroom, and children of the bridechamber. John the Baptist called himself the "friend of the bridegroom". Jesus does not address them as the Bride. Jesus further clearly states that He is coming as the groom returning *from* his wedding, not coming to get His bride. The disciples He was speaking directly to when He spoke these words were all Jewish. They were His friends and His own countrymen. They were men of His family and nation, but they were not the Bride. We will go into this more deeply in the next chapter, but for now, take a moment to recap the main points we have covered as you study the chart of Sardis and the Fifth Age.

Fifth Church: Sardis - Dead Church

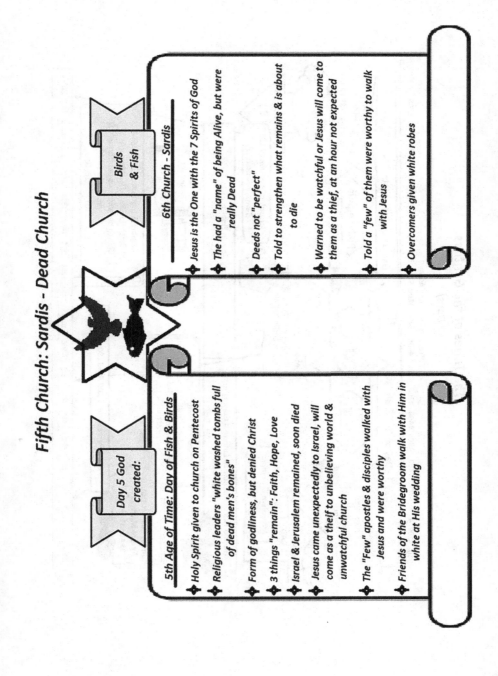

Birds & Fish

Day 5 God created:

6th Church - Sardis

- Jesus is the One with the 7 Spirits of God
- The had a "name" of being Alive, but were really Dead
- Deeds not "perfect"
- Told to strengthen what remains & is about to die
- Warned to be watchful or Jesus will come to them as a thief, at an hour not expected
- Told a "few" of them were worthy to walk with Jesus
- Overcomers given white robes

5th Age of Time: Day of Fish & Birds

- Holy Spirit given to church on Pentecost
- Religious leaders "white washed tombs full of dead men's bones"
- Form of godliness, but denied Christ
- 3 things "remain": Faith, Hope, Love
- Israel & Jerusalem remained, soon died
- Jesus came unexpectedly to Israel, will come as a thief to unbelieving world & unwatchful church
- The "Few" apostles & disciples walked with Jesus and were worthy
- Friends of the Bridegroom walk with Him in white at His wedding

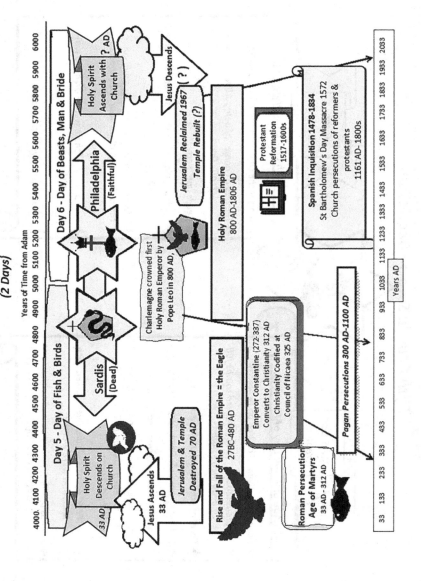

The Times of the Gentiles
(2 Days)

Years of Time from Adam

4000. 4100 4200 4300 4400 4500 4600 4700 4800 4900 5000 5100 5200 5300 5400 5500 5600 5700 5800 5900 6000

Day 5 - Day of Fish & Birds

Day 6 - Day of Beasts, Man & Bride

Holy Spirit Descends on Church

33 AD

Jesus Ascends 33 AD

Jerusalem & Temple Destroyed 70 AD

Sardis (Dead)

Philadelphia (Faithful)

Holy Spirit Ascends with ? AD Church

Jesus Descends

Jerusalem Reclaimed 1967 Temple Rebuilt (?)

(?)

Charlemagne crowned first Holy Roman Emperor by Pope Leo in 800 AD.

Rise and Fall of the Roman Empire = the Eagle 27BC-480 AD

Emperor Constantine (272-337) Converts to Christianity 312 AD Christianity Codified at Council of Nicaea 325 AD

Holy Roman Empire 800 AD-1806 AD

Protestant Reformation 1517-1600s

Spanish Inquisition 1478-1834 St Bartholomew's Day Massacre 1572 Church persecutions of reformers & protestants 1161 AD- 1800s

Roman Persecution Age of Martyrs 33 AD - 312 AD

Pagan Persecutions 300 AD-1100 AD

33 133 233 333 433 533 633 733 833 933 1033 1133 1233 1333 1433 1533 1633 1733 1833 1933 2033

Years AD

CHAPTER 7

Ancient Hebrew Wedding & Revelation

We have been talking a lot about the Bride of Christ, and who she is not. If the predominant congregation of Sardis was not the Bride, who then is the Bride? This would be a good time to look into the ancient Hebrew wedding traditions, because it will unveil so much that is hidden, yet wonderful, to many Gentile believers. Much of the research information I will share was found in the book *Lost in Translation Vol. 1,* written by John Klein and Adam Spears with Michael Christopher. I also found *The Jewish Wedding and Marriage*, by Rabbi David Zaklikowski[1] to be invaluable.

The Proposal:

Prospective Groom arrives at prospective Bride's House with His Father

When a young man decided he wanted to marry, he would go to his father and tell him so. If his father gave his blessing, the two of them would then go to the prospective bride's house together. The groom would carry with him the bride price. This sum serves as compensation to her family for the loss of their daughter. It is also a sum that represents his ability to provide for her and which represents his own inheritance and wealth being bestowed on her. It insures she can never be left desolate. He owes this to

---

[1]   The Jewish Wedding and Marriage. Rabbi David Zaklikowski. Chabad.org.

her even if they should divorce. This is what Jesus did for us when "while we were yet sinners"[2] He died for us, paying the debt for our sins.

In addition to the bride price, the groom would also provide a dowry that was a monetary gift to the bride (often in the form of gold or jewelry) and also gifts for her family. This is what was happening in Genesis when Abraham's servant gave gifts to Rebekah, as well as her family, when he went to betroth her to his master.[3] The groom and his father also carry with them the betrothal cup with wine, and a scribe who will record the marriage covenant and be a witness. Symbolically, this is the role the apostle John is fulfilling in writing the book of Revelation.

The prospective Groom knocks and waits to be admitted

When they arrive at the bride's house, the groom knocks and waits to be let in. We see symbolic representations of this in Song of Solomon 5:2-6, Revelation 3:20, and John 1:11. The Bride has the option of opening the door and admitting them, or not. If she fails to receive him, he turns around and goes away and the engagement does not take place. If she receives him, they all drink the first two cups of wine together while the points of the wedding covenant are being written up.

John 1:11-12 states;

"He came unto His own, and His own received Him not.
But as many as received Him, to them gave He
power to become the sons of God,
Even to them that believe on His name."

In the end of the chapter, we see Jesus calling His disciples, one by one, to follow Him. The first place He leads them is to a marriage ceremony in Cana, where Jesus performs His first miracle by providing wine for them to drink. This is symbolic of the marriage cup.

In Revelation 3:20 we see Jesus "standing at the door and knocking". He then says, *"If any man hear My voice, and open the door, I will come in*

---

2   Romans 5:8
3   Gen. 24:51-51

to him and will sup with him, and he with Me." This again symbolizes the bride accepting the groom, and the ceremonial meal which follows.

The Groom becomes the Redeemer

In the marriage covenant (the Ketubah), the groom promises to honor, provide for (food, clothing, welfare), and support his bride. The groom also agrees to become solely responsible for her debts and any liens against her. This is what redemption means; Jesus covers the debts of our sin and buys back what we have lost.[4]

The bride agrees to provide a dowry which consists of gold, silver and precious things which will provide the furnishings for use in their home together. This was often a portion of the bride price the groom had paid to her father, and which he then gifts to her. Although the bride is responsible to prepare these things, she does so at the expense of the groom. He provides the means, but it is up to her to use that provision and turn it into furnishings for their home. This is where we get the tradition of the "hope chest", which girls used to prepare before their wedding.

"Now if any man build upon this foundation gold, silver, precious stones,
wood hay, stubble: Every man's work shall be made manifest,
for the day shall declare it, because it shall be revealed by fire,
and the fire shall try every man's work of what sort it is.
If any man's work abide which he has built
thereupon, he shall receive a reward.
If any man's work shall be burned, he shall suffer loss,
but he himself shall be saved, yet so as by fire."- 1 Cor. 3:12-15

The Marriage Covenant

Written, Witnessed, and Sealed

Once the marriage contract is completed, it is then sealed with seven seals. This clarifies what is happening in Revelation as seven seals are broken before Christ returns to claim His bride!

---

4   Rev. 5:9; 2 Cor.8:9; Romans 8:1-4.

The bride gives the groom a handkerchief as a token act of acquisition, and the groom hands it back. This seals the deal. This handkerchief symbolizes her handing him herself (her favor and affection and all she possesses), which is now his. This tradition lasted even into the days of knights and ladies when a woman would bestow her handkerchief upon her champion.

When the groom accepts it and hands it back, it symbolizes that he accepts her, and he will come back and take full possession of what is his on the wedding day. This is so beautifully acted out at the empty tomb.

"So they ran both together, and the other disciple did outrun Peter, and came first to the sepulcher. And he stooping down, and looking in, saw the linen clothes lying....
And the napkin, that was about his head, not lying with the linen clothes, but wrapped together in a place by itself." – John 20:4-7

The word translated "napkin" here also means "handkerchief".[5] On the night before Jesus was taken and crucified, paying the price for our sins, He offered the cup of wine to His disciples, declaring it to be the wine of the New Covenant with them. After his death, the disciples wrapped Christ in linen clothes, and placed a handkerchief or napkin over his face. After He rose from the grave, He pointedly returned it to them![6] To Jewish believers they recognized that this act sealed the deal that He was going to return to claim His bride!

"In order to seal all of the stipulated obligations, and to assure that the document (marriage covenant) is not based on speculation, the Rabbis required the legal formality of kinyan, the act of acquisition. Because the bride cannot take possession of all His property at this time, the groom affirms it by a symbolic act called 'kinyan suddar.'

Thus, at the wedding, the rabbi or one of the witnesses gives a handkerchief or other article (but not a coin) in behalf of the recipient, the bride, to the groom. The groom then returns it. Then they record in the ketubah,

5   James Strong, *The New Strong's Exhaustive Concordance of the Bible* (Nashville: T. Nelson, 1990), G4676.
6   John 20:7.

've'kanina' ('and we have completed the act of acquisition'). This symbolic act must be seen clearly by the witnesses, who are the makers of the contract, before they sign to its validity. This act is recorded by a scribe. The ketubah is technically not completed before the kinyan itself is made. If this custom is overlooked it does not alter the ketubah's validity, so long as the witnesses in fact witness the kinyan-transfer of the handkerchief." – Maurice Lamm[7]

How marvelous! The disciples at Christ's burial, acting on behalf of His beloved (the Bride), lay the napkin on Christ. He then gives it back, and they become witnesses to the church of the New Covenant that He has done so. To Gentile believers, the beautiful meaning may remain veiled, but Revelation is the great unveiling of the Truth. How rich, intricate and marvelous the story becomes when we understand the meaning behind every act of the Savior!

After this, the marriage contract must be sealed with seven seals and carefully guarded until the marriage so that none can tamper with it or change any of its stipulations. The father of the groom guards it until the day of the wedding. Only the groom may open and read it.

This is why all Heaven at first weeps when no one is found worthy to open the seals and read from the book in Revelation 5. It means, the wedding cannot take place, for the groom cannot be found. But then, he appears, having accomplished the redemption of the Bride and having paid all her debts! No wonder Heaven rejoices!

The groom opens the seals, and reads the marriage contract before witness before he returns for his bride. This is what we see taking place in the 5th and 6th chapters of Revelation. I have a study of the book of Revelation I am preparing and will go into more of this in depth in that work, but this all serves to help clarify the messages to the churches as well.

---

[7]   Maurice Lamm, "The Jewish Way of Love and Marriage; Celebrating the Jewish Marriage Covenant". Chabad.org.

The Bride & Groom Drink From The Cup

The Cup of Redemption and Inheritance

Once the points of the marriage covenant, detailing the responsibilities of both the bride and groom, have been agreed upon, written up, signed and sealed, a dinner is held to celebrate their engagement. The Bride and Groom drink the third cup of the evening, called the Cup of Redemption and Inheritance. The groom traditionally would not drink wine again until he drinks from the cup with his bride at their wedding.

This opens up richer meaning to what was happening in the evening of the Last Supper, before Christ went to the cross:

> *"And He took the cup, and gave thanks, and gave it to them saying,*
> *"Drink you all of it. For this is My blood of the new testament,*
> *which is shed for many for the remissions of sins.*
> *But I say to you, I will not drink henceforth of this fruit of the vine,*
> *until that day when I drink it new with you in my Father's kingdom."*
> *— Matt. 26:27-29*

The Groom Pays the Bride Price

After the dinner and drinking from the cup, the Groom would settle with anyone who had a lien against the bride's property, paying what was needed to redeem her property.

After the Last Supper, Christ went with His disciples to the Garden where He was betrayed and arrested. He then laid down His life on the cross for us, paying the full penalty of our sins.

The Betrothal is Binding on the Groom

Once the groom makes his offer, and the bride accepts it, the groom cannot change his mind. He is legally liable for all her debts and must fulfill his end of the contract by paying the Bride price, even if the wedding never takes place! He must pay the redemption price before the wedding, not after. Once she accepts him, he can't decide the cost is too high and change his mind. He takes responsibility for all her past debts, as well as her future ones.

There is a beautiful old hymn that celebrates this truth for the church. It's words are;

> *"Jesus paid it all*
> *All to Him I owe*
> *Sin had left a crimson stain*
> *He washed it white as snow."*[8]

At great cost to himself, Jesus paid the full price to redeem us. Not only from our past sins, but of all our sins. He paid it ALL.

This is beautifully illustrated in the book of Ruth. Because Ruth's father-in-law and husband had mortgaged their property before they left for Moab, it was necessary for Boaz to redeem it for her. It was part of the marriage covenant, but the groom must pay up before he takes his bride, not after. The redeemed Bride becomes his wife, but the redeemed property remains the inheritance of the wife and of her children. That is why the other "near kinsman" of Ruth's did not wish to redeem her and her property.[9] To do so would take resources from his present family and children. The price was too high. But Boaz was a rich man, and he had never married. In marrying Ruth, not only did he redeem the inheritance that had been sold away by her first husband, but which was rightly hers through marriage, he also bestowed upon her the full riches of his own inheritance.

The groom figuratively and literally lays down his life for the bride. She is accepted not because she is perfect, but because he loves her. What he asks in return is that she love him and remain faithful. She is purified and redeemed, not by her own actions, but by his sacrificial love.

> *"Husbands, love your wives, even as Christ also loved the church,*
> *and gave himself for it.*

---

8   Mrs. H. M. Hall. "Jesus Paid It All". All-American Church Hymnal. P.383.
9   Ruth 4:5-7.

That He might sanctify and cleanse it with
the washing of water by the word.
That He might present it to Himself, a glorious church,
not having spot, nor wrinkle,
nor any such thing, but that it should be holy and without blemish.
So ought men to love their wives as their own bodies...
For no man ever yet hated his own flesh,
but nourishes and cherishes it, even as the Lord the church" – Eph. 5:25-29

This is what Christ did for us. While we were yet sinners, Christ died for us. We have the option of accepting Him or not, but He paid the price none the less. And He cannot go back on His offer to save us. He assumes all the risk and debt, we receive all the benefit. The groom assumes all the bride's debts, she receives all he is entitled to in his inheritance.

"For you know the grace of our Lord Jesus Christ, that, though He was rich,
yet for your sakes He became poor,
that you thorough His poverty might be rich." – 2 Cor. 8:9

"For He has made Him to be sin for us, who knew no sin; that we
might be made the righteousness of God in Him." – 2 Cor. 5:21

The Groom Prepares a Place for the Bride

After the groom pays the bride price of redemption, the groom then goes away to prepare a place for His bride. Although the wedding has not yet taken place, the couple is considered to be as good as married.

His Father's House, At His Father's Time

Typically, the groom would build a room onto his father's house as the first home for his bride. He would do so under his father's supervision. When the groom's father decided the time was right and that all things were sufficiently ready, he would let his son know it was time to go get his bride.

"Let not your heart be troubled: You believe in God, believe also in Me. In my Father's house are many mansions. If it were not so, I would have told you. I go to prepare a place for you. And if I go and prepare a place fore you, I will come again and receive you unto Myself, that where I am, there you may be also." – John 14:1-3

"But of that day and hour knows no man, no not the angels of Heaven, but My Father only." – Matt. 24:36

"Watch therefore, for you know neither the day nor the hour wherein the Son of Man cometh." – Matt. 25:13

The Bride Makes Herself Ready, and Watches for the Groom

While the groom is away preparing a place for the bride, she has several responsibilities.

First, she must keep herself pure and set apart for him. She is already considered his wife, though the wedding has not yet taken place. There would have to be a divorce decree for them to separate now. Her foremost responsibility is to be true to her love and to keep herself for him. Typically, this separation time would last about a year. This was to prove the purity of the bride. If she were not pure, it would be evident during that time (or within nine months!). It also gave both the bride and groom time to prepare whatever would be needed for their new life together.

She must always be watching and waiting for her groom. Since she doesn't know the exact day or hour he will return, she must always be ready. Jesus promised that He would come again for us, and urged His followers to always be watching and waiting.[10]

During this waiting time, the bride was to be gathering and preparing the things she would need for her new life. Even in more modern times, it has remained a tradition for brides to have prepared a hope chest in which she would keep special items to grace her new home.

Believers of the New Covenant are told to lay up treasures for themselves in heaven. We are told that our acts of faith, hope and love will result in

---

[10]   Matt. 24:42.

riches when Christ returns. Remember, the bride did not typically have to use her own funds for purchasing these items, they were usually gifts. Whatever money she did need to spend for preparation was provided out of the gifts the groom gave her and her family before he left.

This is what Jesus did for the church. He paid for our redemption, but He also left a gift for us in the person and gifts of the Holy Spirit. The treasure we are to lay up in heaven will be provided as we exercise the gifts of the Holy Spirit.

"For the gifts and calling of God are without repentance (meaning He cannot go back on them or change His mind). – Rom. 11:29

"Now there are diversities of gifts, but the same Spirit". – 1 Cor. 12:9

"Wherefore He says, 'When He ascended up on high, He led captivity captive, and gave gifts unto men." – Eph. 4:8

Can the Bride Ever Lose Her Place?

Once the Bride accepts the marriage proposal of the Groom, the only conditions which can now legally nullify the betrothal are:

1. If the bride changes her mind, which she may do at any point up until the wedding;
2. If the bride has intimate relations with another man. However, if she does so, the groom has the option of what to do about it. He could have her stoned, or her could openly shame her and divorce her. He could also choose to quietly divorce her in order to protect her from further penalties. This was the predicament Joseph found himself in when Mary announced her pregnancy, and he knew he was not the father.[11]
3. If the bride betroths herself to another man. Although the woman is free to back out of the engagement at any time before the wedding, to become engaged to another man while still openly

---

[11] Matt. 1:18-24.

remaining engaged to her betrothed would be equivalent to committing adultery, even if the wedding had not taken place.

In every message to each church in Revelation 2-3, the three things Christ rebukes them for are:

1. Leaving their first love. Ephesus had lost her love for Him, and as a result He says she is in danger of "losing her place". This does not mean a loss of salvation. Not all who are saved are the Bride.
2. Engaging in sexual immorality. If the Bride fails to keep herself pure for the groom and engages in intimate relationships with another, the groom can divorce her. The Lord Himself speaks of this in the Old and New Testaments.[12]
3. Eating things sacrificed to idols. Since one of the acts of betrothal involves the bride and groom communing with one another by drinking of the same cup and sharing the betrothal dinner, eating things sacrificed to idols is equivalent to betrothing herself to another. In the New Testament church, those who follow Christ are given the sacrament of communion as a continual reminder of the One to Whom they are betrothed and for Whom they are waiting. When Believers compromise with the world in ways that hurt their conscience and compromise their faith, they are in danger of violating this trust.[13]

The church at Ephesus fell out of love with the Lord. The church at Pergamos was faithful to Him, but she was hanging out with those that hate Him. How can a betrothed woman have friendships with those who hate her beloved? The church at Thyatira went one step further and actually had children by one who hated Him. Jezebel had become an instructor in the church, and "children" (false converts) were produced by her. She seduced the Bride into intercourse with others, and into betrayal of her betrothal vows. The church at Sardis had completely betrayed Him and given herself entirely to immorality and was actively engaged with His enemy. Yet, amazingly, Jesus still holds out His hand to these churches, offering a chance to repent and be forgiven. What incredible love!

---

12   Jeremiah 3:8; Matt.19:9.
13   1 Cor. 11:27-31.

The Groom Returns For the Bride

When his preparations were finished, the groom would let the word leak out that the time was drawing near. The bride, heeding this warning, would make sure there was always a lamp burning in her window, showing she was still up and waiting. Traditionally, the groom would come somewhere between 6 PM (sundown), and midnight.

"Watch you therefore, for you know not when the master of the house cometh; at even, or at midnight, or at the cockcrowing, or in the morning. Lest coming suddenly he find you sleeping. And what I say unto you I say unto all, 'Watch.'" – Mark 13:35-37

"And at midnight there was a cry made, 'Behold, the bridegroom cometh! Go out to meet him!" – Matt. 25:6

Groom Accompanied By His Friends

The groom did not return alone for his bride. He would be accompanied by his groomsmen. These were especially selected friends who met certain criteria: They were all males. They were unmarried virgins. They were all Jews and usually members of the groom's family, or very close friends. They accompany the groom wherever he goes during the whole week of the wedding festival. This gives greater clarity to the 144,000 of Revelation.

"And I heard the number of them which were sealed, and there were sealed an hundred and forty and four thousand of all the tribes of Israel." – Rev. 7:4

"And I looked, and lo, a Lamb stood on the mount Sion, and with Him a hundred forty and four thousand, having His Father's name written in their foreheads... and they sung as it were a new song before the throne, and before the four beasts, and the elders. And no man could learn that song but the hundred and forty and four thousand, which were redeemed from the earth. These are they which were not defiled with women, for they are virgins. These are they which follow

the Lamb withersoever he goes. These were redeemed from among
men, being the firstfruits unto God and the Lamb." — Rev. 14:1-4

In His message to the church at Sardis, one of the things Jesus promises to the few overcomers of this generation of believers is that they will walk with Him in white and that He will confess their names before His Father and before the angels. The special friends of the bridegroom are those of His people who were watching and waiting for His return for His bride, and whom He personally selects, speaking their names before the Father.

When Christ returns, there will be 144,000 Jewish males who will fulfill the role of these friends of the bridegroom. During His time on earth, at His first coming, there were 12 who were specifically, specially selected to walk with Him. That is why He said, specifically to the 12 apostles,

"Let your loins be girded about, and your lights burning.
And you yourselves like unto men that wait for their Lord,
when He will return from the wedding, that when He comes
and knocks, they may open unto Him immediately...
Who then is that faithful and wise steward, whom his lord shall
make ruler over his household, to give them their portion of meat
in due season? Blessed is that servant, whom his lord when He
comes shall find so doing. Of a truth I say unto you, that he will
make him ruler over all that he has." — Luke 12:42-44

The friends of the bridegroom in ancient Hebrew weddings had the responsibility for taking care of whatever the groom needed done for the wedding, including to help seat and serve the guests. They helped with the preparations for the wedding, delivered wedding invitations, and made sure everything went as it should during the whole wedding week, even delivering messages to and from the Bride and Groom to each other. They went with the Groom when He returned to fetch the Bride, and they protected the bridal chamber while the bride made herself ready for the wedding. In short, they acted as special agents of the groom during the time the bride and groom were apart, acting on his behalf, making certain that his will is done.

Could there be a more apt description of the apostles of Christ? They taught others the words of Christ, making disciples. They wrote the gospels and epistles to the churches of the New Testament. Their teachings lead and protect the church to this day. In addition, we have the Holy Spirit, sent from Christ to specifically watch over and care for His Bride. He has never once left us alone.

The Bride is Whisked Away

Sometime during the night, the groom finally comes for the bride, and she is whisked away by him and his friends to a special celebration just for them. The bride and groom, along with their closest friends, would celebrate throughout the night with music and feasting. This was not a feast for all the general wedding guests, but just for the specially selected friends of the bride and groom. In our culture, we would call this the rehearsal dinner the night before the wedding. The rest of the guests would not come until the next day.

The Bride Makes Herself Ready for the Wedding

A few hours before dawn, the groom would leave the bride alone with her bridesmaids so that she could rest for a little while and prepare for the wedding. She would rest for a little while, then bathe and be dressed in white. Keeping all this in mind, consider these verses:

"And when He had opened the fifth seal, I saw under the altar the souls of them that were slain for the Word of God and for the testimony which they held. And they cried with a loud voice saying, 'How long, O Lord, holy and true, dost thou not judge and avenge our blood on them that dwell on the earth?' And white robes were given unto every one of them, and it was said unto them that they should rest yet for a little season, until their fellow servants also and their brethren, that should be killed as they were, should be fulfilled." – Rev. 6:9-11

The Mikveh

One of the ways the bride would make herself ready for the wedding was to "mikveh", which is a ritual bath in which she ceremonially cleanses herself. Traditionally, both the bride and groom would participate in this special bathing ceremony.

Baptism is symbolic of this mikveh. Jesus, the Groom, was baptized by John the Baptist (the friend of the bridegroom)[14], and He desires that His bride follow Him in this ceremony. This is what He meant when Jesus told John that His baptism would "fulfil all righteousness"[15]. Jesus had no sin which He needed to repent of (which is what some believe baptism is symbolic of). His baptism fulfilled the mikveh of the groom, as ours does of the bride. It is symbolic of us being united together with Christ.[16]

This mikveh is always done in running or "living" water with one's head facing the source of the water. Jesus was baptized in the Jordan river. All early baptisms by John, the disciples of Christ, and the early church were done in running water and involved total immersion.

The bride would then be anointed with fragrant oils, and both the bride and groom would be dressed in white. Jesus was anointed with the Holy Spirit after His baptism, and The Holy Spirit, symbolic of holy oil, was poured out on the church (the bride) at Pentecost.[17]

The King and His Queen

The Bride and Groom are considered King and Queen for the week of the wedding celebration. During that time, they are greeted as royalty wherever they go with palm branches, bowing and celebrating. This whole week is a time of celebration and feasting. This is what was happening when Christ was greeted by faithful followers at His entry to Jerusalem. They recognized Christ as their rightful king, and as the Messiah come for His church.

---

[14]   John 3:27-30.
[15]   Matt. 3:13-17.
[16]   Romans 6:3-4.
[17]   Matt. 3:16; Mark 1:10; Luke 3:22; Acts 2:1-4.

"On the next day much people that were come to the feast, when they heard that Jesus was coming to Jerusalem, took branches of palm trees, and went forth to meet Him, and cried, 'Hosanna: Blessed is the King of Israel that comes in the name of the Lord!'" – John 12:12-13

"After this, I beheld, and lo, a great multitude,
which no man could number,
of all nations, and kindreds and people, and tongues stood before the throne,
and before the Lamb, clothed with white robes, and palms in their hands."
– Rev. 7:9

2 Crowns

In preparation of the wedding, upon the bride's head would be placed a golden crown (traditionally in the shape of the skyline of Jerusalem). The groom traditionally also wore a crown, but his would be a crown of roses, with the thorns included! This was to remind him that his marriage would bring both joy and pain, and his love must be prepared to pay that price.

"And when they had platted a crown of thorns,
they put it upon His head,
and a reed in His right hand,
and they bowed the knee before Him, and mocked Him,
saying, 'Hail, King of the Jews!'" – Matt. 27:29

"Henceforth there is laid up for me a crown of righteousness,
which the Lord, the righteous judge, shall give me at that day:
and not to me only, but unto all them also that love His appearing."
– 2 Timothy 4:8

"And when the chief Shepherd shall appear,
you shall receive a crown of glory that fades not away." – 1 Peter 5:4

"Behold, I come quickly.
Hold that fast which you have, that no man take your crown."
– Rev. 3:11

"Let us be glad and rejoice, and give honor to Him,
for the marriage of the Lamb is come,
and His wife has made herself ready.
And to her was granted that she should be arrayed
in fine linen, clean and white:
for the fine linen is the righteousness of the saints.
And he said unto me,
'Write, Blessed are they which are called unto
the marriage supper of the Lamb....
And I saw heaven opened, and behold a white horse;
and He that sat upon him was called Faithful and True,
...His eyes were as a flame of fire, and on His head were many crowns,
and He had a name written, that no man knew, but He Himself...
And the armies which were in heaven followed Him upon white horses,
clothed in fine linen, white and clean..
and He had on His vesture and on His thigh a name written;
King of Kings, and Lord of Lords." – Rev. 19:7-16

"And I John saw the holy city, new Jerusalem,
coming down from God out of heaven,
prepared as a bride adorned for her husband....
And there came unto me one of the seven
angels... and talked with me, saying,
'Come here, and I will show you the bride, the Lamb's wife.'
And he carried me away in the spirit to a great and high mountain,
And showed me that great city, the holy Jerusalem,
descending out of heaven from God." – Rev. 21:2,9-10

The Wedding Ceremony

Finally, the wedding day comes. Traditionally, the actual wedding would take place in the afternoon, or early evening. All the wedding guests assemble at the chosen place, and the groom, attended by his friends, takes his place, waiting for his bride. As the family and friends of the couple proceed to the venue of the wedding, the guests are also dressed in special wedding clothes, and they carry candles or lamps to light the way.

The friends of the couple have been sent to fetch the bride and escort her to the place of festivities from the night before. Both the bride and groom are dressed in white and wearing crowns. As they meet once more, the groom escorts the bride to the "chuppah" (covering). The bride is typically veiled until the groom lifts the veil and reveals her beauty to himself.

I can't help but mention that the book of the Bible which gives the most detail about the wedding of Christ and the church is called the book of Revelation, or "unveiling". In this book, not only is Christ unveiled, revealing His majesty and work throughout all of history, but also the church is fully revealed in her true, glorious identity.

"And He shall send His angels, with a great sound of a trumpet, and they shall gather together His elect from the four winds, from one end of heaven to the other." – Matt. 24:31

7 Blessings

During the wedding ceremony, the groom pronounces the bride "pure, holy, and set apart for Himself." The bride and groom then each speak seven blessings over each other.

In the book of Revelation, there are seven times the Lord speaks a blessing over His people:[18] Specifically, He blesses those who read, heed and obey the words of His prophecy; those which have died in the Lord; those who have kept themselves unspotted from the world; those who are called to the Marriage Supper of the Lamb; those who have a part in the first resurrection; and those who obey the commandments of God. These are the ones who have a right to the Tree of Life and to enter the gates of Heaven. The New Song the redeemed creation sings before the Lord in Revelation 5:12 contains seven blessings:

"Saying with a loud voice, 'Worthy is the Lamb that was slain To receive power, and riches, and wisdom, and strength, And honor, and glory, and blessing."

---

[18] Rev. 1:3; 14:13; 16:15; 19:9; 20:6; 22:7; 22:14.

New Shoes

After the blessing ceremony, the groom removes the bride's shoes and presents her with new sandals. This symbolizes her new inheritance. Ever since the Abrahamic covenant, wherein God promised to give Abraham every place the soles of his feet walked on[19], shoes have been symbolic of one's inheritance. When God told Moses to remove his shoes, He was in essence saying that Moses' fortunes were about to change.[20] When Ruth's near kinsman refused to redeem her or her inheritance, he removed his shoe and presented it to Boaz.[21] By removing the bride's shoes and presenting her with new sandals, the groom is symbolically bestowing upon her his own inheritance, which now would belong to her and her children. Her fortunes have changed.

This also explains the meaning of Christ washing the disciple's feet after Last Supper.

> *"Jesus, knowing that the Father had given all things into His hands,*
> *And that He was come from God and went to God;*
> *He rose from supper, and laid aside His garments,*
> *and took a towel and girded Himself.*
> *After that He poured water into a basin, and began to*
> *wash the disciples' feet, and to wipe them with the towel*
> *wherewith He was girded." – John 13:3-5*

Under His Wings

Finally, the groom spreads his arms around the bride and enfolds her in his "tallit" (prayer shawl, symbolically wings). This symbolizes that she is now under his protection. This is what Jesus was alluding to when He said of Jerusalem;

> *"How often I would have gathered you under My wings,*
> *but you would not." – Matt. 23:37*

---

[19]   Gen.3:17.
[20]   Exodus 3:5; Deut. 11:24.
[21]   Ruth 4:7-8.

CHAPTER 8

The Bride of Christ

Now that we have looked more closely at ancient Hebrew wedding and marriage traditions, what do they reveal about the identity of the Bride of Christ?

The Bride is the One Who Receives the Groom

John said, *"He came unto His own, and His own received Him not.
But as many as received Him, to them gave He
power to become the sons of God,
even to them that believe on His name." – John 1:11-12*

When Jesus came into the world, He went first to His own people, to those who were invited to the marriage, but they did not receive Him. The proposal (which is what being called and chosen are about), then went out into all the world.

*"Go you therefore, and teach all nations,
baptizing them in the name of the Father,
and of the Son, and of the Holy Ghost.
Teaching them to observe all things whatsoever I have commanded you:
and lo, I am with you always, even unto the end
of the world."* – Matt. 28:19-20

But to whom did Jesus physically come? In actuality, He came to believers of every age and day of time. On the first Day, He walked with Adam in the garden and with Enoch.[1] He even appeared to and spoke with Cain.[2]

On the Second Day He walked with Noah. On the Third Day, He walked with Abraham in the plain of Moriah,[3] and appeared to Jacob as he fled his brother.[4] He reveled Himself to Hagar at the well[5], and Sarah outside of her tent.[6] On the Third Day, He revealed Himself to Moses on the mountain and walked in the camp of Israel.[7] He revealed Himself to Joshua on the eve of battle and to Gideon hiding in the threshing floor.[8]

On Day Four, He walked and talked with Daniel by the river, with Elijah on the mountain and in the chariot, and with Ezekiel and Isaiah as the One high and lifted up.[9] In the evening of the Fourth Day, He came as a baby, then as the Lamb of God who walked in Israel with His chosen disciples.

On the Fifth Day He came in the form of the Holy Spirit and walks and talks with all His people, as He does until this day. Best of all, on the Sixth Day He will return.

So, to every age, He came. And some received Him and some did not. In a sense, He "knocked on the door" of every age. The Bride is not the one for whom any of these conditions apply, but the one for whom all of these apply. The family and friends of the groom also receive Him.

The Bride is the One Who Shares the Groom's Cup

After the bride receives the groom, there is a special cup – the cup after the betrothal dinner, from which only she and the groom drink. This is the Cup of Redemption and Inheritance. Jesus lifted this cup up after the Last

---

[1]   Gen. 5:22-24.
[2]   Gen. 4:9-16.
[3]   Gen. 18:1; Gen.17:1; 22:11-14.
[4]   Gen. 32:24-30.
[5]   Gen. 16:6-7.
[6]   Gen. 18:1-15.
[7]   Deut. 23:14.
[8]   Joshua 5:13-14; Judges 6:11-12.
[9]   Daniel 8:1-2; 2 Kings 2:11; Ezekiel 1; Isiah 6:1.

Supper and offered it to His disciples saying, *"This cup is the new testament (or covenant) in my blood"*.[10] He told them to remember Him as often as they drink of it, but that He would not drink wine again until He drinks it with them new in His kingdom. The is the communion of Christ which all New Testament believers drink in remembrance of Him. Only the bride drinks of this cup. To no other church age was this communion given.

But the cup that the Bride of Christ drinks is also the cup of suffering. She follows her Groom, and shares in all His glory, but also all His suffering. She is aligned with His will and His interests on earth. She values what He values, and she is led by His will as she awaits His return.

"He that takes not his cross, and follows after Me
Is not worthy of Me." – Matt. 10:38

"If any man will come after Me, let him deny himself,
And take up his cross, and follow Me." – Matt. 16:24

"There is therefore now no condemnation to those which are in Christ Jesus,
who walk, not after the flesh, but after the Spirit...
they that are after the flesh, mind the things
of the flesh, they that are after the
Spirit, the things of the Spirit." – Rom. 8:1,5

"The Spirit itself bears witness with our spirit,
That we are the children of God,
And if children, then heirs,
Heirs of God, and joint-heirs with Christ
If so be that we suffer with Him,
That we may be also glorified together." – Rom. 8:16-17

"If we suffer (with Him)
We shall also reign with Him." – 2 Timothy 2:12

---

[10] Matt. 26:28.

The Bride Shares the Grooms Baptism

The Bride also shares the Groom's baptism (or ritual washing) that sets them apart and purifies them in preparation for their life together. Jesus Himself submitted to baptism, not in repentance of sin, but in preparation for His betrothal to the church. He commands that all who wish to follow Him also partake of this baptism.[11] Not to wash away their sins, but to mark them as those who have accepted His invitation, and are following after Him.

The Bride Is an Overcomer

In every message to every church in Revelation, the promises and blessings that are promised are bestowed only on those who overcome, not to the church in general. What does she overcome? The temptation to abandon her love and faith. The temptation to engage in immorality. The temptation to have communion with the world in order to reap its benefits. The Betrothed Bride is no longer a free agent, her heart is spoken for. Her will is now lost in His, and her highest aim is to walk in a manner that is worthy of the honor He has bestowed in choosing her. From now on, His will informs every decision she makes. She does this, not from obligation, but from love. Is it possible to be a born again Christian and not be an overcomer? Yes and No.

No, in that one must overcome doubt and unbelief in order to make the decision to accept, by faith, the gift of salvation. In that sense, everyone who accepts that Christ is the Son of God, came in the flesh, died on the cross to redeem us from sin, and rose again to secure everlasting life for us, is an overcomer.

But not everyone who calls upon Christ for salvation is fully aligned with His interests and will on earth. Not all are motivated by love. Love is the only motivation that yields a reward. The only thing Christ asks of His Bride is to love Him and remain faithful to Him. Paul said,

---

[11]   Matt. 28:19; Rom. 6:4; 1 Peter 3:21.

"Though I speak with the tongues of men and angels,
And have not charity (love),
I am become as sounding brass, or a tinkling cymbal.
And though I have the gift of prophecy,
And understand all mysteries, and all knowledge;
And though I have all faith, so that I could remove mountains,
And have not (love),
I am nothing.
And though I bestow all my goods to feed the poor,
And though I give my body to be burned,
And have not (love)
It profits me nothing." – 1 Cor.13:1-3

There are those whose motivation in accepting Christ is simply to make sure they avoid Hell. If that is all they desire, then that is all they will get.

Paul spoke of these when he wrote:

"For other foundation can no may lay than that is laid,
Which is Jesus Christ.
Now if any man build upon this foundation gold, silver, precious stones,
Wood, hay, stubble;
Every man's work shall be made manifest:
For the day shall declare it,
Because it shall be revealed by fire,
And the fire shall try every man's work of what sort it is.
If any man's work abides which he has built thereupon,
He shall receive a reward.
If any man's work shall be burned,
He shall suffer loss:
But he himself shall be saved,
Yet so as by fire." – 1 Cor. 3:11-14

It is clear from the text that Paul is speaking of and to believers. Some have accepted the gift of salvation, but chose instead to build up earthly things and interests. In the parable of the Sower found in Matthew 13, it was the same seed that was received by all the ground. The seed was genuine, but the result varied depending on how that seed was received.

Many are like those who received seed on rocky ground in the parable of the Sower in Luke 8. These are those who joyfully receive the word of God and accept it, but the cares of this world, or riches and pleasures of this life, keep them from being fruitful.

Earthly things will burn when tested. Heavenly things are like gold, silver and precious gems. These do not burn, but become purified by fire. Everyone faces this fire of testing in their lives. Some come out with stronger faith. These are the overcomers. Others do not. They are saved, but they are not overcomers.

Lot is an Old Testament example of a believer "saved so as by fire". He was righteous in that he believed God, not just in His existence but also His word and commands. We know this because the Bible calls him "righteous".[12] When Abraham was pleading with the Lord to spare Lot he said, *"Will You (God) also destroy the righteous with the wicked?"*[13] It was a rhetorical question to which the obvious answer was "no". So, in Gen. 19 we see the angels of God come to Sodom and take Lot and his family out before the city was destroyed by fire. He did not face the fiery trial of destruction, but he only escaped with his life and nothing else.

Though some have only a fire insurance faith, others have gladly received and invested the grace Christ extended to them. They use their spiritual gifts to build up His kingdom. They are motivated by love, and they remain true to His name and Word. They overcome the tests that their love will be put to while they await the coming of The Groom. Their hearts, not just their souls, belong to the Lord.

Revelation 12:11 tells us that we overcome by the blood of the Lamb, by the word of our testimony (confessing Him with our mouth as in Rom. 10:9-10), and by not loving our lives "unto death". This means to value Christ more than we value our own lives. It is "minding the things of the Spirit" more than the things of the flesh. It means being more dedicated to His interests and will than to our own. Those who lose their lives in His life, will find both life and blessing.

---

[12]   2 Peter 2:6-9.
[13]   Gen. 18;23.

"And he that takes not his cross, and follows after Me,
Is not worthy of Me.
He that finds his life shall lose it,
And he that loses his life for My sake shall find it." – Matt.10:38-39

Remember, in His message to the church at Sardis, it was overcomers that were deemed worthy to walk with Him in white!

Are there born again believers who do not love Christ more than their own lives? Clearly. The whole health and wealth movement is built upon the idea that gain is godliness[14] and we can live our best life NOW. Accepting Christ for worldly, self-serving motives will not profit one in the end. Only what is done out of the motivation of love will profit us[15], and yield fruit for eternity.

The Bride is fruitful, because she prepares for the Groom's return by receiving the Gift from Him, and using it to ready herself for her future life with Him. Her motivation is love, and she uses the gift of the Holy Spirit to build His kingdom, and to prepare for His return. We are not saved through works, but those who are chosen by Him have a responsibility to use what He has given us (Holy Spirit) to make ourselves ready for His return and to see His will done on earth.

Peter said in 2 Peter 1 that we believers are given everything we need to prepare for life and godliness. We were given great and precious promises and the divine nature (Holy Spirit). We are to use these to grow in faith, virtue, knowledge, temperance, patience, godliness, brotherly kindness and love.

"For if these things be in you and abound,
They make you that you shall neither be barren, nor unfruitful
In the knowledge of our Lord Jesus Christ...
Wherefore the rather, brethren,
Give diligence to make your calling and election sure.
For if you do these things, you shall never fall.
For so an entrance shall be ministered unto you abundantly
into the everlasting kingdom of our Lord and
Savior Jesus Christ."- 2 Peter 1:8-11

---

[14]   1 Tim. 6:5-6.
[15]   1 Cor. 13.

Again, we see that he is not speaking of salvation being dependent upon works, but the reward is. He says that if we use what the Lord has given us, and grow in our faith, it will not only make us fruitful, but also will guarantee us an abundant entrance in the everlasting kingdom.

We are warned in the book of Hebrews that endurance (what is sometimes called patience, or perseverance) in the faith is necessary if one is to receive the promised reward:

> *"Cast not away therefore your confidence,*
> *Which has great recompense of reward.*
> *For you have need of patience,*
> *That, after you have done the will of God,*
> *You might receive the promise.*
> *For yet a little while, and He that shall come will come,*
> *And not tarry.*
> *Now the just shall live by faith:*
> *But if any man draw back,*
> *My soul shall have no pleasure in him."* – Heb. 10:35-38

There is simply no avoiding the truth that what we do with what we have been given will have eternal consequences. Jesus said, *"If therefore you have not been faithful in the unrighteous mammon (earthly blessings), who will commit to you trust the true riches?"* -Luke 16:11.

The Bride is the One Who Receives the Gift

While many receive gifts from the groom (her family, the wedding guests), only one receives the special dowry that is offered to meet any and all needs that she may have in preparing herself for the wedding – the Bride. As she is preparing for her new home, and for her wedding day, should she find herself in need of anything, she may freely use this gift to supply that need.

> *"And whatsoever you shall ask in My name, that will I*
> *do, that the Father may be glorified in the Son. If you*
> *shall ask any thing in My name, I will do it."*
> *– John 14:13-14*

"You have not chosen Me, but I have chosen you, and ordained you, that you should go and bring forth fruit, and that your fruit should remain, that whatsoever you shall ask of the Father in My name, He may give it you."
— John 15:16

"And in that day you shall ask Me nothing. Verily, verily I say unto you, whatsoever you shall ask the Father in My name, He will give it you. Hitherto have you asked nothing in My name. Ask and you shall receive, that your joy may be full." — John 16:23-24

What day is it that Jesus is speaking of in which believers may now ask for things "in His name"? According to verse 22, that day will be on the day He returns from the grave. The day He sends the Comforter – His own Holy Spirit – to stay with the church and supply all their kingdom needs until He returns.

"But my God shall supply all your need according to His riches in glory by Christ Jesus." — Phil 4:19

The Bride has access to His riches because she is His betrothed, and all He has is hers. The Holy Spirit is the endowment (of which we are endued) of Christ to the New Testament church.

"And behold, I send the promise of my Father upon you. But tarry you in the city of Jerusalem, until you be endued with power from on high." – Luke 24:49

"All things that the Father has are Mine. Therefore said I that He (Holy Spirit) shall take of Mine, and shall show it unto you." – John 16:15

"Wherefore He said, when He ascended up on high, He led captivity captive, and gave gifts unto men (His people)." – Eph. 4:8

"And it shall come to pass in the last days, saith God, 'I will pour out of My Spirit upon all flesh. And your sons and your daughters shall prophesy, and your young men shall see visions, and your

Upon whom was the Spirit poured out? Jews and Gentiles. Young and old. Men and women. No longer is God speaking to the world exclusively through the Jewish nation and Law, but through His Spirit. No longer must people go to the temple in Jerusalem to worship and commune with God. Now true worshippers may worship anywhere in Spirit and in Truth.

The Bride might not have been born of Israel, but she is still of the family because the relationship of a bride to her groom is closer than that of the groom and his sister or family. The Bride takes His name and has the right to ask for things "in His name".

The Bride is the One for Whom the Groom Returns

The Bride is not the only one awaiting the return of the groom. Israel and the Jews are still eagerly awaiting their Messiah. Some recognized Him when He came the first time and are preparing for His return. Others, who did not recognize Him the first time, are still eagerly waiting for His appearance.

In the parable of the ten virgins in Matthew 25, note that all ten virgins are eagerly awaiting the coming of the groom. Prophetically, Israel (at least those who remain true to worship of the one true God) is a virgin. Those who turn from God to idols are called by another name. Although the Pharisees and religious leaders of Israel of Jesus' time did not accept Christ, yet they were all waiting for the Messiah, as are the devout Jews of today. But only five of the virgins had "oil" in their lamps. Oil is a symbol of the Holy Spirit. When the groom arrives, those who have oil in their lamps go into the wedding with the groom, but the others are left behind.

Paul speaks of these things at length in the book of Romans.

"Brethren, my heart's desire and prayer to God for Israel
is that they might be saved.
For I bear them record that they have a zeal of God,

but not according to knowledge. For they being
ignorant of God's righteousness,
and going about to establish their own righteousness,
have not submitted themselves unto the righteousness of God.
For Christ is the end of the law for righteousness
to every one that believes." – Romans 10:1-4

"What then? Israel has not obtained that which he seeks for, but the
election has obtained it, and the rest were blinded." – Romans 11:7

"For I would not, brethren, that you should be ignorant of this mystery,
Lest you should be wise in your conceits,
That blindness in part is happened to Israel,
until the fullness of the Gentiles be come in.
And so all Israel shall be saved.
As it is written, 'There shall come out of Sion the Deliverer,
and shall turn away ungodliness from Jacob." – Romans 11:25-26

"For if the casting away of them (Israel) be the reconciling of the world,
What shall the receiving of them be, but life from the dead?" – Romans 11:15

When Christ returns for His Bride, He will once again reach out to the
nation of Israel. Through the ministry of the 2 witnesses and the 144,000
Jewish men He specially anoints for the task, they will, as a nation, return
to God.

"And I will pour upon the house of David, and upon the inhabitants
of Jerusalem, the Spirit of Grace and of supplications. And they
shall look upon Me whom they have pierced, and they shall
mourn for Him, as one mourns for his only son, and shall be in
bitterness for him, as one that is in bitterness for his firstborn."
– Zechariah. 12:10

"And then shall appear the sign of the Son of Man in heaven. And then
shall all the tribes of the earth mourn, and they shall see the Son of Man
coming in the clouds of heaven with power and great glory." – Matt. 24:30

When Christ returns, who will He return for? He will return not only for those believers who are alive at that time, but for all those who have gone before and have shared His cup and baptism in these two "days".

> *"And He shall send His angels with a great sound of a trumpet,*
> *And they shall gather together His elect from the four winds,*
> *From one end of heaven to the other." – Matt. 24:31*

> *"For if we believe that Jesus died and rose again,*
> *Even so them also which sleep in Jesus will God bring with Him.*
> *For this we say unto you by the word of the Lord,*
> *That we which are alive and remain unto the coming of the Lord*
> *shall not prevent them which are asleep.*
> *For the Lord Himself shall descend from heaven with a shout,*
> *with the voice of the archangel, and with the trump of God.*
> *And the dead in Christ shall rise first.*
> *Then we which are alive and remain shall be caught up together with them*
> *in the clouds, to meet the Lord in the air,*
> *and so shall we ever be with the Lord." – 1 Thess. 4:14-17*

John 14 records that the night before Jesus went to the cross to redeem us, He told His disciples that He was going away, but that He was only going to prepare a place for them and would come back and get them. In the meantime, He would send the Holy Spirit to care for them and supply all they needed to prepare for the kingdom.

The Bride is the One Who Shares the Crown

There are many guests, family and well-wishers at the wedding, but only 2 wear crowns: the Bride and the Groom. There are many that share rule of the kingdom with the King – there are appointed officials, judges, and many in positions of authority, but the only one who shares the crown is the Bride.

Jesus promises crowns for those who follow Him and overcome. And He also warns the church at Philadelphia to care that no one takes their crown. This clearly tells us that not all who are in the church will wear the crown. There is a very real crown to be won, but it can also be lost. Again, this is not speaking of salvation, but of reward. Our souls are not at stake, but crowns are! Only the Bride shares the crown.

The Bride is the One Who Shares the Groom's Name

While all the churches (or congregations) of believers since the First Day of time have been redeemed by Christ and will all share in the kingdom, not all receive the same inheritance. To the church of Sardis (which existed at the time of Christ's walking with them), Jesus promised that only the overcomers would walk with Him in white. As we shall see, there was only one church that was promised His new name, and the name "New Jerusalem". We will look more closely at this church, the church at Philadelphia, in the next chapter, but we have already seen that the "New Jerusalem" is another name for the Bride of Christ'

> *"And I John saw the holy city, New Jerusalem,*
> *coming down from God out of heaven,*
> *prepared as a bride adorned for her husband....*
> *And there came unto me one of the seven*
> *angels... and talked with me, saying,*
> *'Come here and I will show you the Bride, the Lamb's wife." – Rev. 21:2,9*

So, the Bride is both Jew and Gentile. She is made up of men and women; young and old. She is from every tribe, tongue, nation and people. She is the Beloved of Christ. She is the one to whom He came, offering Himself; and she is the one who opens the door to Him. She loves Him and eagerly awaits His return. The Bride is the one who has the Gift. She is the one who drinks of His cup and follows in His baptism. She is the one who knows and confesses His name, and who will take His name.

It is a subject for another study, but Solomon's "Song of Songs" is a beautiful reenactment of this grand love story. The Song from which all songs spring, and the Love from which all loves find their inspiration.

CHAPTER 9

PHILADELPHIA – The Faithful Church

"And to the angel of the church in Philadelphia write,
'These things says He who is holy, He who is
true, He who has the key of David,
He who opens and no one shuts, and shuts and no one opens.
'I know your works.
See, I have set before you an open door, and no one can shut it;
for you have a little strength, have kept My word,
and have not denied My name.
Indeed I will make those of the synagogue of Satan,
who say they are Jews and are not, but lie—
indeed I will make them come and worship before your feet,
and to know that I have loved you.
Because you have kept My command to persevere,
I also will keep you from the hour of trial which
shall come upon the whole world,
to test those who dwell on the earth.
Behold, I am coming quickly!
Hold fast what you have, that no one may take your crown.
He who overcomes, I will make him a pillar in the temple of My God,
and he shall go out no more.
I will write on him the name of My God and
the name of the city of My God,
the New Jerusalem, which comes down out of heaven from My God.

And I will write on him My new name'.
He who has an ear,
let him hear what the Spirit says to the churches." – Rev. 3:7-13

The name Philadelphia literally means "brotherly love", which is the one characteristic above all others that Jesus said would define His church[1]. From His message to this church, it is clear that they lived up to this name. The believers of Philadelphia were not only examples of love to one another, but they also held fast to their love of Christ. They held true to their faith, hope and love even in the face of great opposition by the religious establishment, which pointedly rejected and persecuted them.

True believers of this age are actively persecuted, not so much by the world (which has always been the case), but by the official church. Specifically, those who claim to be the true church and people of God, but are not. In fact, Jesus said they are actually the synagogue of Satan. The persecutors of Philadelphia had the position and titles of religious leadership, but they were actually the enemies of Christ and of all true believers. Though these believers at Philadelphia were under heavy persecution, and had only a little strength, they were authentic, faithful, and effective.

Revelation of Christ: The Holy and True

To the church at Philadelphia, Jesus reveals Himself as He Who is Holy and True. Jesus told His disciples; *"I am the way, the truth, and the life."*[2] There is no shadow or lie in the Father or the Son. Not only is Christ the Faithful Witness, always telling the truth; He is Truth personified. This is significant to the believers of Philadelphia, this Sixth Age of Time, because the predominate characteristic of this age is deception. Jesus repeatedly warned His disciples of the deception of the last days.

"Take heed that no man deceive you.
For many shall come in My name, saying, "I am
Christ' and shall deceive many...

---

[1]   John 13:35.
[2]   John 14:6.

And then shall they deliver you up to be afflicted, And shall kill you,
and you shall be hated of all nations for My name's sake,
And then shall many be offended,
and shall betray one another and shall hate one another.
And many false prophets shall rise and shall deceive many.
And because iniquity shall abound,
the love of many shall wax cold." – Matt. 24:4-5, 9-12

In our day, the battle between what is true and what is false is heating up. Traditional values and beliefs that have guided us for thousands of years are now not merely questioned, but outright denied. So called enlightened and educated people, claiming science as their guide, loudly protest that what used to be right is now wrong, and what was wrong is now right. What the Bible calls sin is now not only tolerated, it is celebrated. Great pressure is placed even on our very young people to espouse the new "woke" values of our day. Sadly, the official stance of many churches is in complete sync with these ideals. Many churches, which once turned the world upside down with the gospel, are now turning truth upside down.

"Woe to them that call evil good, and good evil!
That put darkness for light, and light for darkness,
That put bitter for sweet, and sweet for bitter!
Woe to them that are wise in their own eyes, and prudent in their own sight!
… Which justify the wicked for reward,
and take away the righteousness of the righteous
from him!" – Isaiah 5:20-21,23

Although many scriptures tell us of Christ's truthfulness, there is only one other place in the whole Bible where this title, "Holy and True" is spoken:

"And they cried with a loud voice, saying,
"How long, O Lord, Holy and True,
dost Thou not judge and avenge our blood
on them that dwell on earth?" – Rev. 6:10

Those who are speaking are the souls in heaven who have been martyred for Christ. They are given white robes and told to rest a little longer until the number of their fellow servants and brethren would be fulfilled. It is not a stretch to connect that those who address the Lord as "Holy and True", are the very ones to whom Christ reveals Himself as Holy and True. They are the ones who have laid down their lives for the Truth.

Holiness is the dominant characteristic of Christ throughout scripture. Because He is holy, He desires His Bride to be holy as well.

"But as He which has called you is holy,
So be you holy in all manner of conversation;
Because it is written, 'Be you holy, for I am holy'." – 1 Peter 1:15-16

"Husbands, love your wives,
even as Christ also loved the church, and gave Himself for it.
That He might sanctify and cleanse it with
the washing of water by the word,
That He might present it to Himself a glorious church,
Not having spot, nor wrinkle, or any such thing,
But that it should be holy and without blemish." –Eph. 5:25-27

"Yet now has He reconciled in the body of His flesh through death,
To present you holy and unblameable and unreproveable in His sight."
– Colossians 1:21-22

"Put on therefore, as the elect of God, holy and beloved, bowels of mercies,
kindness, humbleness of mind, meekness and longsuffering." – Col. 3:12

Philadelphia, the sixth church, representing the Sixth Age of Time, also represents the Bride of Christ. Her groom is Holy and True, and He purifies her – not by her own merit, but by His. As Sardis represents the official church of the two days of The Times of the Gentiles, Philadelphia represents the true disciples of Christ in that time. The true followers of Christ are those who are often marginalized and persecuted by the official Church, but who yet remain loyal to Christ.

Keys To The Kingdom

Jesus also reveals Himself to Philadelphia as the One who holds the key of David. He is the one who opens and no man shuts; and who shuts and no man opens. Jesus old Peter;

> *"And I say also unto you, that you are Peter,*
> *and upon this rock I will build My church;*
> *And the gates of hell shall not prevail against it.*
> *And I will give unto you the keys of the kingdom of heaven;*
> *And whatsoever you shall bind on earth shall be bound in heaven;*
> *And whatsoever you shall loose on earth shall be loosed in heaven."*
> *— Matt. 16:18-19*

The keys to the kingdom are associated with the Key of David because it was through David's line the Messiah, king of Judah, would come. Isaiah, speaking prophetically about the coming Messiah said;

> *And the key of the house of David will I lay on His shoulder.*
> *So He shall open, and none shall shut,*
> *And He shall shut and none shall open." — Is. 22:22*

The king, as the supreme ruler, had ultimate control over what went on in his kingdom. He decided who was "in" and who was "out". He decided what would be allowed and what would be prohibited. This was both a figurative, and a literal key.

Locks and keys have been used since ancient times and there are many Old Testament references to them. Typically, the keys of the castle would be entrusted to a senior, high official, whose job it was to conduct the household, or even the kingdom, on the king's behalf. This is the position Joseph held in Pharaoh's household. This is also explains what was happening in the story of Esther. The key to the Persian kingdom was the King's ring. With it one might make any law, even to who lives and who dies. This ring was first entrusted to Haman, the king's most trusted adviser. But after his treachery was revealed, the ring was delivered to Esther, the queen, whose new law delivered her people. Later, Mordecai was given control of the ring, and thus control of the laws of the kingdom.

Just as the king had sovereignty over the kingdom, similarly, a man was considered the king of his castle or home, and was ultimately responsible for what went on there. But in the daily, practical business of the household, the wife was the one entrusted with the keys. Even in ancient times, the wife, as the one who ran the household, was the keeper of the keys.

It was the wife who would direct servants, look after the daily work, and open or lock access to all the household valuables. She possessed total authority over who had access to what. When a woman married and moved into her father-in-law's house (where the groom had prepared special quarters for her), the father's wife was the keeper of the keys. But if for whatever reason she was not present to perform that task, the wife of the eldest son became the one entrusted with the keys. This tradition lasted for many centuries.[3]

In ancient times, the women wore these keys upon their shoulders, later moving them to broaches and even belts. It is from this custom that the tradition of the chatelaine of the castle came.[4] This gives further insight to the phrase "the key of the house of David will I lay on His shoulder"[5], as that is where keys were worn. It also is symbolic of bearing the responsibility on one's shoulders.

So, when Christ represents Himself as the One who holds the keys, and then told Peter that He would bestow upon him and His Church these keys, it is symbolic of the New Testament church being His Bride. The only ones who would be entrusted with these keys were the King (or husband); a high ranking, trusted steward of the household; or the wife.

Acknowledgement: I Know Your Works and Faithfulness

Jesus commends the church at Philadelphia for their works and acknowledges that they have remained faithful to His name, despite heavy persecution. He doesn't list a long line of accomplishments, in fact, He says she has only a "little strength", yet His message to this church is the most

---

3   Glens Davies, Lloyd Llwellyn-Jones;(2007), Greek and Roman Dress From A to Z. Rutledge, 2007 : Eve L'Ambra, Roman Women. (2001)Cambridge University Press pp 116-117.

4   History of Keys; historicallocks.com.

5   Isa. 22:22.

tender expression of love of all the messages. He doesn't love her for her list of accomplishments. He loves her because she has remained faithful to Him.

In Psalm 91 we hear the Lord sing of blessedness of those who put their love and trust solely in Him:

> *"Because he has set his love upon Me, Therefore will I deliver him.*
> *I will set him on high because he has known (been loyal to) My name.*
> *He shall call upon Me, and I will answer him.*
> *I will be with him in trouble,*
> *I will deliver him, and honor him." – Psalm 91:14-15*

Notice, it isn't because they are so great and capable or righteous in themselves, but because they love Him and have remained true to His name. Jesus doesn't berate this church for having only a little strength, but rather commends them for it! His strength is made perfect in our weakness, and the Lord does not look for mighty heroes, but for ones who will steadfastly love Him and rely on Him.

Philadelphia has done the one work Christ is most looking for in His church: she has held on to Him. She has remained faithful to His name, and she is holding on fast to His Word. She is counting on Him for everything, and that is what He most desires. Christ is not looking for a Bride who does things "for" Him, but one who does all things "through Him". He most desires that we fully rely on Him, looking to Him to be the hero of our story; the One who will provide, rescue, redeem and love us.

The Bride is not faultless because she is strong and perfect, but because she loves and is loved. She relies fully on that love.

> *"Who shall lay anything to the charge of God's elect? It is God that justifies.*
> *Who is he that condemns? It is Christ that died,*
> *yea rather, that is risen again,*
> *Who is even at the right hand of God, who also makes intercession for us.*
> *Who shall separate us from the love of Christ?*
> *Shall tribulation, or distress, or persecution,*
> *or famine, or nakedness, or peril, or sword?*
> *As it is written, For thy sake we are killed all the day long;*

We are accounted as sheep for the slaughter.
Nay, in all these things we are more than
conquerors through Him that loved us.
For I am persuaded, that neither death,
nor life, nor angels, nor principalities, nor powers,
nor things present, nor things to come,
nor height, nor depth, noir any other creature
shall be able to separate us form the love of God,
which is in Christ Jesus our Lord." – Romans 8:33-39

The Open Door

Jesus also said He would set before them an open door, which no man can shut. The door is likely connected with the keys to the kingdom. Jesus said He would open this door, and no one would be able to shut it – though some would certainly try. This door is symbolic of the kingdom, understanding, and opportunities. An open door is an open opportunity to access something.

This has special significance to the church of this Age because true believers are not only expelled from many congregations, but are told that they are not loved, chosen or the people of God. Many religious establishments claim the right to say who can get into Heaven or not. The official Church says, "No one can get into Heaven but by me". Jesus says, He alone decides that.

When Paul began his ministry, the first convert to Christianity in Europe was a woman named Lydia. (So this whole "Christian thing" in Europe began in a women's Bible study! Just saying.) Of her Paul wrote,

"And a certain woman named Lydia, a seller
of purple, of the city of Thyatira,
which worshipped God, heard us. Whose heart the Lord opened,
that she attended unto the things which were spoken of Paul." – Acts 16:14

Speaking of ministry opportunities to spread the gospel Paul wrote:

"But I will tarry at Ephesus until Pentecost.
For a great door and effectual is opened unto me,
And there are many adversaries." – 1 Cor. 16:8-9

"Furthermore, when I came to Troas to preach Christ's gospel,
And a door was opened unto me of the Lord." – 2 Cor. 2:12

"Praying also for us, that God would open unto us a door of utterance,
To speak the mystery of Christ, for which I am also in bonds." – Col. 4:3

The Lord threw open the doors for the Gentiles to access the kingdom of God through Jesus Christ. The New Testament church was given the commission to go into all the world, teaching all nations the gospel of Christ. And the Lord promised, though many would oppose and try to stop them, this door would remain open until His return. The church which Christ established was never the door, but the messenger. They are the ones whose job it is to deliver the invitation to the whole world that Christ has made a way for us. But power corrupts, and all too often, the messenger desires to become the message. This is the state of many which claim to be churches.

No Rebuke or Condemnation

For the church of Philadelphia, which represents the Bride of Christ, there is no rebuke. She is not blameless because of her own righteousness, but because Christ loves her and gave Himself for her. He Himself becomes our righteousness.

"There is therefore now no condemnation to them which are in Christ Jesus,
Who walk not after the flesh, but after the Spirit...
Who shall lay anything to the charge of God's elect (chosen ones)?
It is God that justifies.
Who is he that condemns?
It is Christ that died,
Yea rather, that is risen again, who is even at the right hand of God,
Who also makes intercession for us." – Romans 8:1,33-34

Though she receives no rebuke from Christ, this church suffers much abuse from the world and especially those who claim to be God's representatives.

Philadelphia has much in common with the other suffering church; the church at Smyrna.

The church of Smyrna represented the Second Age of Time in which Noah lived. The church at Philadelphia represents the Sixth Age of Time in which Jesus will return for His Bride. Jesus said,

> *"But as the days of Noe (Noah) were,*
> *So shall also the coming of the Son of Man be.*
> *For as in the days that were before the flood*
> *They were eating and drinking, marrying and giving in*
> *marriage, until the day that Noah entered into the ark,*
> *And knew not until the flood came and took them all away,*
> *So shall also the coming of the Son of Man be." – Matt. 24:37-39*

The Synagogue of Satan

Both these churches (Smyrna and Philadelphia) not only suffer persecution, they suffer it from the same group: by those who say they are Jews, but are actually of the synagogue of Satan.

It is important to note that Christ is NOT saying that Jewish synagogues are Satanic. The exact opposite is true. It is through the nation of Israel that God has chosen to reveal His Word and His Son – literally Himself. The response of true Christians to the nation of Israel should be one of love and gratitude.

This relationship is illustrated in the Old Testament book of Ruth. Although the story of Ruth is actual history, it is also illustrative of Christ and His relationship with the Church. Ruth is symbolic of the New Testament church, and Naomi is symbolic of Israel.

Ruth was a Gentile woman who married into a Jewish family. After her husband died, Ruth remained attached to her mother-in-law, Naomi. She determined to follow Naomi wherever she went and to worship her God. Ruth cared for Namoi and worked long, hard hours to provide for them. Naomi saw all of Ruth's hard work, but she knew a better way.

She told Ruth that what she needed was a Redeemer. She then instructed Ruth on where to find him and how to meet him. Ruth followed Naomi's instructions, and it led her to her Redeemer, who would also become her husband.

This is the relationship of Israel and the church. All the scriptures came through the Jews. Jesus said, "salvation is of the Jews." All the prophets and the apostles were of Israel. As we follow the teachings of the Bible, it leads us to the Redeemer. We realize we do not need to work for our salvation, we need a Redeemer who will cover us and provide for us. As Christians, we should love the nation of Israel because it is the family of our Redeemer. We should be grateful because their scriptures lead us to know God. When our Groom comes, the church and Israel will dwell together with Him as one family. We should love them, even if they do not yet love us, because they are the earthly family of Christ.

So when Jesus speaks of this group in Smyrna as being of the Synagogue of Satan, He is referring to those who say they are Jews, but are not. They say they are the people of God, but they are not the people of God. They claim to have a relationship with God, but in actuality they are in relationship with Satan. Whether they realize this or not is uncertain – but whether they realize it or not, the reality is the same.

These are they of whom Christ said,

"Woe unto you, lawyers!
For you have taken away the key of knowledge.
You entered not in yourselves,
and them that were entering in you hindered." – Luke 11:52

The reference to lawyers here is not the same group that we call lawyers today. In Christ's time, lawyers were those who were teachers and enforcers of the Law of Moses. They were often those who obey in the letter and not in the Spirit. Those who claim to be experts in God's will, but who do not even know Him.

This was gone into in greater detail in the chapter on Smyrna, but both churches suffer at the hands of those who claim to be God's representatives on earth. It is not just the world that persecutes them, but the established religious leaders. In this Sixth Day, persecution of believers, and even their execution, is a dominant theme of Age. The number one persecutor of those who have died as martyrs is the official church in Rome. Even many of those they canonize now as saints were people they themselves persecuted and killed. They are like the Pharisees of Christ's day, of which Christ said,

> *"Woe to you! For you build the sepulchers of the prophets,*
> *and your fathers killed them.*
> *Truly you bear witness that you allow the deeds of your fathers:*
> *for they indeed killed them, and you build*
> *their sepulchers." – Luke 11:47-48*

It is not coincidental that the two churches for which Christ had no rebuke were also the two which suffered the most persecution, and which are linked to each other in prophecy. Jesus said the days just before His return would be "as in the days of Noah". Since this was covered in more detail in the chapter on Sardis, I will only remind you that the days of Noah were characterized by deception, immorality, and perversion. It is clear from prophetic passages in both the Old and New Testaments that the persecution that would arise in the last days would come largely from religious systems, not just from a secular world. When the secular, political state and the church become the same thing, great abuse and persecution follow.

Command: Hold On To Your Crown!

The believers of the church at Philadelphia are commended for holding fast to their faith, and they are encouraged to continue to hold fast to what they have so that no one can take their crown. The unsettling thing about this is that the implication is clearly made that this crown could be lost. Those who believe that once you accept Christ is doesn't matter what you do, are grossly uninformed about what the Bible actually says. One's immortal soul may be saved, but one may still suffer loss. There are crowns at stake.

In the ancient Hebrew wedding ceremony, we saw that it is the bride who wears a crown, along with her groom. The apostles Paul, James, Peter and John all wrote of this crown the Bride would receive at the coming of her Groom.

"For I am now ready to be offered, and the time of my departure is at hand.
I have fought a good fight, I have finished my course, I have kept the faith.
Henceforth there is laid up for me a crown of righteousness,
Which the Lord, the righteous judge, shall give me at that day.
And not to me only, but unto all them also that love His appearing."
—Paul (2 Tim.4:6-8)

"Blessed is the man that endures temptation.
For when he is tried, he shall receive the crown of life,
Which the Lord has promised to them that love Him." – James 1:12

Another way the church at Philadelphia and the church at Smyrna are linked is that Smyrna is the only other church to which a crown is promised:

"Fear none of those things which thou shalt suffer.
Behold, the devil shall cast some of you into prison, that you may be tried,
And you shall have tribulation ten days.
Be thou faithful unto death,
And I will give you a crown of life." – Rev. 2:10

To both churches, the receiving of a crown is closely associated with following the Lord even in times of suffering and persecution. If we have remained faithful to the Lord, following Him even in difficult times, the One who wore the crown of thorns for us will reward us with a crown of gold.

Warning: I'm Coming Quickly!

The only warning given in the message to this church is addressed to those who have mistreated His beloved. To them He warns that there is humiliation, suffering and tribulation coming when He returns.

To the church, there is no warning, and no "or else" given. As long as the Bride holds faithful to her Groom, she can never be rejected. Instead, Jesus says, *"Behold, I come quickly!"* This is the first time in all the messages that those words are spoken as a promise rather than a threat. To the church at Ephesus, Pergamos, and Sardis those words were definitely spoken as a warning that when He comes, they were not going to like what happens. Jesus speaks to those churches as one might speak to disobedient children.

But to the church at Philadelphia, Jesus says in essence, "Hold on Beloved, … I'm coming quickly!" He speaks to this church as a betrothed husband would speak to His beloved wife who is being disrespected and mistreated. No rebuke. No criticism. No condemnation. Just assurance of His love and that He is coming to the rescue soon.

His words remind me of the scene in The Last of the Mohicans when Hawkeye has to temporarily leave Cora, the woman he loves, in the hands of the enemy in order to save her. He hates to leave her, and she is fearful of his going, but it is necessary. He looks into Cora's eyes and says, "Stay alive, no matter what occurs. I will find you. No matter how long it takes, no matter how far. I will find you." And you know He will come back for her, no matter what he has to endure, no matter what she has to endure, he will come back and rescue her.

Encouragement: I Will Protect You!

Jesus tells the church at Philadelphia that because they have "*kept the word of My patience*", He is going to keep them from the "*hour of trial (or temptation) which shall come upon all the world to try them that dwell upon the earth.*" The word "keep" used here is the Greek word "tereo". It means to "to attend to carefully, to take care of, to guard or protect, to hold fast"[6]. Because she has kept true to Him, He will keep her from what is coming on the earth.

We have been talking much about Days and what those represent. But the Bible also speaks about an Hour that is coming. An hour is a shorter period of time than a Day, but it too is characterized by a defining motif.

---

[6]   James Strong, *The New Strong's Exhaustive Concordance of the Bible* (Nashville: T. Nelson, 1990), G5083.

Jesus responded in several situations in which others were urging Him to some action with *"My hour has not yet come."*[7] When speaking of His second coming, He said, *"of that Day and Hour no man knows".*[8]

The Hour of Trial

Jesus refers to the time of His second coming and the events that follow as "the day and the hour".

"But of that day and hour knows no man,
No, not the angels of heaven,
But My Father only." – Matt. 24:36

"Therefore be you also ready
For in such an hour as you think not,
The Son of Man comes." – Matt. 24:44

The second half of what is called the Tribulation Period by many Bible scholars, is referred to as an hour in scripture, although it is actually 1260 days, or three and a half years.

"And the ten horns which you saw are ten kings,
which have received no kingdom as yet,
But receive power as kings one hour with the Beast." – Rev. 17:2

"And there was given unto him a mouth speaking
great things and blasphemies,
And power was given unto him to continue
forty and two months" – Rev. 13:5

It is for another study on the book of Revelation to go into this in more detail, but during the first half of the Tribulation Period, which are the days of the first six trumpets, there will be many who are converted and come to Christ, even in the midst of great persecution. The New Testament

---

7   John 2:4.
8   Matt. 24:36.

church is already raptured, but the testimony of the two witnesses and of the one hundred and forty-four thousand will result in the Gospel being preached all over the world. Many will be killed for their faith during this time, but nevertheless, many will believe.

The church of Philadelphia would include all the believers of the New Testament church; from every nation and language on earth. But at the end of this Age, there will be the conclusion of the 70th week of Daniel, which pertains specifically to the nation of Israel. During this "week" (seven years), the Lord will wrap up and fulfill the final prophecies given to Israel, and many will turn to Christ. This Sixth Day of Time; the Age of the church of Philadelphia, will see persecution on a global scale unlike anything the world has ever experienced before, but it will also see the revelation and power of God unlike any generation of believers has ever seen.

There may be some who will object to including those who come to Christ during the Tribulation period with the New Covenant believers on this Sixth Day of Time. But both groups will come to Christ during this millennia. I do not believe that both groups make up the Bride of Christ (tribulation age believers remain on earth during the Trumpet judgments, which the New Covenant age believers are already absent for), but both groups will take part in the heavenly kingdom and escape the hour of wrath that will come upon the whole world.

I believe this is what Christ was talking about when He told the parable of the 10 virgins in Matthew 25. In the parable, there are ten virgins who are awaiting the return of the bridegroom. Note, they are not the Bride (there is only 1 bride), but they are waiting for the Bridegroom. They are virgins, which in prophetic language symbolizes those who worship the true God, and not idols. Israel, and especially Judah, are represented as virgins in prophecy. They are awaiting the Groom, which is symbolic of Messiah. Five of these virgins have oil (symbolic of the Holy Spirit, which is given to the church) in their lamps and five do not.

Suddenly, at midnight, the cry came, "Behold the bridegroom comes! Go out to meet Him!" Those with oil (Holy Spirit) in their lamps "go out" (symbolic of the rapture of the church) to meet the Groom. While the foolish virgins then scramble to go and get oil as well, the bridegroom comes and those who are ready go in with him to the marriage, and the door is shut.

Although many will come to Christ during the first half of the Tribulation Period, there will be no converts during the last three and a half years. The door in Heaven is closed, and it is the Hour of Judgment that will come upon the whole world. The Seal Judgments involve a quarter of the earth. The Trumpet Judgments cover one third (although the whole world will feel the effects), but the Bowl judgements are upon the whole world. This is not a study of the book of Revelation, but what we are concerned with here is that the church at Philadelphia is told they will be kept from this Hour, and it is the generation of unbelievers that see the second coming of Christ – in the Sixth Day of Time – that will also experience this Hour.

"I Have Loved You"

The sweetest promise of any Christ made to the churches, is His assurance that He will openly, publicly, and unashamedly proclaim His love for them to all the world . The Greek word translated "love" here is the word "agapao"[9], and it means" to take pleasure in, to prize above all others, to be unwilling to abandon or to do without, to have preference for, to desire". Because she has held on to Him, He will hold on to her. She has remained true to His name, and He will proudly proclaim her name. This is what the Groom does for the Bride. Jesus pointedly said that He would do so in front of those who had persecuted her.

As we have seen, this church is rejected and maligned by those who say they are Jews and are not. The clear indication is that this church is predominately non-Jewish. Paul said, writing of and to the New Testament church:

> "I will call them 'My people', which were not My people,
> And her 'Beloved', which was not beloved.
> And it shall come to pass, that in the place where it was said unto them,
> 'You are not My people',
> There shall they be called the children of the living God." – Romans 9:25-26

---

9   James Strong, *The New Strong's Exhaustive Concordance of the Bible* (Nashville: T. Nelson, 1990), G25.

Paul goes on to explain that the Gentiles, who were once not the people of God, have now attained the promises of God by grace through faith. He further states that Israel, who were once called the people of God, as a nation, had not found the righteousness they sought because they sought it by their own works and merit and not by grace. God's grace was never meant to exclude or to choose one race or nation over another, but to open wide the door to all people, of every tribe, nation and tongue. All the merit is His, all the blessing is ours.

To any believer who has suffered any form of persecution for their faith: whether it be by being ostracized (which is so painful, especially to the young), to being discriminated against and maligned, to being outright persecuted economically and physically, this verse is their great hope and faith. As they weep into the night, they comfort themselves with knowing, "One Day, they'll know I'm not what they say. I know I'm loved, and One Day, they will too." Persecution has many forms, and your persecution may seem trivial to others, but Heaven is watching and taking note. Christ will not just cause those who have persecuted His Beloved to know that He has loved Her, He will cause those who tormented her to come and bow at her feet. Wow!

Writing prophetically of this time of great persecution, the prophet Malachi wrote:

"You have said, 'It is vain to serve God'
And 'What profit is it that we have kept His ordinance,
and that we have walked mournfully before the LORD of hosts?'
And now we call the proud happy.
Yea, they that work wickedness are set up,
Yea, they that tempt God are even delivered.
Then they that feared the LORD spoke often to one another,
And the LORD harkened and heard it,
And a book of remembrance was written before Him
For them that feared the LORD, and that thought upon His name.
'And they shall be Mine', says the LORD of hosts,
'in that day when I make up My jewels,
And I will spare them, as a man spares his own son that serves him.
Then shall you return, and discern between the righteous and the wicked,
Between him that serves God and him that
serves Him not." – Malachi 3:14-18

The promise of our Lord is ours to claim. Even just speaking to others about the Lord, encouraging them and reminding them of His truth, is enough to be remembered and rewarded. Believers may be ostracized and rejected here, but they are famous in Heaven. Books are written and read about them in Heaven! All of Heaven is watching and cheering on the church, that is enough to keep the faith[10].

Jesus is watching over His church closely. The Father Himself loves us, and notes every pain, every sorrow, every sacrifice, no matter how small. No act of faith and love is too small to be noted.

> *"And whosoever shall give to drink unto one of these little ones*
> *A cup of cold water only, in the name of a disciple,*
> *Verily I say unto you,*
> *He shall in no wise lose his reward." – Matt. 10:42*

One day, it will be worth it all. Paul said,

> *"For I reckon that the sufferings of this present time*
> *Are not worthy to be compared with the glory*
> *which shall be revealed in us...*
> *What shall we then say to these things?*
> *If God be for us, who can be against us?...*
> *Who shall separate us from the love of Christ?*
> *Shall tribulation, or distress, or persecution,*
> *Or famine, or nakedness, or peril, or sword?...*
> *Nay, in all these things we are more than*
> *conquerors through Him that loved us.*
> *For I am persuaded, that neither death, nor life,*
> *Nor angels, nor principalities, nor powers,*
> *Nor things present, nor things to come,*
> *Nor height, nor depth, no any other creature,*
> *Shall be able to separate us from the love of God*
> *Which is in Christ Jesus our Lord." – Romans 8:18,29-31,35,37-38*

---

[10]   Heb. 12:1-2, 22-24.

Promise to Overcomers: Go Out No More

Jesus makes many beautiful and wonderful promises to the overcomers of this church of the Sixth Day. First, He promises that He will make them a *"pillar in the temple of My God, and he shall go no more out."* In Biblical terms, the people "came in" to worship and "went out" to war. Jesus is promising that the overcomers, who have had to fight so many battles and temptations here, will never have to "go out" again.

Saying that they would be in His temple (or abode) and never have to go out also has the connotation that they are not visitors in His house, but part of the household. The family who dwell in the house do not ever have to leave. His home will be their home.

Pillars of the Temple

What did Jesus mean when He said overcomers would be pillars in His temple? Paul reminds us that we, the New Testament Age believers, are the temple of the Living God[11]. In a prophetic Psalm, David writes:

> *"I will sing a new song unto thee, O God*
> *Upon a psaltery and an instrument of ten strings*
> *Will I sing praises unto thee...*
> *That our sons maybe as plants grown up in their youth;*
> *That our daughters may be as corner stones,*
> *Polished after the similitude of a palace." – Psalm 144:9, 12*

When I was in Israel in 2016, we visited a wonderful archeological site at Magdala. There we toured a special chapel that had been built to commemorate the ministry and miracles of Christ. In the chapel, there were a number of pillars, and each pillar was dedicated to a different woman of the Bible who had followed Christ. We enjoyed walking from pillar to pillar, reading the names inscribed on each one, and celebrating the women of faith who had gone before us. Then we came to one final pillar, which had no name inscribed on it. We were thrilled when we were

---

[11]   1 Cor. 3:16.

told that this pillar was dedicated to us; to all the women today who choose to walk with Christ. The temple of Christ in heaven is made up of His people, and our very selves become the pillars!

In Revelation 15 we are told something very special about the temple of God in heaven. The events described take place at the end of the Trumpet judgments, but before the Bowl judgements. First, we see a great multitude of people in heaven; those who had gotten the victory over the beast and his mark, and they all have harps and are singing. We are told that the temple of God in heaven is opened. Remember, we are the temple, and Jesus said to the church of the Sixth day that He would place before them an open door. But a little later, we see that seven angels come out of the temple with the seven final judgments for earth – the Bowl judgments. Then John writes:

> "And the temple was filled with smoke from the
> glory of God, and from His power;
> And no man was able to enter into the temple,
> Till the seven plagues of the seven angels were fulfilled." – Rev. 15:8

This is a closed door. This is one way we know that no one will be "saved" during the final half of the tribulation period. During the Trumpet judgments, we are told what is happening on earth to two groups of people: those who take the mark of the Beast, and those who do not. But during the Bowl judgments, there is only one group of people recorded: those who refuse to repent and glorify God. There is never any mention of any repenting and turning to God during this time. The door to heaven is Closed.

As in the parable of the 10 virgins, there will come a day when Christ returns for all those who are ready – Jew or Gentile alike. But there will also come a day when it will be too late to repent and turn to Him. Today is the day of decision, because the time is very short. We are already at the end of the sixth day!

The Bride's Name Revealed

Jesus told the church at Philadelphia that when He comes, He will write on them His new Name and the name of the New Jerusalem – which we are told is actually the Bride of Christ[12].

The study of the New Jerusalem will have to wait until we study the book of Revelation together, but the Bride of Christ is clearly revealed as being the New Jerusalem. Hebrews 12: 22 calls it the "heavenly Jerusalem", and mentions briefly those who dwell there:

"But you are come unto the mount Sion,
And unto the city of the living God, the heavenly Jerusalem,
And to an innumerable company of angels,
To the general assembly and church of the firstborn,
Which are written in heaven,
And to God, the judge of all,
And to the spirits of just men made perfect,
And to Jesus, the mediator of the new covenant..." - Heb. 12:22-24

We see there are individuals from several different groups who are mentioned as being in heaven: angels, the church, the spirits of just men made perfect, God and Jesus. The "just men made perfect" is a reference to Old Testament saints and the righteous of Israel. We are told in Gen. 6:9 that Noah was a just man, David made many references to believers in Israel as the just (as opposed to sinners and the unrighteous), and Joseph, Mary's husband was called a just man[13], as was John the Baptist[14].

Paul states;

"For not the hearers of the law are just before God,
but the doers of the law shall be justified." – Romans 2:13

Here again, equating those who are obedient to the law of God as the just. The point to all this being that not everyone in Heaven is the Bride, but the Bride is known as the New Jerusalem there.

---

12   Rev. 21:1-3, 9-10.
13   Matt. 1:19.
14   Mark 6:20.

The earthly Jerusalem is the capital city of Israel. It is the homeland of those who are born of Abraham, Isaac, and Jacob. It is the city of the Jews, those born on earth of the chosen family. The heavenly Jerusalem is for those who have been born again. They may not be born of Abraham's body, but they are born of Abraham's faith, and have their names written in Heaven.

"For he is not a Jew, which is one outwardly,
Neither is that circumcision, which is outward in the flesh,
But he is a Jew, which is one inwardly:
And circumcision is that of the heart,
In the spirit, and not in the letter,
Whose praise is not of men, but of God." – Romans 2:28-29

"For the promise, that he should be the heir of the world,
Was not to Abraham, or to his seed through the law,
But through the righteousness of faith...
Therefore it is of faith,
That it might be by grace,
To the end the promise might be sure to all the seed,
Not to that only which is of the law,
But to that also which is of the faith of Abraham,
Who is the father of us all." – Rom. 4:13, 16

A New Name

The final promise to the overcomers of the church of Philadelphia is that Christ will share with her His New Name. On whom else but the Bride does the Groom bestow His new name? This promise was not made to any other church – only the church of the Sixth Day – the church of the New Covenant – made up of believers from every tribe, tongue, nation and people.

Philadelphia, Symbolic of the Sixth Age: The Day of Beasts, Man & the Bride

Historically, the Sixth Age of time began around 1033 A.D. and continues until the 2nd coming of Christ. This is our present time. Although that is when the Sixth Day began, Philadelphia is one of the two churches which make up the Times of the Gentiles. Both Philadelphia and Sardis exist within these two days. Sardis represents those who have the label "Christian", but deny the Word of God and corrupt the teachings of Christ. When Jeus addressed Sardis, He said, "I know your works." Full stop. No other comment on her works. She was full of works. Sardis is all about works. She thinks her works will earn her eternal life, but she is dead. Philadelphia represents those who do not rely on their own strength, but on Christ for their salvation. To Him alone belongs all the praise and glory. They remain faithful to Christ, even in times of persecution. They are the ones who obey Christ's command to "Take up your cross and follow Me."[15]

The New Testament Church Age (synonymous with the times of the Gentiles) began on the day of Pentecost when the Holy Spirit was given to all who followed Christ – Jews and Gentiles alike[16]. From the very earliest days of church history, even as the New Testament was being written and the apostles were still alive and teaching, there were two factions in the church. There were those who were loyal to the Word of God and the gospel as it was taught by Christ and the apostles; and those who came in with heretical ideas, and the desire to have preeminence over the church[17]. Their corrupt teaching emphasizes gaining power and wealth rather than godliness.

The first thousand years of the Church Age (33AD – 1033 AD) was dominated by the growing force of the Catholic church, and the waning power of the Roman Empire. At the beginning, the church was persecuted by Rome, and the pagan world. Many of the first bishops died as martyrs for the cause of Christ and the gospel. By the end of that Age, however, Rome and the Church had merged into the Holy Roman Empire, dominated by the Catholic church in Rome. The merging of church and

---

[15]   Matthew 16:24.
[16]   Acts 2.
[17]   1 John 1:9; Acts 20:29; Matt. 7:17; Jude 1:3-4, 17-21; 1 Timothy 4:1-3.

government accomplished what persecution could not. Christians, who once laid down their lives rather than bow to idols, were now taught to bow and venerate statues of the saints, icons, relics. Scripture, once held in high esteem, was now actively suppressed by the official church. The absolute power of the popes and the institutionalized church in Rome, corrupted its leadership and abused its people. That was the time of the Dark Ages, and many were martyred for their faith and loyalty to the Word of God at the hands of the Church.

As we have studied in the chapter on the Sixth Age in Part 1 of this book, at the dawn of the Sixth Age, nation states began to emerge. The world was no longer under the absolute control of one global political power. A growing number of nations claimed sovereignty over themselves. However, all these nations were still heavily controlled and influenced by the official Church at Rome. The pope had become a king maker. Crusades and Inquisitions sought to control the world through force, intimidation and even death. And all this destruction was supposedly done in the name of Christ. One can hardly think of greater blasphemy than to torture and kill the children of God, and claim to be doing it in the service of our Heavenly Father.

Each of these emerging nations adopted as its symbol an animal – real or mythical. There is the English Lion, the Scottish Unicorn; the Russian Bear, and the American Eagle, just to name a few. As on the sixth day of creation, in which God created all the many animals, this Age sees the rise of many national beasts. It will culminate with the rise of The Beast of Revelation, and the coming of the Son of Man for His Bride.

As this new Age of Reformation and Enlightenment grew, two significant things happened; the Word of God became more widely available to people in the language of the common man, and the world opened up for people to travel and settle the far reaches of the earth.

The invention of the moveable type printing press, made the Bible more accessible to everyone, not just the clergy or the rich. When the Bible was translated into the common man's language, for the first time people were able to read the Bible for themselves. They began to question unbiblical teaching and authority.

"When they compared the beliefs and practices of the early church and the teachings of the Bible to those of the church in their own day, (they)

found glaring differences... Many people were shocked to discover that
a number of the most common practices of medieval Christianity (for
example, the veneration of relics and the sale of indulgences) were not
found in either the New Testament or the post-apostolic church." [18]

Because reading the scriptures weakened their authority and ability to define truth, the Catholic church of Rome vehemently opposed the reading and distribution of the Bible.

The growing access to the word of God led the Reformers to try to purify doctrine and teaching within the Catholic church. When this was met with persecution and inquisition, the Protestants left the church all together.

"Outspoken reformers like John Wycliffe in England, and John Huss
in Bohemia challenged papal authority and claimed that if popes did
not conform to the bible in their teaching and behavior, they should not
be obeyed... (they) criticized the sale of indulgences and his own king's
military alliance with the pope. In the end, politics and theology conspired
at the Council of Constance, which condemned both men. Huss was
burned at the stake in 1415; and because Wycliffe had already died in
1384, officials had to disinter his body to carry out the council's order.
They burned his corpse and threw the ashes in the Swift River." [19]

The driving force of the Protestant Reformation was a renewed focus on Scripture as authority rather than the clergy. As the Age of Exploration opened new lands, the persecutions from the official church, which was now hand in hand with the government, led to a great protestant migration to the New World.

This history of both the Church and most of the Western world could be described as a war between the church of Sardis and the church of Philadelphia. Sardis believes she holds the power to give eternal life to whomever she chooses and that she is the sole representative of God on earth. Philadelphia holds true to the inerrancy of scripture, and that salvation is in Christ alone. Certainly, many of the wars that have been

---

[18]   Publishers Preface, Thomas A'Kempis. *Imitation of Christ.* (1999) Nashville, Tennessee. Thomas Nelson, Inc.

[19]   (Kempis, 1999) Publisher's Preface.

fought, especially in the early part of this millennia, were so-called "holy wars".

This is not to say that all abuse of power and corruption lie solely within one church or denomination. The tendency to abuse power, deny the faith, and chase after wealth and prestige is not unique to one religion. The abandonment of the Bible as the standard of truth, and the compromise with the world on issues of morality knows no denominational or cultural bounds. The Lord looks on our individual hearts, not on our denominational affiliation. Jesus said, "I am He which searches the minds and hearts, and I will give to every one of you according to your works."[20] Sardis and Philadelphia don't represent the Catholics and the Protestants. They represent institutionalized religion, with all its abuses and worldliness; and true, authentic followers of Christ.

Despite the schism in Christianity, the faith itself continued to grow and spread around the world. With the growth of Christianity, also came the growth of new opposition. At the dawn of the 20th century, theoretical Science began to pose real opposition to traditional faith. Humanism and Evolutionary thought gained strength, and a new kind of persecution and suppression began to overtake believers. In this Sixth Age, as creationism and the Bible is rejected, the teaching that man is not only just another beast, but also evolved from beasts, gained popularity and general acceptance. In a very real sense, it is the Age of the Beast. This is the Sixth Day. This is the culture which surrounds the church of Philadelphia.

In conclusion, the Sixth Age of Time began around 1033 AD and continues until the present. No one knows for sure WHEN the Day will end, but we know HOW it will end!

The order of creation on the sixth day, was the animals, man, and finally the woman. In the same order, this Sixth Day will culminate with the Rise of The Beast of Revelation, and the return of the Son of Man for His Bride, the Church.

To this church, Christ had no rebuke or warning. Because of His redeeming blood shed on the cross, there is no condemnation for the Bride (those who walk after the Spirit, and not after the flesh.[21]).

---

[20]   Rev. 2:23.
[21]   Romans 8:1

"Blotting out the handwriting of ordinances that was against us,
Which was contrary to us,
And took it out of the way,
Nailing it to His cross."- Colossians 2:14

This age of believers will suffer great persecution by those who are against Christ, which sadly would include some claim to be His voice on earth. Before this Day is over, there will be global persecution of all who hold true to Jesus Christ and His Word. World leaders will merge their nations into a One World Government, and one world religion will take the place of all the various faiths. This unified government and religion will venerate the Beast, the one who heads both government and religion. Anyone who fails to profess allegiance to them will be persecuted, and even killed. Like Rome and the Romanized church before them, this hybrid national church will tolerate no opposition. But God has always had His people. There will be true followers of Christ, even in this age. They will be conspicuous for their love of Christ, adherence to Scripture as the Word of God, and faithfulness to the purity of the Gospel.

Jesus said He has put an open door in front of the true believers of this Age, and no one can shut it – not even those who claim to be His agents and who claim to have the power to shut us out. When Jesus promises to make the overcomers like pillars in His temple in heaven, and they would never again have to go out, it has a particularly poignant meaning to those who were forced out of the official church because of their loyalty to Christ and the Word of God.

To believers of this Age Jesus says, "Behold I come quickly". He is coming to rescue His Bride. When He comes, He will cause all those who maligned them to bow at their feet and to know that He has loved them.

Jesus promises the overcomers of this church that when He comes for them, they will receive a crown, the name of "New Jerusalem" (which is the name of the Bride of Christ according to Revelation), and share with them His New Name. This – the church of Philadelphia, is clearly The Bride.

Sixth Church: Philadelphia - Faithful

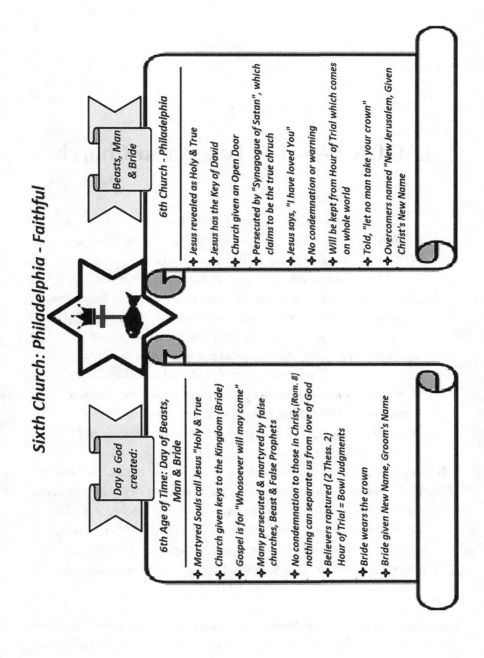

Beasts, Man & Bride

6th Church - Philadelphia

- ❖ Jesus revealed as Holy & True
- ❖ Jesus has the Key of David
- ❖ Church given an Open Door
- ❖ Persecuted by "Synagogue of Satan", which claims to be the true church
- ❖ Jesus says, "I have loved You"
- ❖ No condemnation or warning
- ❖ Will be kept from Hour of Trial which comes on whole world
- ❖ Told, "let no man take your crown"
- ❖ Overcomers named "New Jerusalem, Given Christ's New Name

Day 6 God created:

6th Age of Time: Day of Beasts, Man & Bride

- ❖ Martyred Souls call Jesus "Holy & True
- ❖ Church given keys to the Kingdom (Bride)
- ❖ Gospel is for "Whosoever will may come"
- ❖ Many persecuted & martyred by false churches, Beast & False Prophets
- ❖ No condemnation to those in Christ, (Rom. 8) nothing can separate us from love of God
- ❖ Believers raptured (2 Thess. 2) Hour of Trial = Bowl Judgments
- ❖ Bride wears the crown
- ❖ Bride given New Name, Groom's Name

CHAPTER 10

LAODICEA – The Lukewarm Church

"And to the angel of the church of the Laodiceans write,
'These things says the Amen, the Faithful and True Witness,
the Beginning of the creation of God:
'I know your works, that you are neither cold nor hot.
I could wish you were cold or hot. So then, because you are lukewarm,
and neither cold nor hot, I will vomit you out of My mouth.
Because you say, 'I am rich, have become wealthy, and
have need of nothing'—and do not know that you are
wretched, miserable, poor, blind, and naked—
I counsel you to buy from Me gold refined in the fire, that you
may be rich; and white garments, that you may be clothed,
that the shame of your nakedness may not be revealed; and
anoint your eyes with eye salve, that you may see.
As many as I love, I rebuke and chasten. Therefore be zealous and repent.
Behold, I stand at the door and knock. If anyone hears My voice and opens
the door, I will come in to him and dine with him, and he with Me.
To him who overcomes I will grant to sit with Me on My throne, as
I also overcame and sat down with My Father on His throne.
"He who has an ear, let him hear what the Spirit says to the churches.'"
– Rev. 3:14-22

Laodicea was a town in the Roman province of Asia. Just a few miles away
was the town of Colossae, which is why in his letter to the Colossians,
Paul mentions that he wants them to share the letter with those at

Laodicea[1]. It seems likely that the gospel came to Laodicea, if not from Paul directly, then from his converts in the nearby cities of Ephesus or Colossae. What is evident from the text is that the church of Laodicea was rich, full, and had need of nothing.

The name "Laodicea" literally means "Justice or Power of the People or Laity".[2] This church is the living embodiment of the verse, "everyone did what was right in his own eyes"[3]. But God is looking for men like David, who "did what was right in the eyes of the Lord"[4].

Laodiceans and Nicolaitans

One can't help but notice the similarities between the meaning of the names Laodicea and Nicolaitans. Laodicea means "power of the people", and Nicolaitan means "power over the people". Under the teaching of the Nicolaitans, there were those lording it over the people to oppress them. Here, the people themselves reject authority and are rich, wealthy, and have need of nothing – at least in their own eyes.

The Example of Korah

There are two Old Testament references that seem to echo what was happening in this church – at least in attitude. The first is found in Numbers 16:1-3:

> "Now Korah ..., took men; and they rose up before Moses with some of the children of Israel, two hundred and fifty leaders of the congregation, representatives of the congregation, men of renown. They gathered together against Moses and Aaron, and said to them, "You take too much upon yourselves, for all the congregation is

---

1 Colossians 4:13-16.
2 James Strong, *The New Strong's Exhaustive Concordance of the Bible* (Nashville: T. Nelson, 1990), G2993.
3 Judges 17:6, 21:25.
4 1 Kings 15:5.

holy, every one of them, and the LORD *is among them. Why then*
do you exalt yourselves above the assembly of the LORD?"

Korah was of the lineage of Levi. As such, he had a calling as one
who served in the tabernacle and assisted the priesthood of Aaron. Yet he
decided that neither he, nor any of the children of Israel, needed to follow
the leadership of Aaron and Moses. He reasoned that they were God's
people and just as holy as Aaron and Moses. In his own mind, he was
rich and wealthy and had need of nothing. By the time God had finished
explaining things to him, it had cost him and his whole family their lives.
It is a dangerous thing to behave presumptuously before the Lord.

The Example of Babylon

The second example is even more poignant. It is a prophecy against
Babylon because they lived in pleasure and trusted in their own greatness
and wealth. It is found in Isaiah 47:8-11:

"Therefore hear this now, you who are given to pleasures,
Who dwell securely, Who say in your heart,
'I am, and there is no one else besides me;
I shall not sit as a widow, Nor shall I know the loss of children';
But these two things shall come to you In a moment, in one day:
The loss of children, and widowhood. They
shall come upon you in their fullness
Because of the multitude of your sorceries,
For the great abundance of your enchantments.
"For you have trusted in your wickedness; You have said, 'No one sees me';
Your wisdom and your knowledge have warped you;
And you have said in your heart, 'I am, and there is no one else besides me.'
Therefore evil shall come upon you; You shall not know from where it arises.
And trouble shall fall upon you; You will not be able to put it off.
And desolation shall come upon you suddenly, Which you shall not know."

This same attitude is also seen in Psalm 10:2-7 where the wicked trust in their pride and prosperity and not in the Lord:

"For the wicked boasts of his heart's desire;
He blesses the greedy and renounces the LORD.
The wicked in his proud countenance does not seek God;
God is in none of his thoughts.
His ways are always prospering; Your judgments are far above, out of his
sight; As for all his enemies, he sneers at them. He has said in his heart,
"I shall not be moved; I shall never be in adversity."
His mouth is full of cursing and deceit and oppression;
Under his tongue is trouble and iniquity."

Gain Does Not Equal Godliness

This church confused material wealth, power and prosperity with godliness. They assumed that because they were not in adversity, then they must be pleasing to God. They fit the description of those with false teaching that Paul warned Timothy to watch out for:

"… men of corrupt minds and destitute of the truth,
who suppose that godliness is a means of gain.
From such withdraw yourself. Now godliness with contentment is great gain.
For we brought nothing into this world, and it
is certain we can carry nothing out.
And having food and clothing, with these we shall be content.
But those who desire to be rich fall into temptation and
a snare, and into many foolish and harmful lusts which
drown men in destruction and perdition.
For the love of money is a root of all kinds of evil,
for which some have strayed from the faith in their greediness,
and pierced themselves through with many sorrows." – 1 Tim. 6:5-10

If persecution and trials have a tendency to purify a church and weed out those who are not authentic, then it seems evident that wealth, prosperity and ease tend to breed hypocrisy and corruption- which we definitely see in this congregation. Smyrna and Philadelphia received no rebuke, Laodicea received no commendation. They were not necessarily outright evil, they were merely lukewarm and unconcerned. Like the frog in the pot that is slowly brought up to a boil, they did not even recognize their peril.

Revelation of Christ: The Beginning of Creation

Christ reveals Himself as the Amen, the Faithful and True Witness, and the Beginning of the creation of God. As we have seen in the messages to every church, how Christ reveals Himself also reveals what is going on in that time. Here, He is "the beginning of the creation of God".

I believe that the church of Laodicea is symbolic of the church on earth during the Millennial Reign of Christ. This is not those who have already been raptured and transformed into their Heavenly bodies from the previous ages, but rather the people who remain after the Tribulation and their children. They recognize Jesus as the "Amen", because He has had the last word in the Tribulation. They recognize Jesus as the "Beginning of the Creation of God", because He has restored the earth to the way it was in the beginning of creation. We'll go into this in more detail in the final section of this chapter, but this is so evident in every aspect of His message to Laodicea.

Acknowledgement and Rebuke: You're Lukewarm

Much like the church in Sardis, the acknowledgment and rebuke of Christ were practically the same thing. Christ could not mention their works without immediately rebuking them. Jesus said to them, "You're neither cold nor hot. You're lukewarm."

Nothing can be so offensive to one who is passionately in love than to be met with indifference. Outright rejection would be easier to take. The Lord feels this as well.

Warning: I Will Spew You Out of My Mouth!

For their lukewarmness, Christ said He would spew or vomit them out of His mouth. It is interesting to note a couple of things in this message: First, in order for Christ to spew them out of His mouth, they would have to be in His mouth already – which would indicate that their name was one He knew.

Secondly, to every other church there is the phrase "I come quickly" – uttered either as a warning or as a promise, but indicating that Christ was on His way. But to this church He says in essence "I'm here". "I'm standing at your door, knocking." And they were people He loved – He tells them, "As many as I love I rebuke and chasten", which He certainly was doing. These were people who believed they were already in relationship with Him because of their blessings. They did not realize they were blind, naked, poor and wretched.

Command: Repent

Christ's command, His solution to their spiritual poverty, is the same as it was to every other church: repent. They have an open invitation; He is knocking, but they have to choose to open the door.

Like every church, each individual must choose Christ for himself. And each person, having chosen, must then overcome the spirit of the age in which they live, and bring forth fruit of their faith.

Gold Tried in the Fire

Jesus advised the church at Laodicea that they need to produce "gold tried in the fire", which means that like believers of every other age, they must be willing to persevere in their faith. Following Christ may be easier during this time than it had been at any other time in history, but at the end of this Day, they will again have to go against the prevailing culture, which will rise up against Christ.

This used to just amaze me, because I had always believed that people only reject Christ because they just don't know Him. That it is because they just don't see Him. I thought, like the foolish rich man in Luke 16, that if only they could see someone rise up from the dead, they would believe. But the Lord said they will not. They did not believe when Lazarus rose, nor when Christ rose, nor will they when all the dead in Christ rise! Revelation 20:4 says that during this time those who had been killed for the cause of Christ will rise again and be part of Christ's government of the earth. Despite peace and plenty, people will rebel against this rule at the end of the age.

Get White Raiment from Me

Jesus said they needed to procure white garments to cover their nakedness. In prophetic language, nakedness is being in a fallen state without covering for ones sins. Rev. 19:8 tells us that these clean, white garments represent the righteous acts of the saints. A righteous act is any act based on faith in God's promises. When we are fully persuaded that God will do exactly what He says, and we act according to that belief, that is a righteous act.[5]

Satan managed to lure Adam and Eve into rebellion against God, even while they were living in the Garden of Eden, and he will manage to do so at the end of all ages, to those living in the restored earth. Just as Adam's fall resulted in him being aware of his nakedness, those in the millennial reign of Christ, who are not part of the raptured church or resurrected saints, will also need a solution for their spiritual poverty and nakedness.

Encouragement: I Rebuke You Because I Love You

If there were any words of encouragement from Christ to this church, this age of believers, it is this: that He loves them. The truth He is speaking may sound harsh, but He assures them that "As many as I love, I rebuke and chasten", and He urges them to take heart from this, and repent. He is standing right at their very door. He is knocking. He has not abandoned them and given them up. If they are willing, He is willing to commune with them.

---

5   Romans 4:21-24.

Jesus Isn't Coming... He's There!

Notice: to this church Jesus says, "Behold, I stand at the door and knock." To every other church He says, "I am coming", but to this church, He is here! He is right there with them, and His invitation to join Him is once again open to any who will "open the door" to Him.

Promise to Overcomers: You Will Sit With Me on My Throne

Overcomers would be granted the right to sit with Christ on His throne, just as He sat down with His Father on His throne.

"God, who at various times and in various ways
spoke in time past to the fathers by the prophets,
has in these last days spoken to us by His Son, whom He has appointed
heir of all things, through whom also He made the worlds;
who being the brightness of His glory and the express image of His person,
and upholding all things by the word of His power,
when He had by Himself purged our sins,
sat down at the right hand of the Majesty on high." – Hebrews 1:1-3

"But this Man, after He had offered one sacrifice for sins forever,
sat down at the right hand of God,
from that time waiting till His enemies are made His footstool."
– Hebrews 10:12-13

This final generation of believers will be granted the privilege of ruling and reigning with Christ, just as believers form the first six ages were. At first glance, this doesn't seem fair. They have a much fuller revelation of Christ than any other age had, and endured much less toil and suffering.

The Parable of Laborers in His Vineyard

I believe this tension is what Christ was teaching about in Matthew 20. He tells a kingdom parable about a man who hires laborers to work in his vineyard. He sends some out at the beginning of the day with the promise of pay at the end of the day. Later he goes out at the third hour, and again at the sixth hour, and the ninth hour, each time finding more people to send to work in his fields. Then at the eleventh hour he goes out again.

> *"And about the eleventh hour he went out,*
> *And found others standing idle, and said unto them,*
> *'Why stand you here all the day idle?'*
> *They said unto him, 'Because no man has hired us.'*
> *He said unto them, 'Go you also in to the vineyard....'*
> *So when even was come, the lord of the vineyard said unto his steward,*
> *'Call the laborers and give them their hire,*
> *Beginning from the last unto the first...."* – Matt. 20:6-8

Jesus goes on to say that every worker received the same reward – the last the same as the first- which did not sit well with those who had been working longest. They grumbled that they had born the burden and heat of the day, and so they should not get the same pay as those who came to work later. But the good man of the house said,

> *"Is it not lawful for me to do what I want with my own?*
> *Is your eye evil because I am good?*
> *So the last shall be first,*
> *And the first last;*
> *For many be called, but few chosen."* – Matt. 20:15-16

When Jesus established His New Testament church, there were many Jews who did not think Gentiles should be included with them in the blessings and promises of God. Israel had been toiling for God for centuries, why should the heathen now be allowed to be co-heirs with them? But the Lord was doing a new thing. He was breaking down walls and healing the division that had endured since the Tower of Babel. There, tongues divided nations. Now the Holy Spirit came and bridged the chasm between people of different tongues and nations. Now they would all be called the people of God.

The believers of the Seventh Day may not have to bear the heat that believers on the Sixth Day, or Second Day did, but they will have to make the choice to serve the Lord, the same as all the others, and they will be rewarded with a place in His eternal kingdom as well.

Laodicea, Symbolic of the Seventh Age: The Day of Rest

On the Seventh Day of Creation, God rested (or ceased) from all His work of creating. He blessed the seventh day and commanded that people should always remember it, and keep it holy.

The Seventh Day of Time, begins with Christ returning to the earth to set up His thousand-year reign, and ends with Satan being released and once again stirring up the nations against Christ. During this time, the earth will experience rest from all the wars, upheaval and labor pains it has endured during the sixth day. The church of Laodicea is symbolic of this age.

During this Age, the world is once again restored to its pre-fall conditions. Isiah prophesied of the kingdom of the coming Messiah,

> *"The wolf also shall dwell with the lamb,*
> *And the leopard shall lie down with the kid,*
> *And the calf and the young lion and the fatling together,*
> *And a little child shall lead them.*
> *And the cow and the bear shall feed,*
> *Their young ones shall lie down together,*
> *And the lion shall eat straw like the ox.*
> *And the sucking child shall play on the hole of the asp,*
> *And the weaned child shall put his hand on the cockatrice's den.*
> *They shall not hurt nor destroy in all My holy mountain,*
> *For the earth shall be full of the knowledge of the Lord,*
> *As the waters cover the sea."- Isaiah 11:6-11*

Isaiah continues his prophecy about this time after the Tribulation:

> *"And I will rejoice in Jerusalem,*
> *And joy in My people,*
> *And the voice of weeping shall be no more heard in her,*

nor the voice of crying.
There shall be no more thence an infant of days,
Nor an old man that has not filled his days,
For the child shall die an hundred years old,
But the sinner being an hundred years old shall be accursed.
And they shall build houses, and inhabit them,
And they shall plant vineyards, and eat the fruit of them…
For as the days of a tree are the days of My people,
And mine elect shall long enjoy the work of their hands.
They shall not labor in vain,
Nor bring forth for trouble,
For they are the seed of the blessed of the Lord,
and their offspring with them.
And it shall come to pass, that before they call, I will answer
And while they are yet speaking, I will hear.
The wolf and the lamb shall feed together,
And the lion shall eat straw like the bullock,
And dust shall be the serpent's meat.
They shall not hurt nor destroy in all My holy mountain, says the Lord."
– Is. 65:19-25

Laodicea is full and has need of nothing because there is no more curse upon the land. All things have been restored, and yet they too, like people of every age, will have to choose whom they will serve. Zechariah 14 speaks of this time as being a time of peace and plenty, but also that there will begin to be those who kick against the rules and law of the kingdom. So much so that according to Revelation 20, at the end of the thousand years, Satan will once again be able to stir up the nations against Christ.

I cannot help but notice similarities between Christ's message to this church and words He spoke to His disciples concerning His second coming:

Let your waist be girded and your lamps burning,
And you yourselves be like men who wait for their master, when
he will return from the wedding, that when he comes and knocks
they may open to him immediately. Blessed are those servants

whom the master, when he comes, will find watching. Assuredly,
I say to you that he will gird himself and have them sit down
to eat, and will come and serve them." – Luke 12:35-37

Notice the parallels. In both messages, Jesus comes and knocks for admittance. And where was He coming from? His wedding. He is not coming to His bride, but to His friends. What does Jesus advise them to do? To have their "waists girded". In the message to Laodicea, He advised them to procure white garments that they may be clothed. I believe both passages are addressed to those who will be on earth at the end of the Millennial reign of Christ.

The great challenge for those living during this age will be to realize that, although they are blessed with living in a peaceful, rich age, they still need to be saved. It is much harder for good, affluent, happy people to realize their spiritual poverty than it is for oppressed, or even wicked people. Because their need isn't obvious or pressing, it is easy for them to assume it doesn't exist.

Jesus doesn't warn them of His imminent return, because He has already returned. He is standing right there at the door, knocking.

Seventh Church: Laodicea - Lukewarm

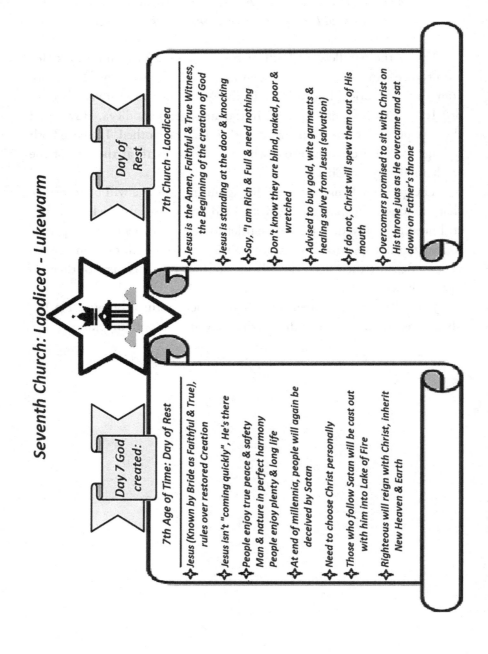

Day of Rest

7th Church - Laodicea

- Jesus is the Amen, Faithful & True Witness, the Beginning of the creation of God
- Jesus is standing at the door & knocking
- Say, "I am Rich & Full & need nothing
- Don't know they are blind, naked, poor & wretched
- Advised to buy gold, wite garments & healing salve from Jesus (salvation)
- If do not, Christ will spew them out of His mouth
- Overcomers promised to sit with Christ on His throne juas as He overcame and sat down on Father's throne

Day 7 God created:

7th Age of Time: Day of Rest

- Jesus (Known by Bride as Faithful & True), rules over restored Creation
- Jesus isn't "coming quickly", He's there
- People enjoy true peace & safety Man & nature in perfect harmony People enjoy plenty & long life
- At end of millennia, people will again be deceived by Satan
- Need to choose Christ personally
- Those who follow Satan will be cast out with him into Lake of Fire
- Righteous will reign with Christ, inherit New Heaven & Earth

CHAPTER 11

Echoes of the Past, Reflections
of the Future

The premise I proposed at the beginning of this book is that the seven days of creation are literal, but also symbolic of seven ages of time, each age being a thousand years. But there is another interesting pattern to be seen that Jesus Himself pointed out.

Jesus said that the end times would be "as in the days of Noah". Noah lived in the 2nd age of time. The end of the age which Christ was speaking about is the end of the 6th age of time. Using this as a guide, we can match up the three Days before Christ with the three Days after Christ and find startling similarities.

The First and Seventh Days

In the First Day of time (the days of Adam), the earth was in a pristine, unspoiled state. Man lived in the Garden of Eden and walked with God there. There was peace and harmony in nature, with nothing causing harm or hurt. People lived to be the age of trees.

In the Seventh Day of Time (the millennial reign of Christ), all these conditions will be true again. God will dwell on earth with mankind and will restore the earth to its former glory. Nature will be healed, and people will again live to be very old. The scripture says that the one who dies at the age of 100 will be considered to have died as a child.

In the First Day of time, this pristine state was spoiled when Satan, in the form of a Serpent invaded the Garden and influenced mankind to rebel against God and His word. In the Seventh Day of time, Satan will again invade the restored earth and try to usurp the Lord's authority. Revelation 12:9 identifies him as, "the great dragon... that serpent of old, called the Devil and Satan, who deceives the whole world."

The Second and Sixth Days

In the Second Day of time (the days of Noah), the earth experienced a world-wide cataclysm that destroyed all life on earth. The righteous were "taken up" to safety before this great judgment. That Day also saw the rise of a one-world government, religious system, and all-powerful ruler. He ruled over a nation called Babel. During this Day God divided the nations by giving them different languages.

In the Sixth Day of time the earth experiences these same events, but in reverse! The day begins when the Holy Spirit gave the gift of "tongues", which God gave to spread the gospel to all the earth. In Noah's day, different tongues caused the nations to separate. At Pentecost, the Holy Spirit caused people of all languages to come together and hear the Gospel. On this Day, there will again be the rise of a one-world government, led by a great despotic ruler. His kingdom is called Babylon in the book of Revelation. It will culminate in a world-wide cataclysmic judgment that destroys everything, while the people of God escape by being "taken up".

The Third and Fifth Days

In the Third Day of Time (the Days of Abraham and Moses), God called one man out of the nations to establish a new covenant and a new people. He began with one family with 12 sons, and in just a few generations they grew to be a mighty nation.

In the Fifth Day of Time (the early church age), God sent one man (Christ) into the earth to establish a new covenant, and to create a new people. He began with 12 disciples, and in just a few generations, they multiplied to the point where they turned the world upside down!

The Fourth Day

The Fourth Day of Time stands alone and above all the others. It is the central light of the Menorah. It is the Day of the King and the Cross. The Day that ties all the days before with all the days after. It is the center point of History, and the Day that marks the change in Time from which all nations still mark their calendars. It was the Day that changed everything.

CHAPTER 12

The Quest Continues

We have come to the end of our journey together, but we have by no means come to the end of our quest! There is still so much treasure to be found, this is just the beginning!

I love puzzles of all kinds, and one of my favorite pastimes is putting together jig saw puzzles. When we first dump all the pieces on the table, there are so many colors and shapes, and no discernable order or pattern. The task looks overwhelming, even impossible, at first glance. But then we begin to sort through the pile looking for the edge pieces, and slowly, we get our outline defined. Once all the edge pieces are in place, we have a framework in which to place all the other pieces. There is still a lot of work sorting and culling, but the pattern has become a lot more discernable.

You and I have started in Genesis, and ended in Revelation, but we have only just established the outline of this wonderful puzzle. There is a whole, wonderful world of text to explore, but now we can see where to place the other pieces.

I do not claim to be a prophet, but I am going to make a prediction. A prediction about you. If you have stayed with me throughout this treasure hunt, you are not going to be able to read scripture the same way you did before. Even if you don't completely agree with all the conclusions I have drawn, from now on, you are going to start seeing things in scripture you never noticed before. You will pick up a verse, and hold it to the light; and you will suddenly have an idea of where it belongs in the larger framework. Things will begin to fall into place. From being a book full of random, unconnected verses, you will begin to see patterns and order. This will happen even if you aren't trying to make it happen. Once the edge pieces are all in place, the rest is easier.

When I had finished my study of the seven days and seven ages, I started seeing the pattern repeated all over the Bible. It opened up scripture for me that I had never understood before.

If you will allow me, I would like to take you on one more exploration before we finish, because it illustrates what I am saying, and it is just too good not to share!

I have always found the Song of Songs a mystery. I have read through it many times, and have read some excellent commentaries on it, but none of them have ever fully satisfied my mind. There are certainly many wonderful parallels and teachings to be gotten from its study, but the book has always remained an enigma for me. Until after I finished my Seven Ages study.

This next chapter will not be an in-depth study of the book of the Song of Songs. It is just an assaying test of what treasure this ground still holds. I hope it will inspire you to dig more deeply to see what you can find for yourself.

CHAPTER 13

The Song of Songs

Solomon's Song of Songs, is supreme among songs in the same way Christ is "Lord of Lords" and "King of Kings". It is The Song, not only above all other songs, but it is also the Source from which all others songs flow.

"Both the singers and the players on instruments say,
'All my springs are in You." – Psa.87:7 NKJV

This Song reveals the Romance of the Ages; the love story of the Creator and His People. As we read through its chapters, we see unfolded the same story the Days of Creation and the Messages to the Churches tell.

In the Song of Songs, the young woman is symbolic of the church (God's beloved people) in every Age of Time.

The Song Begins

In the opening scene, a young woman suddenly appears and begins to sing:

"Let him kiss me with the kisses of his mouth –
for Thy love is better than wine…
Thy name is as ointment poured fourth,
Therefore do the virgins love Thee." – Song of Songs 1:2-3

The word "kiss" here is the Hebrew word "nashaq"[1], which means "to put together, to touch gently, to arrange, put in order, to join mouth to mouth, to meet together, to kiss". The word "ointment" is most often used in Scripture for anointing oil, by which people and objects are made consecrated unto God's use. It is symbolic of the Holy Spirit, who is poured out on Believers, making them holy to the Lord. Wine is symbolic of both the Spirit, and the blood[2], for both give life. The life of the body is in the blood[3], but by the breath man became a living Soul.

When we compare this to the opening scenes in Genesis, the similarity is striking. In Genesis 1:2, we are told the Spirit of God "moved upon the face of the waters"; the picture is of the Spirit hovering over the new creation, about to be born.

God speaks (breathes out His Word), and everything is formed. Then comes the crowning, glorious moment in creation, when God forms a man and woman "in His own image".

And the Lord God... breathed into his nostrils the breath of life,
and man became a living soul." – Gen. 2:7

The image evoked is of God giving man the "kiss of Life". He breathed from His mouth into Adam's nostrils, and His Spirit entered this piece of clay, and he became a Living Soul! He opens his eyes, and begins to sing The Song!

"Thy love is better than wine...
Thy name is as ointment poured forth,
Therefore do the virgins love Thee." – Song of Songs. 1:2-3

Who are these virgins who love Him, and who are also part of the Song?

---

[1]   James Strong, *The New Strong's Exhaustive Concordance of the Bible* (Nashville: T. Nelson, 1990), H5401.
[2]   Eph. 5:8; Luke 22:20.
[3]   Gen. 9:4; Gen. 2:7.

Where were you when I laid the foundations of the earth?...
When the morning stars sang together,
and all the sons of God shouted for joy?" – Job 38:4,7

The Old and New Testament tell us that the angels in Heaven sing over creation, and rejoice to see God's work on earth. Jesus said that the angels in heaven neither marry, nor are given in marriage, so they are virgin creations. The principle actors in this story are taking their places.

The new creation, beloved of the Lord now sings:

"Draw me, we will run after Thee.
The king has brought me into His chambers,
We will be glad and rejoice in Thee.
We will remember Thy love more than wine,
The upright love Thee." – Song of Songs 1:4

"And the LORD God planted a garden,
Eastward in Eden,
And there He put the man whom He had formed...
And the LORD God took the man,
And put him into the garden of Eden
To dress it and to keep it."-Gen. 2:8, 15

In this first Age of Time, Adam was not the only one drawn away. The phrase "draw away" means "to be drawn, led or lifted away"[4].

"And Enoch walked with God,
And he was not, for God took him."- Gen. 5:24

Where did God draw him away to? "Into His chambers".

But back to our principle story: Notice that the pronouns have changed to "we". Adam is joined by Eve, and together they sing and rejoice in the Lord.

---

4   James Strong, *The New Strong's Exhaustive Concordance of the Bible* (Nashville: T. Nelson, 1990), H4900.

The Mood Shifts

Suddenly, the rejoicing young woman changes her tone. A dark note enters the song. She has become self-conscious and shy:

"Look not upon me,
Because I am black,
Because the sun has looked upon me.
My Mother's children were angry with me.
They made me the keeper of the vineyards,
But mine own vineyard I have not kept." – Song of Songs1:6

"And the eyes of them both were opened,
And they knew that they were naked,
And they sewed fig leaves together,
And made themselves aprons.
And they heard the voice of the LORD God
Walking in the garden in the cool of the day.
And Adam and his wife hid themselves
From the presence of the LORD God
Amongst the trees of the garden.
And the LORD God called unto Adam, and said unto him,
'Where art thou?'
And he said, 'I heard Thy voice in the garden,
And I was afraid, because I was naked,
And I hid myself." – Gen. 3:7-10

God made man the keeper of the garden, but they sinned, and became ashamed of their skin and hid themselves. The "mother's children" were the angels, the other sons of God. The angels were angry that man had not kept their vineyard, and had left their first love.

Outside of the garden, man now had to toil by the sweat of his brow under the hot sun to provide for himself. He had lost his first place and failed to keep his own garden, but he was still loved. And he still longed for fellowship with the Father. But, whereas before God walked with him in the garden, now he wonders:

"Tell me, O Thou whom my soul loves,
Where You feed, where You make Your flock to rest at noon,
For why should I be as one that turns aside
By the flocks of Your companions?" – Song of Songs 1:7

In answer to her question, her Beloved answers:

"If you do not know,
O thou fairest among women,
Go you way forth by the footsteps of the flock,
And feed your kids beside the shepherd's tents." – Song of Songs 1:8

The Lord showed Adam and Even that the way to restored fellowship would be through the blood of the Lamb, which He Himself would provide. The Lord took the skin of the slain lamb and provided a covering for Adam and Eve. They understood from this that the way back would be through the Lamb.

Their son, Abel became a keeper of sheep as well, but his brother Cain was a "tiller of the ground". They each brought their sacrifices to worship the Lord. God accepted Abel's lamb, but He did not accept Cain's offering of fruit. The way back into fellowship would not be through the sweat of our brow (works), but through the blood of the Lamb. When Cain became angry, the Lord reasoned with him, showing him the way. In essence, *"If you don't know… go by the footsteps of the flock"*.

In the Song of Songs, it is the young woman asking where to find her Beloved. In Genesis, it is the Lord asking where His beloved has gone.

"And the LORD said unto Cain,
'Where is Abel your brother?" – Gen. 4:9

Cain became angry with his brother (another brother angry with his mother's child), and killed him. As a result, God marked Cain's skin, and Cain too lost his place. We don't know if the mark darkened his skin, as some have alleged, but we do know that it caused him to remain separate from others.

The Vineyard is Lost, But Not Their Love

The first stanza of the Song closes with the King assuring the young woman that she is still beautiful to him, and the young woman wistfully reminiscing :

"Behold, You are fair, my Beloved,
Yes, pleasant. Also our bed is green,
The beams of our house are cedars,
and our rafters of fir."- Song of Songs 1:16-17

Though much has been lost, their love is still strong. The place where they once were together (the garden) had a bed of grass, and rafters of trees. The garden is but a memory, but they still share fellowship together under the trees.

This is not meant to be a verse by verse study of the Song of Songs, so I will more quickly highlight the rest of the chapters. If you are looking for a place to "dig" next, this wonderful book would be a great place to study next.

Life Outside of the Garden

The second chapter of the Song of Songs highlights the events in the Second Age of Time: Noah's time.

The young woman is now living in the valley, and she sings:

"I am the rose of Sharon,
And the lily of the valleys." – S. of S. 2:1

The lily of the valley, and the rose of Sharon are both common wild flowers. She had been cultivated for the garden, but now she is living in the wilds. But her Beloved reassures her:

"As the lily among thorns,
So is My love among the daughters." – S.of S. 2:2

Noah, alone in his generation, found "grace in the eyes of the Lord". Noah stood out from all the "thorns" (thorns and tares are always symbolic of the unsaved) of his generation, as a lily (symbol of purity). He was a man who walked with God, was just in his dealings and pure in his generations.

The Banqueting House

She sings of being weak or sick, and asks her Beloved to strengthen and sustain her with provision. Her beloved brings her into his banqueting house, and his banner over her was love. This is symbolic of the Lord bringing Noah into the ark and sustaining him there on provisions during the Flood. Without a doubt, during all the tossing and turning of the horrific storm, Noah and all those with him experienced sea sickness! But they were also doubtless sick at heart. Everyone and everything they had ever known was gone. But the Lord sustained them.

The Rain is Over

"The voice of my Beloved!
Behold, He comes leaping upon the mountains,
Skipping upon the hills!...
My Beloved spoke and said unto me,
'Rise up, My love, My fair one,
And come away!
For lo, the winter is past,
The rain is over and gone.
The flowers appear on the earth,
The time of the singing of birds is come,...
The fig tree puts forth her green figs,
And the vines with tender grape give a good smell.
Arise, My love, My fair one,
And come away!" – S. of S. 2:8, 10-13

The symbolism is so obvious, one need hardly comment (but I will!). What a joyous day it was when Noah looked up and saw that the rain had ended! The time finally came when things began to grow upon the earth again, and the aroma must have been intoxicating.

First the Lord had caused Noah to "rise up and come away" in the ark, and then He instructed Noah when it was time to "rise up" and come out of the ark at last. Noah had looked trough the window and saw that the rain had stopped and the sun was shining. Compare that to verse 9 here, *"He looks forth at the windows, showing himself through the lattice."*

Noah then releases the dove, which comes back to him with the olive branch in her beak: symbolic of peace, rest, and new life budding. Genesis 8 tells us that the ark came to rest upon the mountains. The Beloved now sings to His love:

> *"O My dove,*
> *That art in the cleft of the rock,...*
> *Let Me see your countenance,*
> *Let Me hear your voice,*
> *For sweet is your voice..."* – S. of S. 5:14

Seeking Him In the City and Highways

Chapter three opens with the young woman rising up and going on a quest to find the One her soul loves. She seeks him in the city streets and highways. She doesn't know where she is going, because she is not seeking a place, but a person. He is her quest.

> *"I will rise now, and go about the city in the streets,*
> *And in the broad ways I will seek him whom my soul loves.*
> *I sought him, but I found him not."* – S. of S. 3:2

This third chapter is symbolic of the Third Age: The Age of Abraham, Isaac and Jacob. The Age in which Israel sojourned in the wilderness on the way to the Promised land.

> *"Now the LORD had said unto Abram,*
> *'Get out of your country, and from your kindred,*
> *And from your father's house,*
> *Unto a land that I will show you."* - Gen. 12:1

"By faith, Abraham, when he was called to go out into a place
which he should after receive for an inheritance, obeyed.
And he went out, not knowing where he was going....
For he looked for a city which has foundations whose
builder and maker is God." – Heb. 11:8,10

Then the young woman encounters watchmen (angels are called "The Watchers" in Daniel), and inquires if they have seen her love. She sings:

"It was but a little that I passed from them,
But I found him whom my soul loves.
I held him, and would not let him go,
Until I had brought him into my mother's house,
And into the chamber of her that conceived me." – S. of S. 3:4

After fleeing from his brother Esau, Jacob stayed with Laban for many years. Finally, it was time for him to go home to his father and mother's house. While he was on the way, the Angel of the Lord met him, and Jacob "wrestled" with him, holding on with all his might. Jacob refused to let Him go until He blessed him. After the blessing, Jacob travels on, and eventually returns to the house of his father and mother in Hebron. You can read about all this in Genesis 32-35

In The Wilderness

Now a whole chorus of young women begin to sing:

"Who is this that comes out of the wilderness like pillars of smoke,
Perfumed with myrrh and frankincense...?" – S. of S. 3:6

When the children of Israel left Egypt to return to the promised land, they sojourned in the wilderness for forty years, led by a pillar of smoke by day, and a pillar of fire by night.

The chorus of young women go on to sing about Solomon's "bed", and how it travels with men holding swords and is adorned with gold, silver and purple. In the description of the Ark of the Covenant, which traveled with the children of Israel in the wilderness, it was guarded by armed soldiers, and was adorned with gold, silver and purple. They sing of Solomon, who is the king of Israel at the time the Song of Songs was written, but the true king of Israel at was the Lord Himself[5]. His bed (the place where he rests) was the Ark, on which the glory of God rested.

She Has Found Him!

The next verse of the Song is sung mostly as a solo by the young man – the Beloved and King. There is no more seeking, they are together at last, and they revel in each other's presence. He extols her beauty and goes into detail of how he finds every part of her lovely.

This Age was the time of the Kings and Prophets. Israel is wandering no longer, and she meets with the Lord in the magnificent temple of Solomon. At the end of this Age, Christ is born, and begins His ministry, calling His disciples to follow Him. At His birth, and at His death, He is worshipped with frankincense and myrrh.

The Beloved sings:

> *"Until the day break,*
> *And the shadows flee away,*
> *I will get Me to the mountain of myrrh,*
> *And to the hill of frankincense....*
> *Come with Me from Lebanon, My spouse,...*
> *Look from the top of Amana,*
> *From the top of Shenir and Hermon,*
> *From the lions' dens,*
> *From the mountains of the leopards." – S. of S. 4:6,8*

The Lord Jesus Christ traveled the hills and lanes of Israel with His disciples, and particularly concentrated His ministry in the north, which is the location of all these hills. He invited His disciples to "Come, and follow Me".

---

5   Isaiah 43:15.

The Beloved compares his love to a garden and names nine kinds of fruit and spices that are in her. In Galatians 5:22-23, Paul lists nine "fruit of the Spirit" which will be in those who are Christ's. The Beloved then goes on to say that His love is "all fair… there is no spot in thee" [6]. He says she is "a well of living waters and streams". Compare this to these verses:

"Husbands, love your wives, even as Christ also loved the church,
And gave Himself for it, that He might sanctify and cleanse it
With the washing of water by the word.
That He might present it to Himself, a glorious church,
Not having spot, or wrinkle,
Or any such thing, but that it should be
Holy and without blemish." – Eph. 5:25-27

"He that believes on Me, as the scripture has said,
'out of his belly shall flow rivers of living water." – John 7:38

The young woman, moved by His lavish praise and declaration of love sings:

"Awake, O north wind,
And come, thou south,
Blow upon my garden,
That the spices thereof may flow out.
Let my Beloved come into His garden
And eat His pleasant fruits." – S. of S. 4:16

Compare that to:

"And suddenly there came a sound from heaven,
As of a rushing might wind,
And it filled all the house where they were sitting…
And they were all filled with the Holy Ghost…" – Acts 2:2-3

---

[6]   Song of Solomon 4:7.

The Beloved Goes Away!

In the first verse of this chapter, the Beloved is singing his last lines before he goes away. He sings:

> *"I am come into my garden, my sister, my spouse.*
> *I have gathered my myrrh with my spice.*
> *I have eaten my honeycomb with my honey,*
> *I have drunk my wine with my milk.*
> *'Eat, O friends. Drink, yes,*
> *Drink abundantly, O beloved."* - S. of S. 5:1

In His final night with His disciples before He goes to the cross, Jesus eats with them and says:

> *"And as they were eating,*
> *Jesus took the bread, and blessed it, and brake it,*
> *And gave it to the disciples, and said,*
> *'Take, eat; this is My body.'*
> *And He took the cup, and gave thanks, and gave it to them saying,*
> *'Drink you all of it. For this is My blood of the*
> *new testament..."* – Matt. 26:26-28

Seeking Him Again

The scene now shifts again, and we see the young woman waking up. Her beloved is standing at the door and knocking, urging her to let him in. Having just studied the messages to the churches, we cannot fail to recognize the words and scene of Jesus saying;

> *"Behold, I stand at the door, and knock.*
> *If any man hear My voice, and open the door,*
> *I will come in to him,*
> *And will sup with him, and he with Me."* – Rev. 3:20

Having also just studied the ancient Hebrew wedding customs, we can readily recognize that what is happening: here is a marriage proposal!

She goes to let him in, but she is too late. While she has been sleeping, He has come and gone. This is symbolic of Israel, who did not respond to Christ when He came. When she goes out into the night to look for him, she is assaulted. The watchmen, who were supposed to be keeping the walls, wound her and take away her veil. This is all symbolic of what happened to Jerusalem after Christ's death and resurrection. Those who were supposed to be watching for the Messiah (the priests and Pharisees of Jesus' day), become the ones who persecute and kill those who are seeking to follow the Messiah. As a result, the temple is destroyed, and the city is laid waste.

But this does not deter the young woman. She continues to seek him, and she does not hide her love from scoffers or the daughters of Jerusalem, though they neither know nor care about him. They ask her,

"What is your beloved more than another beloved?
They want to know what makes him so special that she would risk so much to find him.

She answers them by singing of how beautiful and wonderful he is, testifying of all his perfections to them.

Others Begin To Seek Him

The young woman's description and testimony of the perfections of her Love is so compelling, that now those who scoffed at her earlier ask;

Where has you beloved gone,
O thou fairest among women?
Where is thy beloved turned aside,
That we may seek him with you.!" – S. of S. 6:1

This is the mission of the New Testament church: to testify of what great things the Lord has done for us, and to go into all the world and make disciples of everyone.

The young woman says that her beloved has gone to his garden, to "gather lilies". Remember, he called her a lily. In this time, Christ has gone to heaven, but He is still seeking "lilies", and gathering in all who will respond to his call. Even though they are temporarily separated, the young woman confidently sings, *"I am by beloved's and my beloved is mine."* She is confident in his love.

The Beloved is so pleased with her confidence in his love that he breaks into rapturous song over her beauties. He calls her "My undefiled", and "the only one". He sings:

> *"Who is she that looks forth as the morning,*
> *Fair as the moon, clear as the sun,*
> *And terrible as an army with banners?"* – S. of S. 8:10

She is "one" and the "only one", yet she has become like a mighty army, awesome and majestic.

> *"After this I beheld, and lo a great multitude,*
> *Which no man could number,*
> *Of all nations, and kindreds, and people, and tongues,*
> *Stood before the throne, And before the Lamb,*
> *Clothed with white robes, and palms in their hands."* – Rev. 7:9

Raptured!

The young woman now sings:

> *I went down into the garden of nuts to see the fruits of the valley,*
> *And to see whether the vine flourished, and the pomegranates budded.*
> *Before I was aware,*
> *my soul made me like the chariots of Amminadib."* – S. of S.6:11-12

As she is going about her business, tending to the garden and making sure the fruit was growing as it should, she is suddenly snatched away as if in a chariot!

The name "Amminadib" is really two Hebrew words: "'am", meaning "nation, people, kindred, persons"; and "nadib", which means "inclined, willing, noble, generous, princely"[7]. So, the text could be read: "My soul was taken away as if in a chariot with all the noble, willing people from every nation and kindred"!

The young women of Jerusalem now cry out:

"Return, return, O Shulamite!
Return, return, that we may look upon thee!" – S. of S. 6:13

And her Beloved answers them:

"What will you see in the Shulamite?
As it were the company of two armies." – S. of S. 6:13

The is the first time the word "Shulamite" is used. It comes from the Hebrew word "salam" and means "peaceful one, or one who is in a covenant of peace"[8].

The church, the beloved of the Lord, will suddenly be taken away, and when she does, the world will be in fear and turmoil. The Beloved says she is the one who has entered into a covenant with Him, and she is now at peace. The reference to her being like a "company of two armies", indicates that believing Israel, and believing Gentiles are now One.

Beautiful Bride

Completely enraptured with his bride, the Beloved sings;

"How beautiful are your feet with shoes, O prince's daughter!" – S. of S. 7:1

Hopefully you recognize the meaning of this comes from the ancient Hebrew wedding ceremony, in which the Bride is given new shoes by her

---

[7]   James Strong, *The New Strong's Exhaustive Concordance of the Bible* (Nashville: T. Nelson, 1990), H5971, H5081.

[8]   James Strong, *The New Strong's Exhaustive Concordance of the Bible* (Nashville: T. Nelson, 1990), H7759.

Beloved. This indicating that she has a new inheritance and future. Her fortunes have changed!

The majority of the chapter is the Beloved singing over the beauties and perfections of his new bride.

Then the new bride says to her beloved:

> *"Come, my Beloved,*
> *Let us go forth into the field,*
> *Let us lodge in the villages,*
> *Let us get up early to the vineyards,*
> *Let us see if the vine flourishes,*
> *whether the tender grape appears…" – S. of S. 7:11-12*

After the long night of the Tribulation is over, Christ will return to the earth with His Bride, to establish His kingdom on earth.

The Bride and Groom Return

The first verse of chapter eight gives us another hint about the Bride. She sings:

> *O that Thou wert as my brother…"*

She so longs to be a part of His family, but she is not of His people. But He has a better way to make her a member of His family – He will marry her!

Chapter eight continues the song from the last chapter. Then those who have been left behind look up and see the happy couple returning:

> *"Who is this that comes up from the wilderness,*
> *Leaning upon her Beloved?" – S. of S. 8:5*

The Bride answers the question by declaring;

> *"I am a wall, and my breasts like towers.*
> *Then was I in His eyes as one that found favor" – S. of S. 8:10*

Jesus promised the overcomers of the church that He would make them like pillars in His temple. The Bride is the temple of the Lord.

She then goes on to say that Solomon (the king and her Beloved), must come and dwell in her vineyard and that he "must have a thousand". This is a picture of the thousand-year reign of Christ in the New Jerusalem (the Bride of Christ), which the book of Revelation speaks of. Revelation 21 goes into great detail about the Bride of Christ, including descriptions of her wall and towers.

CHAPTER 14

The Next Chapter is Yours!

Now, this really is the end of our journey. The next chapter is yours to write. I wish I could be with you on your quest. I know there will be many thrilling moments of discovery; and a few frustrating dead ends too. It won't always be easy or neat: treasure hunting never is. But for those who persist, the reward is far beyond anything it will cost you. My prayer for you echoes the prayer of Paul for the church at Ephesus. I pray:

> *"That the God of our Lord Jesus Christ,*
> *The Father of glory,*
> *May give unto you the spirit of wisdom and revelation*
> *In the knowledge of Him.*
> *The eyes of your understanding being enlightened,*
> *That you may know what is the hope of His calling,*
> *And the riches of the glory of His inheritance in the saints." – Eph. 1:16-18*

May your eyes behold wondrous things in His word[1].

---

[1]   Psalm 119:18.

BIBLIOGRAPHY

A Commentary on the Old and New Testaments. Vol. 5 [Book]/ auth. John Trapp. -Eureka, Cal.: Tanski Publications, 1997.

A Dictionary of Greek and Roman Antiquities/ auth. James Yates. // in the public domain.- pp.1044-1046.

A Survey of Israel's History [Book]/ auth. Leon Wood. – Grand Rapids, Michigan: Zondervan Publishing House, 1970, 1975.

Ancient Christian Martyrdom [Online]/ auth. Dr. Philip Irving Mitchell. // Dallas Baptist University. – 2001. -www.3dbu.edu>Mitchell.

Antiquities of the Jews [Online]/ auth. Titus Flavius Josephus. // Complete Josephus Collection. – August 8, 2001. – www.charlesrivereditors.com.

Are GMOs in My Food? [Online]/ auth. Farm Aid// GMOs – What Eaters Need to Know Fact Sheets. -March 17, 2016. -www.farmaid.org.

Bible Study Tools [Online] / auth. Blair Parke. // Ichthys, the Christian Fish Symbol: 5 Origin and History Facts. – 2022. - www.Biblestudytools.com.

Christian History Issue #23 [Journal] / auth. Mark Galli. // Christianity Today. – 1990.

Commentary on Matthew: The Gospel of the Kingdom [Book] / auth. Charles Haddon Spurgeon. – London: Passmore and Alabaster, 1893.

Creationism and the Early Church. Chapter 5 "The Sons of God" [Online] / auth. Robert I. Bradshaw – 1998. – www.robibradshaw.com.

Reason & Faith: Do Modern Science and Christian Faith Really Conflict? [Book] / auth. Roger Forster & Paul Marston. – Eastbourn: Monarch Publications, 1989.

First Council of Nicaea [Online] // The Encyclopedia Britannica. – Jan. 2024. – Britannica.com

Fox's Book of Martyrs [Book] / auth. John Fox. Edited by William Byron Forbush, D.D.– Philadelphia, Chicago: The John C. Winston Company, 1926 (first published in 1563).

Genesis: An Expositional Commentary Volumes 1, 2 and 3 [Book]/ auth. James Montgomery Boice. – Grand Rapids, Michigan: Zondervan, 1987.

Greek and Roman Dress from A to Z. 1st Edition. [Book] auth. Lloyd Llewellyn-Jones, Glenys Davies. – London: Routledge, 2007.

Hebrew For Christians [Online]/ auth. John J. Parsons. : hebrew4christians.com.

Historical Locks [Website], History of Keys. Auth. Assa Abloy. April 28, 2008. Historicallocks.com.

Holy Bible, New Living Translation, NLT [Book]. – Carol Stream, Ill.: Tyndale House Publishers Inc. Used by permission., 1996, 2004, 2007.

Is There Water in Space: An Extensive FAQ [Online]// Orbital Today. – October 8, 2022. – orbitaltoday.com.

Jesus Paid It All [Hymn]/ auth. Mrs. H.M. Hall // All-American Church Hymnal.

King James Bible, KJV. [Book]: Oxford University Press. Public Domain, 1945/1769.

Largest Ever Hoard of Anglo-Saxon Gold Found in Staffordshire [article] / auth. Kennedy Maey. – London, UK: The guardian, 2009.

Lost In Translation Vol. 1 [Book] / auth. John Klein, Adam spears, Michael Christopher. – Bend, OR: Klein & Spears, 2014.

Lost In Translation Vol. 1 Rediscovering the Hebrew Roots of Our Faith [Book] / auth. John Klein, Adam Spears. – Bend, OR: Klein & Spears. - 2007.

Marsha Blackburn asked Ketanji Brown Jackon to define 'woman'.; Science says there's no simple answer. [Online] / auth. Alia E. Dastagir // USA TODAY, Health and Wellness. – March 24, 2022. – www. usatoday.com.

Most Americans Believe in Intelligent Life Beyond Earth [Online]/ auth. Courtney Kennedy & Arnold Lau. // Pew Research Center. – Jund 30, 2021. – pewresearchcenter.org.

New International Version, NIV [Book] / auth. International Bible Society. – : Biblica, Inc., 1973.

New King James Version, NKJV [Book]. Thomas Nelson, Inc. Used by permission, 1982.

Oxford Scholars Consult the Stars for Date of Crucifixion to 33 A.D. [Journal] / auth. Thomas O'Toole. // The Washington Post. – April 20, 1984.

Pontius Pilate in History and Interpretation [Book] / auth. Helen K. Bond. : Cambridge University Press, 1998.

Religion Wing/ Judaism/ Jewish Holidays & Festivals / Rosh Hashanah [Online] / Judaism 101 //Jewish Virtual Library. – 1998 – 2024. – jewishvirtuallibrary.org.

Roman Women [Book] auth. Eve L'Ambra. (Cambridge University Press, 2001),

Scofield Reference Edition Bible, King James Version [Book] / Scofield notes. Auth. Rev. C.I. Scofield D.D. – New York: Oxford University press, 1945.

Septuagint (LXX) / auth. (CCAT) Pennsylvania Center for Computer Analysis of Texts // Septuagint Greek Old Testament. Blue Letter Bible Septuagint text.

Strong's Exhaustive Concordance of the Bible [Book] / auth. James Strong. Reference Library Edition – Iowa Falls, Iowa: World Bible Publishers.

Symbolism of the Fish/ auth. Maurice Hassett. // Catholic Encyclopedia. – New York: Robert Appleton Company, 1913.

Tashlich, the Symbolic Casting Off of Sins [Online] / auth. Lesli Koppelman Ross. // My Jewish Learning – 2024. – myjewishlearning.com.

Thayer's Greek Lexicon, Electronic Database : BibleSoft, Inc. 2011.

Thayer's Greek- English Lexicon of the New Testament [Book]/ auth. Joseph H. Thayer. – Grand Rapids, Michigan: Baker Book House, 1977.

The First Book of the MaCabees [Book Section] from *The Apocrypha or Deuterocanonical Books of the Bible* / auth. Various // Halcyon Press Ltd., July 7, 2011.

The Book of Jasher / auth. Anonym. – Scotts Valley, CA; copyright by IAP, 2009.

The Books of Enoch: Complete Edition – 3ʳᵈ Ed. [Book] / editors: Paul C. Schnieders & Robert H. Charles – Las Vegas, 2012.

The Catechism of the Catholic Church, Simplified [Online] / Mary Foundation // Catholicity. -MaryFoundation@catholicity.com

The Holy Bible, New International Version, NIV [Book]; Biblica, Inc. Used by permission, All rights reserved worldwide., Copyright 1973, 1978, 1984, 2001.

The Jewish Calendar, A Lunar Eclipse and the Date of Christ's Crucifixion [Article] / auth. Colin Humphreys & W. Waddington. :Tyndale Bulletin. 43.10.5375/001c.30487, 1992.

The Jewish Way of Love and Marriage; Celebrating the Jewish Marriage Covenant [Online] / auth. Maurice Lamm. // Chabad.org

The Middle Ages in Europe. The Holy Roman Empire [Online] / auth. Biel // World Civilizations (HIS101). https://courses.lumenlearning.com.

The New Strong's Exhaustive Concordance of the Bible [Book] / auth. James Strong S.T.D., LL.D. – Nashville:, Thomas Nelson, 1990.

The Rise of Christianity [Book] / auth. Rodney Stark. – San Francisco: Princeton University Press, Harper, 1996.

Tiberius [Online] // Wikipedia. – Sept. 23, 2023 – en.m.wikipedia.org.

Verse by Verse Study of Gen. 10-12 [Report] / auth. Chuck Smith. / Blue Letter Bible Commentaries, 2000.

What the Bible Says About Two Passover Observances at Time of Jesus [Online] / auth. David C. Grabbe. // from Forerunner Commentary/ 1992-2024/ Bible Tools/ bibletools.org.

Printed in the United States
by Baker & Taylor Publisher Services